Patri...

The Sportswriter

Twenty Years of Award-Winning Sports Journalism

First published in Great Britain in 1996 by
Virgin Books
an imprint of Virgin Publishing Ltd
332 Ladbroke Grove
London W10 5AH

*A catalogue record for this book
is available from the British Library.*

ISBN 0 7535 0086 8

Typeset by SX Composing DTP
Printed and bound by Cox & Wyman Ltd, Reading, Berks

For Julie

Contents

Introduction and Acknowledgements

VICTOR RAILTON WAS A man of simple tastes. He liked fish and chips, West Ham United and tea so strong you could stand a spoon in it. A football writer of the old school, he would spend endless hours on the telephone, bending managerial ears and conjuring a flow of exclusive stories for the *London Evening News*. But he didn't like Abroad. He didn't care for the part of his job which involved air tickets. Most of all, he hated World Cups. In Vic's view, World Cups amounted to little more than weak tea, skinny chips and people who had never been to Upton Park. And so, one spring morning in 1978, he called me at home.

'I've got a lovely little skive for you,' he said. 'Argentina. World Cup. Loads of words every day, all over the back page of the *Evening News*. And if you go, I can stay at home. Do us a favour, my son; take the job, eh?'

A few weeks later, I found myself standing in a small room while two soldiers, bulging with pistols, searched my luggage, inspected my passport and asked pointed questions about my political views. Eventually, they were satisfied. 'Welcome to Buenos Aires,' they said.

Looking back down the years, that greeting was an invitation to the treadmill: World Cups, Olympics, title fights, Test matches, rugby internationals and the rest. Some invitation, some treadmill.

Ian Wooldridge, a good friend and respected colleague, once wrote that sports writing is an equable arrangement by which a newspaper pays you for doing what you were going to do in any case. My daughter Mary expressed a similar thought long ago. When she was five years old, she came home from school and said, 'Our teacher wants to know what we're going to do when we grow up;' A pause, and then, 'Daddy, what are *you* going to do?'

The truth, as people like Wooldridge know all too well, is that sportswriters never really do grow up. We travel the world in a certain style, watching the gods at play and attempting to convey the pleasure it produces. And not only do we watch the great ones, we actually get to meet them. A trawl through the chapters of this book yields a selection of names almost too precious to drop: Ali, Piggott, Tyson, Busby, Blanchflower, Ovett, Coe, Greaves and Finney. Now it would be stretching the truth beyond tolerance were I to claim a close relationship with all these notables. For instance, I never found the nerve to call Busby 'Matt', while in the course of my last cosy chat with Mike Tyson the garrulous fellow managed to mumble a grand total of 33 words. But we do, occasionally, get the chance to speak with them, to listen to their tales, and to marvel at how grown men and women can achieve a kind of heroic stature by excelling at children's games.

The trick, of course, is to find somebody willing to send you on these desirable excursions, and in this I have been particularly fortunate. Starting with Peter Watson at the *Evening News* and moving on via Vic Wakeling, Doug Jackson, Alan Hubbard, Ken Haskell and Jon Ryan to my present boss Roger Kelly at the *Mail on Sunday*, I have enjoyed nothing but encouragement from an immensely talented band of sports editors. Successive editors have been similarly generous, from Louis Kirby at the *News* and *Evening Standard* to the *Mail on Sunday* editors Bernard Shrimsley, Stewart Steven and Jonathan Holborow. I am enormously grateful.

Then there are the sub-editors. Anybody who has even attempted to chisel out a column on a regular basis will appreciate precisely what he owes to those newspaper professionals who handle the copy, smooth out the errors and generally keep the author out of the libel courts. I thank them as I thank Pete Silverton of *Night & Day* and Mal Peachey of Virgin who came up with the idea for this book. And if I had the space, I would thank by name all those colleagues, from broadsheet to tabloid, from the haughties to the naughties, with whom I have enjoyed so many long days and late nights across the world. I value their companionship more than I can say.

But the biggest debt by far is owed to my family. As the son of a sportswriter, I have always known that the job is quite impossible without the unswerving support of a close-knit family. Like the other Pat Collins before me, I have been richly blessed. My deepest thanks are due to Michael, Daniel, Mary and Patrick. And most especially to Julie, my wife.

Looking back on this introduction, I seem to have painted an improbably rosy picture. Travel the globe, enjoy the best of sport, hob-nob with your idols, then rattle out a few words to justify the journey. Some think it an idyllic existence; others disagree.

A few years ago, on a flight from London to Los Angeles, I found myself sitting next to a chartered accountant. He was a man in love with his calling, and he wanted to share that love with a financial illiterate. In the course of ten and a half hours, he instructed me in the mysteries of cash flow and cost benefits, he described the joys of capital gains and corporate efficiency and, if memory serves, he drew a canny line between tax avoidance and tax evasion. He was on his way to an accountants' convention in San Diego, and he couldn't wait to get there.

When we arrived in Los Angeles, we reached up to the overhead compartment to collect our briefcases. 'By the way,' said my financial friend, 'I haven't asked you what you do?' I explained that I was a sportswriter, there to cover the Los Angeles Olympics. He frowned sympathetically. Then he tapped my arm. 'Never mind,' he said. 'Somebody's got to do it.'

1978

If everything had gone to plan, the Scots would have become champions of the world in Argentina. They had the players, or so it was said. Certainly they had hordes of fervent followers. And they had the manager. Ah, the manager! Ally MacLeod was a decent dreamer who had assured his countrymen that the World Cup was theirs for the taking. Sadly, he was wrong. Scotland came home after three matches, and the inquests lasted for months.

In fairness, the Argentines scarcely noticed their departure. Enchanting people who were beset by rampant inflation and governed by a band of Ruritanian thugs, they had placed all their hopes in their football team. And at the close of a memorable tournament, the team repaid the nation's trust.

Soon after returning from South America, I travelled to South Wales to meet a personal hero . . .

'Mucking It Up When It Matters'

London Evening News, 5 June 1978

THE GENERAL RETREATED to the hills outside Cordoba, reflected long and deeply upon the reasons for defeat and emerged into the early-morning sunlight with his considered conclusion . . . the blame, it seemed, lay exclusively with the troops.

In the past few weeks the Scottish manager Ally MacLeod has revealed himself as an inept tactician, an inadequate strategist and an indifferent diplomat. The man makes so many mistakes that it is difficult to isolate one as being of absolutely critical importance.

But I believe that his blank and brazen refusal to accept any part of the responsibility for the humiliation which overtook his Scottish team in the Chateau Carreras Stadium on Saturday may yet prove his most expensive error.

It was quite bad enough that he selected the team which was lamentably ill-equipped to represent itself at this level of competition, but to absolve himself of the consequences of that selection is far, far worse.

'I'm convinced I picked the right team,' he said. 'And there was nothing wrong with the tactics, if only they'd carried on playing as they played in the first 15 minutes.

'But then they got casual, they played without fire. Eight of the team did not play to their ability. Normally you expect to carry three, but eight: that's amateur stuff.'

After the way he picked and prepared his team for Saturday's match, it ill-becomes MacLeod to toss around jibes about amateurism.

And the timing of the insult is even worse than its content, for the man has in charge several players whose international experience derisively exceeds that of their manager.

They know how poorly they played. They also have one or two ideas about why they played so poorly.

And at a time when morale will have to soar to stratospheric heights if the situation is to be retrieved, one could detect quite audible rumblings of discontent in the camp.

I said in this column on Saturday that Peru's ability would surely exceed their reputation.

As understatements go, it was a beauty.

They revealed explosive pace, astonishingly instinctive control and a tactical awareness which was a stunning rebuke to those who had regarded them as a bunch of insignificant strolling players.

Marcos Calderon, the menacing, massive-shouldered Peruvian manager, had travelled extensively to watch the Scots and analyse their deficiencies.

MacLeod, on the other hand, had seen a few video-tapes of the Peruvians and has been saying for months that he wasn't too bothered about scouting missions – his sole concern was the preparation of his own team.

One remark from Scotland's captain Bruce Rioch crystallised the results of that policy: 'What really took us by surprise was the pace of their wingers. Tremendous pace, they had. We were amazed.'

The point does not need elaboration.

You will, by now, have seen the details of the Scottish disaster analysed and argued over a thousand times on television.

But you had to have trudged away from that elegant stadium with the despondent Scots to realise just how bitterly their glittering expectations had been abused.

They felt let down as never before, and instinctively they sought solace in whisky and self-pity.

Laments were sung, curses were uttered, the amber liquid began to flow and slowly that wry, bitter, self-mocking humour began to emerge like a genie from the glasses.

'We always do it, we always muck it up when it matters,' said one man who had spent his RAF gratuity on the journey across the South Atlantic to cheer on the lads.

'You don't mind getting beaten, but not playing, not showing anything, that's really hurtful.'

He then returned to his declared intention of: 'Beating them Peruvians five-nothing at singing' and he was working doggedly towards that end as dawn rose over the city of Cordoba.

It was a lovely irrational gesture and it perfectly represented the mood of most of the Scots over here.

A team which was so thoroughly outclassed by Peru may well

take the required victory over Iran but will surely not possess sufficient resources to survive against the Dutch in Mendoza next Sunday.

MacLeod states the task quite simply.

'We have got to win our next two games handsomely, no ifs or buts,' he said. 'Then we've got to hope that the other results go in our favour.'

Then he lets himself down with a piece of nonsense about: 'Every game now is a battle of Bannockburn.'

If he really believes that, if he approaches his task in that spirit, then the Scots may as well begin their packing right now.

For nothing could prove more disastrous than the policy of sending good, intelligent players into these two critical games with adrenalin pumping insanely and long-forgotten battle cries ringing in their ears.

They must approach them responsibly, restore a measure of balance to their mid-field, re-think their sterile, fatuous ploy of aiming every attack at the head of Joe Jordan, and hope against hope that something can be salvaged from the wreck of their ambitions.

Sadly, the signs are that they are already beyond salvation.

Pride, Patriotism and Player-Power

London Evening News, 12 June 1978

THEY TOOK IT out of Ally's hands last night. With little except their sanity and self-respect to play for, the footballers of Scotland assumed control of their own destinies.

And the result is that the Scots are departing from this World Cup merely seething with frustration instead of sagging with remorse.

I have good reason to believe that the strategy and selection policy which lay behind the 3–2 victory over Holland was conceived and enforced by the team's senior professionals in a dramatic display of player-power.

Ally MacLeod was told precisely how his team intended to play against the Dutch and given the names of the players who would be required to carry out those intentions. Left without a realistic option, MacLeod went along with the wave of feeling.

Thus, for the first time in the tournament, the Scots entered a match fully aware of the size of their task and deeply confident of their ability to master it.

When you looked into the grey, drained faces of the Scottish players last night, you realised just how close they had come to mastering it in a manner which nobody had believed was possible.

Landed with the absurd proposition of having to beat Holland by three goals, the Scots contrived a situation which saw them firmly in the market for a miracle, holding a two-goal advantage with 26 minutes of the game remaining.

The fact that they could not discover the extra goal which would have killed the Dutch will infest Scottish nightmares for years to come. The fact that they came so close to that discovery will always remain a bright source of pride.

For the strategy had been superb. Graeme Souness, whose inclusion in the side was two games overdue, operated from deep. He chipped and floated a stream of perceptive passes to utilise the running power of Joe Jordan and Kenny Dalglish. Bruch Rioch got himself into the forward positions from which he is most effective. Asa Hartford and Archie Gemmill beavered unsparingly in the mid-field while Tom Forsyth and the impeccable Martin Buchan were totally dominant in the centre of the defence.

Having said all that – and mindful of an already perceptible Scottish feeling that one fine display has wiped out all that has gone before – it should be pointed out that the Dutch were almost unbelievably poor.

With the exception of their players of glittering quality – Rudi Krol, Wim Jansen and Johnny Rep – they were an indifferent impersonation of the side which fell just a step short of the ultimate prize four years ago.

Scotland ignored the Dutch attempts to stifle the pace of the game, had a Kenny Dalglish goal disallowed after 13 minutes for a barely detectable push, then conceded a penalty in the 35th minute when Stuart Kennedy toppled Rep. Rob Rensenbrink struck the kick punishingly.

With Johann Neeskens departing injured in the 11th minute and Wim Rijsbergen crippled by the Jordan tackle which was to end his match prematurely, Scotland secured equality just before half-time when a Souness cross was knocked down by Jordan's head and Dalglish collared a murderous half-volley.

A Gemmill penalty in the 47th minute, after Souness had been shoved in the area, gave rise to optimism and a marvellous Gemmill goal in the 64th, when he buzzed in and out of tackles like a demented clockwork mouse, gave birth to euphoria.

But the Dutch have too many good players to offer a completely abject surrender and at the back of one's mind there always lurked the fear that sooner or later they would exploit the international inadequacies of Alan Rough in the Scottish goal. So it proved.

Krol played a short forward pass to Rep, there was a brief run, a brute of a 30-yard drive and there was Rough, waving a forlorn farewell to the tournament, while an entire nation glared at television screens and murmured might-have-beens.

In a stadium of quite stunning beauty, with the looming Andes providing a dramatic backcloth, the team which had travelled to this continent on a tide of rampant patriotism and unbounded aspiration had died a brave but inexorable death.

MacLeod, it must be said, handled the post-mortem with dignified sensitivity. I believe that he genuinely felt he was destined to

carry the World Cup home to Glasgow. The process of his international education has therefore been particularly painful.

The man had been through too much agony, faced too many ugly
realities to pursue any question of resignation last night. But my feeling is that he will jump before the Scottish Football Association are
given the chance to push him and that resignation will not be long
delayed.

So this flawed and frantic Scottish crusade is over. Now they must
prepare for the long journey home, for whatever welcome may await
them in Glasgow.

How shall we remember it? Will it be for the Willie Johnston
dope scandal, for the pain of false promise wrecked by reality, for
the unceasing stream of headlines and rumours or for the cruel
paradox of final victory yielding ultimate defeat?

For my part, it will be none of these things. My abiding memory
of Scotland's World Cup campaign of '78 will be of a broad Scottish
accent complaining: 'The London office is driving me mad. My
Sports Editor says I'm not turning in enough stories for the money
he's paying me.'

The words are the traditional heartcry of the harassed reporter.
In this case, they were spoken by a Scottish footballer.

'El Reverso Forecasto'

London Evening News, 15 June 1978

L
IKE SO MANY good ideas, it was born in a bar. It was the kind of bar you happen across in downtown Buenos Aires, with a poster proclaiming the birth of the Irish Republic on one wall, a rather forlorn sign saying 'Scotland for the World Cup' on another, and in a corner, the man from the Guardian singing Sussex By The Sea in raucously indifferent baritone.

As I recall, it was during the Guardian man's second chorus that my friend Harry suggested a day at the races.

Now as my friend Harry is conceivably the worst judge of horse flesh in Western Europe, and as my knowledge of those noble animals extends to an awareness that they have a leg at each corner, the excursion suddenly became inevitable.

So it was that we found ourselves out at Palermo, armed with an incomprehensible race card, a bundle of vulnerable Argentinian pesos and my friend Harry's equine expertise.

Apart from the track itself – a brown, unlovely circle which oozed clouds of dust for a mile and a half – you might just have been on one of England's most distinguished courses.

The punters exuded that neurotic air of quiet desperation which marks the breed the world over. And in the press room a group of characters torn straight from the pages of Damon Runyan argued incessantly over a poker game.

A remarkable body of men, the Argentine racing press. They absolutely insisted on providing us with the winner of the first three races. After some misgivings, my friend Harry endorsed their opinion and an investment of 10,000 pesos left us clutching an enormous bundle.

And that, regrettably, was where ambition took over. 'Next race,' said Harry, 'we'll hit them with a reverse forecast.' 'A what?' I inquired. 'Leave it to me,' said the finest judge of horse flesh in the Americas.

The amiable little fellow who was running our bets was summoned and in impeccable Spanish Harry ordered: 'Reverso Forecasto – four and ten.' The man went away with a puzzled smile and a lot of money.

We sauntered across to the owners' bar to watch the race, Harry assuring the assembled racing brains of Argentina that on the basis of faultless information, we were about to bring off the most devastating coup that the country's racing has seen.

No. Ten made the pace from the start and, after a brisk 1,600-metre sprint, won the race with yawning ease. Harry, by then, was peering at the cloud of dust which enveloped the rest of the field.

As they reached the line, one enormous beast thrust his head in front of the pack – No. Four. People came flocking to shake the hands of the English experts who had travelled 7,000 miles to demonstrate how the game is played in the first division.

One or two actually applauded as we strolled towards the man whom, the statisticians assured us, was about to hand over no less than 260,000 pesos.

He greeted us with a smile which was suspiciously sympathetic. And offered us 5,000 pesos. 'The rest?' said Harry. 'El remaindero?' It transpired that Harry's Spanish had proved less than faultless. Instructions had been misunderstood. The 'reverso forecasto' had become a place bet on No. four.

The rest of the meeting was a sadly unrelieved disaster. Harry's fancy in the next race was beaten by what they call the 'minima', or half a nose. My attempt at inspired selection pinned our dwindling bundle of pesos on an animal which ran so slowly that they seriously considered delaying the start of the following race.

The hospitality remained both warm and lavish. Dinner invitations were extended by two of Argentina's leading owners and accepted with gratitude, but Harry's thoughts were still revolving around El Reverso Forecasto.

'A day at the races,' he said. 'Whose bloody idea was it, anyway?'

Arlott: The Voice of Summer

London Evening News, 21 July 1978

THE DAY IS WARM and sultry. Sweat is running in rivers from the fast bowler's forehead and the elderly members in their private stand are loosening belts a notch or two to accommodate the lunch-time excesses of new potatoes and warm beer.

Yet John Arlott, padding around the outfield as he escorts his guest to the pavilion restaurant, is encased in a large raincoat, as if to advertise his basic mistrust of the British summer.

Strange that such a man should reveal such lack of trust in the season, since without him I really believe that we should cancel the British summer and spend three or four months seeking an acceptable substitute to fill the gap between spring and autumn.

To most of us Arlott is, and always has been, the voice of summer. And if the game which God invented in a moment of commendable inspiration is not always accompanied by sun-splashed days, fast, true wickets, keen young boys scribbling every stroke into score-books and old men murmuring memories of Woolley and Hammond, then it can still offer Arlott to remind us of its enduring charm and fascination.

Since 1946, long before any of today's sports commentators had been introduced to a microphone, Arlott has been interpreting with wit and considerable wisdom that intricate ritual which is our summer game.

And he has done it with such distinction that somehow his soft Hampshire burr has become woven into the very fabric of the game, blending quite perfectly with its air of satisfying tranquillity.

He rejects that description as we peer through the pavilion windows at Cardiff to watch some merciless Somerset batsmen expose the limitations of Glamorgan's bowlers.

'Not tranquil,' he says. 'Never that. It can be a savage, violent game, a cruel game. There's none so vulnerable as the opening bat who walks out there with 11 men after his blood and two umpires hovering to see he doesn't escape. Or the bowler who's being carted all over the place by a batsman in form. Or the fielder who's trembling beneath a skier that he's got to catch.

'It never was a tranquil game, and least of all today. I often wonder what Sir Pelham Warner would say if he were to walk into Lord's one Sunday when there was a full house watching limited-over cricket sponsored by a tobacco firm. The old chap would have a fit.'

Yet despite its changing circumstances, it remains a game which encourages reflective, elegant use of the language. In this aspect, Arlott is still without peer.

I recall that he once described Colin Cowdrey as having 'persuaded' a cover drive to the boundary. With one word he had painted the perfect picture. He shrugged off the recollection: 'There's a very large English vocabulary and somewhere there's absolutely the right word. It's simply a question of finding it, that's all.'

I also asked him about one or two of his fellow commentators down the years who have attempted to emulate his genius. There was the story of the man who attempted to inject some colour into a county match by concluding every few passages of description with the phrase: '. . . as the sun sets slowly in the West.'

Arlott eventually came to the microphone and announced: 'The sun is still setting slowly in the West and if it should start to set anywhere else, I shall be the first to let you know.'

'True story,' Arlott recalls. 'The chap took it rather well. At least, I think he did.'

Yet if cricket is his passion, it has yet to become his obsession. Unlike some of his contemporaries, he does not believe that life should be lived exclusively within a 22-yard strip of turf.

He once remarked that the British 'treat sport too seriously and life too lightly,' and just eight years have passed since he tried to reverse that process at considerable personal sacrifice.

You will remember those agonising months which preceded the proposed South African tour of England in 1970. They were the months when you took sides, believing either that it was wrong to play against a team selected on grounds of race or that the importance of the game transcended anything which was happening in the outside world.

Arlott, to the everlasting admiration of those of us who shared his view, decided that he wanted no part of the tour and declined to commentate on any of the matches on the grounds that threats of demos and disruption would make it quite impossible for cricketers to play the game he wanted to talk about.

He remembers the period with some bitterness. 'It cost me the unrelenting hostility of two-thirds of the cricket Establishment,' he says, 'but not, I'm proud to say, of the players themselves.

'I had a stream of foul, virulent letters. People would cut me when they saw me at matches, or they'd make loud, pointed comments within my hearing. I wasn't asked to a lot of functions I'd attended for years, which only confirmed my view about the kind of people who'd been asking me anyway.

'But I'm still certain I was right. That series was impossible from the start and the authorities were stupid not to see it.

'I also happen to think I'm right about the present crisis, the Packer Affair. I don't like what's happened, but it isn't going to go away so you've got to sit down and try to find a few things you don't disagree on. You won't help the game by starting a battle.

'Perhaps Tony Greig's the saddest figure in it all. He acted as a recruiting agent while he was still captain of England.

'He used the status the Establishment had given him to mobilise forces against the Establishment. That was regrettable, and the pity was that he was too self-centred to realise the hatred and bitterness he would cause.'

But the politics of the game do not detain him for too long and he looks up as a ripple of applause announces the arrival of Ian Botham at the wicket.

'A remarkable young man, this one,' he says. 'He's going to be a great cricketer because he'll never discover that it's a very complex game. A great asset, that. He'll either do tremendous things today or he'll give us a first-ball anti-climax.'

And with that, Botham gave a sharp return chance off his first ball and in the ensuing confusion ran out his partner who had just scored 145.

Arlott laughed almost until the tears came. 'Did you hear the calling for that run?' he asked. 'Reminds me of that fellow who played for Oxford, Fellows-Smith. He was the author of the famous call: "Yes . . . No . . . Wait . . . Sorry . . . Oh, bugger it!"'

Still chuckling at the memory, and at the incident which had evoked it, he left the restaurant to stroll back around the outfield, buttoning his raincoat against the warm summer afternoon.

1979

A marvellous March afternoon on Limerick racecourse, with John Treacy striding home at the head of the world's finest cross-country field. The lingering memories are of the celebrations, which lasted for several days, and of Treacy's desperate agitation when large numbers of his countrymen attempted to pump his hand long before he had completed the course.

Came November, and I was meeting another hero. Football will continue to produce its share of great players, fine writers and passionate talkers. But there was only one man who possessed all three gifts in extravagant measure. Chances are we shall never see the equal of Danny Blanchflower.

'Canonised or Crucified'

London Evening News, 26 March 1979

As the citizens of Limerick peered through a grey Irish dawn and cursed the devil who invented strong drink, the little fellow responsible for their condition was preparing to board a trans-Atlantic jet.

John Treacy, slender, pale and painfully shy, was returning to his temporary home in Providence, Rhode Island, after proving himself the finest cross country runner in the whole wide world.

And if you doubt his right to that title, then you were not among some 25,000 of his countrymen who stood in driving rain and cheered every step of his 7 mile journey through a bog known as Limerick Racecourse yesterday afternoon.

A nation whose sporting victories are usually delivered by four-legged runners had heaped huge expectations upon Treacy's slim shoulders.

'Your man'll be canonised or crucified out there today,' remarked one observer with uncomfortable accuracy before the start of the World Cross Country Championship event.

But when the green-vested figure came striding through the mist and rain for the very last time – and had his chances imperilled by a couple of hundred gleeful lunatics who invaded the course with the quaint idea of shaking his hand! – you knew that the expectations had been richly justified.

By the simple expedient of getting out in front after a mile and a half, piling on the pace and inviting the world's best cross country runners to argue over the minor placings, Treacy had triumphantly defended the world title he won in Glasgow last year.

And defended it so convincingly out there in the racecourse mud that you almost believed the man who swore that the champion 'could have covered the last mile with Jonjo O'Neill on his back.'

Indeed, so expansive was Limerick's mood last night that nobody was lamenting the fact that the English runners, by scoring solidly if unspectacularly, had denied Ireland the team title.

Led through by Shaftesbury Harrier Julian Goater in ninth place and the Geordie Mike McLeod at 14, England packed Andy Holden, Nick Rose and Bernie Ford at 20, 21 and 22 and rounded off with young Nick Lees in 33rd place to beat Ireland by 79 points, with the Russians back in third position.

But since athletics is essentially about individuals rather than teams, the Englishmen were in no mood for celebration last night.

McLeod, in fact, described the course in a phrase which can find no place in a family newspaper.

'The mud was that bad, you couldn't keep your feet,' he complained. 'The real track runners didn't have a chance. A firm course would have produced a different winner.'

It was a theory best spoken softly in those parts for Treacy, whose talent was produced in the Waterford village of Villierstown, and is currently being refined at an American college, had run himself into the realms of folklore.

You had known it was going to be one of those magnificently chaotic afternoons from the moment you entered the racecourse and heard a loudspeaker appealing for the services of 'Someone who can open doors without resorting to the use of a key.'

The athletes, it seemed, were locked out of their dressing rooms. A Limerick lock-picker was quickly forthcoming.

The chaos continued in the tiny and hopelessly overcrowded grandstand where VIPs took on the gentlemen of the Press in an amiable tussle for seats, only to discover that their breath in the cold air misted over the viewing window and obliterated the early races.

This misfortune resulted in a mass exodus to the bar, where sympathetic men dispensed hot whiskey and tall stories.

A splendid anarchy settled over the company, as one of Ireland's leading politicians found when he made his belated arrival.

'Do we have a seat for the Minister of Foreign Affairs?' came the anxious inquiry. 'Give him a drink and tell him to fight for a place like the rest of us,' was the response.

And they did, and he did.

Nobody quibbled, nobody complained. Everyone was trying so hard to please and everyone had come to see John Treacy beat the world.

And when he loped in ahead of Poland's Bronislaw Malinowski, Alexander Antipov of Russia and Tony Simmons of Wales, it seemed entirely appropriate that 25,000 people should abandon themselves to ecstasy.

The 21-year-old champion was perhaps the one man around who was completely unaffected by the emotion of the occasion.

Settling his 9st. frame upon a bench in the jockeys' weighing room, he appeared a trifle surprised at all the fuss he'd caused.

'It was really quite easy. Easier than last year,' he explained.

'Maybe I was a bit inspired, running in front of my own people, but I just broke early and stayed there. It's easier when you're out on your own.'

He went on: 'The conditions helped. I prayed for rain last night and down it came. I felt really good then.

'The only time I was worried was when I fell over with two laps to go. Just a tumble, like, nothing serious, then when the crowd came on at the end, I thought they were going to tread on me.

'No, I didn't react to the pressure. I'm not the sort of fellow that gets bothered by pressure.

'I'm not bothered by celebrations, either. I'm going back to America tomorrow, so tonight I'll have a quiet evening out with my mother and father. Let everyone else do the celebrating.'

Well, the people of Limerick took him at his word. While John went off to get himself hugged by his mother – 'He's done great things for our village,' she said. 'It's known all over Waterford' – the people who had screamed him to victory went away to comfort their throats.

They talked of his future glories: how he's going to complete the cross country treble next year and how he's certain to wipe the floor with the Olympic 10,000 metres field in Moscow.

Easy, premature, rose-tinted talk it was; but you couldn't blame them.

Their agonies of the morning after will be quickly forgotten, but the courage and talent of John Treacy had given them an enchanted afternoon they will remember for ever.

The Last Great Romantic

London Evening News, 29 November 1979

W HEN DANNY BLANCHFLOWER was manager of Chelsea, a player approached him to complain that training had become too repetitive.

'That,' said Danny, 'is because we are after a repetitive performance.' Then he tried to illustrate his point.

'A concert pianist sits at the piano and runs his hands up and down the keys. Five hours a day, every day. Very repetitive.

'Then he goes along to the concert, sits down to play and he's perfect. Every time. That's what I'm after.'

Danny smiles at the memory. 'The lad just stared at me. I don't know if I got through. But it seemed the best way to explain consistency to him.'

I tried to imagine the player returning to his team-mates: 'I've seen the boss about the training and he went on about some bleeding piano player. Do you reckon he was having me on?'

It is the kind of reaction Danny has been provoking for decades. Nobody has better represented the honourable, decent and romantic side of the game, and nobody has sent away more people shaking their heads and wondering: 'Was he having me on?'

Last week he decided to turn in his job as manager of Northern Ireland.

Last month, he decided to step down as manager of Chelsea.

And last night he was to be found in the clubhouse of the Royal Wimbledon Golf Club, spinning parable and paradox.

At a time when the game has developed a thirst for self-destruction, reserving most of its best action for the High Court, Danny seemed a good man to talk to.

'I'm not sad to be out of the game,' he said. 'I was never in football management as a career. If I had been, I'd have gone into it years ago.

'No, I was asked to help Chelsea and I did. And if I didn't make

17

them much better, I certainly didn't make them any worse.

'As for Northern Ireland, I took on the job because I owed a lot of debts to Irish football and over the past few years maybe I've paid some of them off.

'Certainly I am not disillusioned with the game because I never had too many illusions to start with. Perhaps I'm a wee bit sad about the money side of things. Football was never a money game. They brought in professionalism because they wanted players to work harder and become better. Now, to a great extent, money has taken over.

'Some managers are in it just for the money. You can't really blame them. Many of them are wrongfully sacked, a fair amount are wrongfully employed. It's precarious, so they grab it while they can. And players get obsessed with it too. They do well out of the game, but they are looking to earn from all kinds of sources.

'All that nonsense some of them give you about not talking to the Press unless they get paid. When I started you were grateful to grab a reporter and make him listen to you. Of course, the Press are daft to stand for it, but I don't like it.

'Obviously, not all players are the same. I remember when I was at Chelsea, and Luton came on trying to buy Ron Harris. I arranged it that Ron should have the fee, about £15,000. But when I told him about it he turned down the move. "If you don't mind," he said, "I think I'll take my chances here."

'I was delighted with that. The fellow really wanted to play for us. Money wasn't everything. He went on to play some good stuff, too. A far better player than I'd given him credit for. You see, you find out the genuine ones. It helps, too, if you are open with them. I used to tell them everything.

'If a club came on wanting to buy Ray Wilkins, Garry Stanley or the gateman, whoever, I'd have them in and tell them about it.

'"Hey," I'd say, "Shamrock Rovers are in for you. Do you fancy it?" And if you were honest with them, you had a right to expect honesty in return. I wasn't often disappointed.

'Sometimes you could be so honest that they didn't have a comeback. When I first started managing Northern Ireland, one of the lads came to me to ask about the size of the bonus.

'"Bonus?" I said. "We've got no money and we don't win matches. Therefore there's no bonus and no problem." He had a chuckle and I never heard any more about it.'

You sense that some of Danny's apparently cavalier sentiments must have fallen incongruously upon ears conditioned to believe that only victory is acceptable and defeat represents disaster.

'Of course, Chelsea are a peculiar club in many ways,' he says. 'West Ham get 26,000 Cockneys turning up every week and they all sing Bubbles on good days and bad and they don't believe any other club exists. That's stability.

'But Chelsea's so near to the West End that it's influenced by its environment. You get lots of showbiz types turning up and the club does the social bit very well. Sometimes the social side is better than the football. You have to try to balance things out without destroying either.

'I was glad when I could help them, but when I realised how young the team was and just what a long-term job it was going to be, I told the chairman to find a younger man.

'We were still good friends and it was better to go too soon than too late. Still, I enjoyed it all. It's such a marvellous game; so simple, yet always challenging you to understand it.

'I was thinking back the other day to the early days at home when I played for the youth team at Glentoran with fellows like my brother Jackie, Jimmy McIlroy and Billy Bingham. How we'd talk football without stopping and on Sunday evenings how we'd go round to the homes of people who ran the teams, to talk some more.

'And I thought of men like Stan Cullis and Harry Storer who were in the Midlands when I played for Villa and how we'd meet once a week and argue about the game till one or two in the morning.

'And Arthur Rowe, who was the reason I joined Spurs. And Bob Paisley at Liverpool, an impressive, decent man.

'Then I read what Tommy Docherty said about all managers being liars and cheats.

'It made me angry for a moment, but I looked at it rationally and I thought "Ah, well, if the fellow admits he's a liar, why should I believe him about anything?"'

It was the same Docherty who once remarked that: 'Football is a rat race and the rats are winning.'

I left the golf club last night reassured that while Danny Blanchflower is still around the rodents won't have things all their own way.

1980

An Olympic year bedevilled by politics. The Americans boycotted the Games of Moscow, and Prime Minister Thatcher urged Britain's athletes to follow their lead. To their enormous credit, the British Olympic Association resisted their government's pressure, and in doing so they helped to save the Olympic movement. The Games were largely sombre, yet ultimately successful. The Soviet propaganda victory never materialised; instead the world was given an extraordinary insight into a dying system.

Later in the year, Muhammad Ali was punched to the brink of oblivion on an odious evening in Las Vegas. And London lost a fine newspaper.

'Until They Fired the Tear Gas'

London Evening News, 13 June 1980

THE YOUNG MAN WAS about 19 years old; a plump, fair-haired lad from Hampshire who wore owlish spectacles and an England football shirt.

He was shocked and bewildered and a little drunk, and we found him on a bench outside the Stadio Communale last night.

'It was all right until they fired the tear gas,' he said, and repeated it over and over again. Then he winced and clutched at his back, and that was when we saw the wound.

It was 18 inches long, slashed open by a stiletto blade, and the blood was seeping through his tattered shirt and drenching the seat of his trousers.

A young Italian, seeking some small revenge for English assaults on his countrymen, had caught the fat lad as he left the stadium. So now he sat there, waiting for the ambulance, and he started to cry because he was a long way from home and his wound was beginning to hurt.

Soon they took him away, speeding along the broad avenues of Turin, where the noxious tang of gas still hung in the air, the siren of his ambulance swelling the vile chorus of a dozen riot trucks which screeched around the city.

It was a small, insignificant incident. Yet somehow it encapsulated all the ugliness, the obscenity and the mindless cruelty of an appalling evening.

If the men who control England's football team had decided last night to pack their bags, apologise to their hosts and lead their players away from the championships their fans had defaced, then few could have condemned the decision.

Instead, we shall continue in the competition, preparing ourselves for the match with Italy on Sunday when that same stadium will be packed with the most hostile crowd any English team has ever faced.

The possibility of renewed and still more terrible violence is too obvious to require elaboration.

It is impossible adequately to convey the feelings of contempt and revulsion which we experienced in that imposing stadium last night.

The signs had been there long before the start of the match, when hordes of arrogant, drunken English youngsters had lurched through the city chanting their hatred of the 'wops'.

An English goal, the product of an admirable individual thrust from Ray Wilkins in the 26th minute, brought a flurry of Union Jacks from the fans at the popular end.

A retaliatory Belgian goal from Jan Ceulemans three minutes later provoked a riot.

The rabble threw aside their flags and surged about the terraces in search of Italian spectators. From the sanctuary of the grandstand, I watched a slight, grey haired man savagely kicked and beaten by a gang of six booted thugs.

I watched young Italians flung to the ground and viciously assaulted by our brave ambassadors. I saw two middle-aged ladies, dazed and hysterical, punched and spat upon by hooligans who were far beyond reason or control.

Then I watched the same warriors flee in terror from the swinging truncheons of the steel-helmeted riot police.

And suddenly we were all involved in the madness as, with a dull, ominous thump, canisters of tear gas were lobbed into the bedlam of the terrace and a soft breeze carried a nauseating wave of smoke across the pitch and stadium, temporarily blinding Ray Clemence and causing the game to be adjourned for four minutes.

The match went on, the most important England has played in more than a decade. You registered a few fleeting impressions; the ever-increasing stature of Wilkins, the tidy diligence of Kenny Samson.

But somehow it all seemed irrelevant and impossibly trivial, as if we were being asked to enjoy the deck games on the Titanic.

A group of furious Italians started to harangue the English journalists, the memory of our recent criticism of Juventus fresh in their minds. 'Who are the animals now?' they screamed. 'Stand up and look at the real animals.'

Nobody could offer them an argument.

The mayor of Turin, Signor Diego Novelli, bustled through to declare himself 'angry and alarmed,' promising to double the police presence for Sunday's match. We recognised the necessity and blushed at the shame.

Then we went off to talk with Ron Greenwood, and we loathed

even more the malevolent fools who had disfigured such an important occasion in the life of that decent man.

But we sensed that he, like the rest of us, realised that the relevance of the match had long since drifted away on a cloud of that gas which pricks the eyes and sets the stomach spinning.

Over the past few years, English football has lost a series of battles to the boots and fists of its most furious followers.

Last night it lost a war. And the evidence of defeat could be seen in the automatic weapons which jutted from speeding riot cars, in the terrified face of the Italian boy who was too frightened to scream as he sheltered with his father in a stadium doorway.

And it could be seen most vividly in the blood which oozed from a young man's back and spread a dark, ugly stain across the white shirt of England.

'Red Corner . . . Rabani Chulam . . . Afghanistan'

London Evening News, 21 July 1980

H E WAS A SLIM, vulnerable man, with stubble on his chin and a mop of black hair which bounced as he ducked beneath the ropes.

And he was apprehensive. His eyes darted everywhere, but only once did he glance at the thin khaki line of Soviet army officers who sat straight-backed and totally still on three sides of the ring.

Quickly he looked away, staring down at the blue canvas. And he ignored the applause which clattered around the great hall off the Prospekt Mira when they announced his presence: 'Red corner . . . Rabani Chulam . . . Afghanistan.'

A shriek of a klaxon, a curt wave from the portly East German referee, and out shuffled the first Afghan to enter Olympic competition since his country was overrun by the brother officers of those men who sat at the ringside.

You found yourself praying for him: 'Please be a fighter. Please be a puncher. Please do yourself justice.'

Emotive, irrational prayers . . . and they died within five seconds when poor Rabani threw his first, foppish jab. You knew, right then, that he couldn't fight; that his appearance among the Olympic featherweights was more of a gesture than a threat.

More importantly, his opponent knew it. He was a squat Korean, shaped like a pillar-box and just as difficult to hurt.

The soldiers looked on without interest as the Afghan was jolted and chastised by a stream of right hand punches. His nose started to trickle blood, his brain began to despair of the orders it was issuing to his legs, he received two compulsory counts from the referee.

And within two minutes and 13 seconds of the second round, his Olympic career was over. The referee had decided that Rabani Chulam from Afghanistan must be spared further punishment. And those with an eye for a parable could appreciate the irony.

The crowd offered him a sympathetic cheer, while the soldiers continued to stare straight ahead. Just another Olympic loser. Just another victim.

The tale of Rabani Chulam illustrates the strange ambivalence which is constantly present in this sadly beautiful city.

At one moment you are swept along with the sense of pride which the Muscovites feel in having organised these Games so superbly.

The guides, the interpreters, even fellow travellers on the Metro beam broadly when you congratulate them on the stunning magnificence of the opening ceremony.

They smile their thanks when you remark upon the scope and beauty of their stadia, even when they can't quite understand the nature of the compliment.

Henry Cooper, here as a radio commentator, shook his head as he walked into the massively opulent boxing hall. 'It's not Manor Place Baths, is it?' said our favourite Londoner. And they guessed that he was impressed.

You sense, too, that they love their sport, from the few moments of spontaneity permitted.

When the punches started flying among the featherweights yesterday, the advice came bellowing from the stalls: 'All the work . . . be first . . . jab and move . . . come on, come on, my son.' It didn't need translation. It really could have been the old Manor Place patrons offering legal aid.

We were even given the exquisite irony of the Olympic boxing tournament being introduced from the ring by an *American* army colonel.

As you may imagine, American accents are fairly thin on the ground in these parts. American soldiers are even thinner.

But there was Col. Dan Hull – in his capacity as President of the Olympic Boxing Committee and looking a little like the younger Eisenhower – captivating his audience with a charming little speech of welcome.

Lovely moments, and you float happily along with them until reality intrudes.

It may arrive in the form of an athlete jogging out a few training miles in a track suit which bears the emblem 'Czechoslovakia.'

It may be a boxer called Chulam, slumping into a corner with his chin sagging upon the letters 'Afg.'

Or it may be a line of young men, clad in khaki with brass buttons gleaming, staring unblinking into the middle distance, while other young men act out their dreams at the Moscow Olympics.

Leaving His Mark on Moscow

London Evening News, 25 July 1980

A FEW MOMENTS BEFORE noon yesterday 27 radio stations and two television channels regretfully informed the people of Nicaragua that Leonel Teller was a loser.

For the past four years, the tall, curly-haired athlete had been preparing his body for the exorbitant demands of the 400 metres hurdles.

He was eager and ready and, when he set off from the airport at Managua two weeks ago, he carried with him the dreams of 2½ million of his countrymen.

Those dreams dissolved in a handful of seconds on the track of the Lenin Stadium.

'Get to your marks,' said the starter. Leonel, out in lane eight, moved to his mark. 'Set,' barked the starter. Leonel didn't move. He hadn't heard the order.

Crack! the pistol blasted, and the young man looked up to see other men running past him. A trackside judge waved urgently at Leonel, pleading with him to start running. But, when he looked up, the other athletes were distant figures disappearing over distant hurdles.

He waved his arms briefly in the air, stared down at the track and shuffled off through the dressing room tunnel.

After four years of dedication and a journey of 10,000 miles, Leonel's Olympics were over.

In years to come, people will pass him on the streets of Managua and they'll nudge their friends and say: 'You know who that is? That is Leonel Teller.' And their friends will remember him as the famous man who left his mark on the Olympic Games by failing to leave his mark.

The Olympics, you see, loves its losers. And while we were enthralled and excited by some admirable track and field performances, we kept a warm corner of the memory for the ones who were beaten.

How, for instance, shall we ever forget Motlalepula Thabana, who is, on his day, the finest 10,000 metres runner in Lesotho. Yesterday was not his day.

The ruler of that tiny, land-locked state in Southern Africa – His Majesty King Moshoesho the Second – had sent off young Mot to take on the world. When he was lapped for the first time, long before halfway, we sensed that the world was winning.

He had travelled 6,000 miles to run like a man climbing a flight of stairs. His pace degenerated from merely slow to semi-static. He was lapped once more, then once again. But he remembered the instructions of good King Moshoesho, so he gritted his teeth and trudged on.

He finished, eventually, in 40min. 01.5sec., almost 12 minutes behind the winner of the heat. But the stadium cheered him home.

Motlalepula Thabana was an Olympian.

At least Mot was able to run off the track. Poor John Treacy was carried away from that same race on a stretcher. A pale, painfully slim man, he had pushed himself beyond endurance in his efforts to stay with the pace through 90 degrees of heat.

His legs finally betrayed him 200 yards from home, when he tottered and swayed and drifted into soothing oblivion.

I recalled watching him win the world cross country title on a storm-tossed Sunday afternoon in Limerick two years ago. His mother was beside herself that day. 'My John,' she said. 'He's done great things for our village. He's made it famous all over Waterford.'

I wondered what were that Irish mother's thoughts last night, as her son recovered from his agony in a Moscow hospital bed.

Then there was Thipsamay Chanthaphone. Now he was a special case. Leonel was sad, Mot outclassed and Treacy was tragic. But Thip was stupendously incompetent.

He came all the way from Laos to contest the 20 kilometre walk. 'Contest' is perhaps a misleading word, since he entered Lenin Stadium rather more than half an hour after the last man had waggled home.

Suddenly, this rigorously-organised programme was disrupted by the presence of a tiny Laotian in green shorts and a white vest, picking his way through 800 metres runners and asking directions for the finishing line.

After two wrong turnings, the slowest walker in Olympic history crossed the line without noticing, and he seemed about to undertake a lap of honour when he was led away by a bewildered official.

The smile never left his face. There, you thought, is a man who will never know failure. For, as he disappeared from view, waving to 80,000 instant fans, something about the set of his shoulders seemed to be saying: 'Now all I've got to do is cut 57 minutes off my time and who knows . . .'

There were no tears from Thip, for he was one of nature's survivors. It was different for Tessa Sanderson, who came to these Games with genuinely golden ambitions and froze dramatically with the occasion. 'I blew it,' she said. 'I just died. I can't believe this has happened to me. Now I'll have to start my life all over again.'

And she went back to the village to cry herself to sleep and wonder just how she managed to squander all those years of sweat and sacrifice.

Angela Littlewood also had tears in her eyes last night. In a final field of 14 shot-putters, she had taken 13th place. A loser if ever there was one. So why was she wearing the happiest smile this city has seen since it heard that Joseph Stalin had been summoned to his maker.

'I did what I came to do,' said the Charlton school-teacher. 'I reached the final. I broke the British record and I didn't make a fool of myself. I could have stayed out there for ever. I'm so pleased . . . honestly, I just couldn't tell you.'

Angela had every reason for her delight. She is a hefty girl who has worked desperately hard this past year to generate the power required for this explosive event.

But she has remained a woman, a female female. And your heart went out to her last night as she stood among the grotesque Amazons of Eastern Europe like a tot who has strayed into a sideshow.

'I was really overawed at first,' she said. 'God, those Bulgarians. Aren't they *awful*? But I remembered the telegram from my coach, John Hillier. "You're the best we've got," he said. "Remember that and just do your thing."'

So she ignored the cannonballs which the freaks were launching past the 20 metres mark. She ignored the awesome superiority of the gold medallist, Ilona Slupianek, the East German who was shamefully reinstated to amateur athletics after being suspended for drug-taking.

And with her final putt she pushed out the shot to 57ft. 6¼in., 1ft. 2¼in. beyond the British record.

A loser? Some would say so. But, if you had seen the joy in Angela Littlewood's face last night, you would have derided the description.

Angela and Mot, Leonel and Thip; human beings all. They have earned their places in that warm, happy corner of Olympic memory.

Death of a Meal Ticket

London Evening News, 3 October 1980

A S BEDLAM RAGED AROUND him, Muhammad Ali sat quietly in his corner, lost in a private world of pain. And Larry Holmes fought his way across the Las Vegas ring to be at his side.

The champion leaned over the broken fighter and whispered in his ear: 'I love you, man. I respect you. You're my brother. Any time you need me, I'll be there.'

But Ali never heard the murmured consolation. He never heard the announcer boom: 'Ali fails to answer the bell for the 11th round.' He never heard the self-pitying screams of his camp followers as they mourned the death of a meal ticket.

He simply sat and recruited the last dregs of his energy and pride, and perhaps he prayed that oblivion would descend and spare him the struggle.

They formed a cordon around him and helped him from the ring, the familiar entourage punching and kicking their way across the converted parking lot which had served as his professional graveyard.

And as he shuffled away, a blue-haired matron in a pink jump suit climbed upon her 500-dollar seat and screamed: 'You quit, Ali! Ya fink, you quit.'

He deserved better than that. For two decades he has exerted the kind of fascination which no other athlete ever possessed. We have loved him for his extraordinary virtues and willingly overlooked his faults. He is a part of all our pasts.

And he should not have said farewell in a casino parking lot, exposing his broken talent to the pathetic snipers of a tawdry town.

Yet he had carried so many along with him. Wilfully rejecting form and logic, some of us had come to believe that the old illusionist could disappear for two years, shed 33lbs and – four months from his 39th birthday – engage the most lethal heavyweight in the world with genuine hope of success.

He had enlisted our emotions, the way he has always done. And, as we gathered at the ringside beneath the luminous monstrosity called Caesar's Palace, we gazed around at the hookers and high-rollers, the sober-suited Moslems and the hard-eyed men in brown shirts with revolvers slapping on hips, and we forced ourselves to believe that another miracle was at hand.

Ali looked so young, so fit as they ushered him into action; skipping past the stars, past Gregory Peck and Cary Grant, past the rotund Sinatra, past the sad, slumberous figure of Joe Louis who sat in a wheelchair and contemplated the only heavyweight whose name history will whisper in the same breath as his own.

Then we saw Holmes; serious, intent and flatly rejecting Ali's clumsy attempts to overpower his senses, the way he had overpowered Liston and Foreman and so many, many others.

And we realised that the old man had nothing to offer but an illusion. The conjurer had lost his sleight of hand and the act was about to fall apart.

Behind Ali's corner the garish casinos of the Las Vegas Strip peered over the heads of the paupers in the distant 50-dollar seats.

Behind Holmes, we could see the mountains rising above the purple darkness of the Nevada Desert. Illusion against reality. The plastic against the permanent. Ali against Holmes.

All the clowning and the faking, the tricks stolen from memory's scrapbook, could not conceal the fact that Ali was taking a slow, inevitable and utterly comprehensive beating.

'There was no happiness for me in that,' said Holmes later. 'No happiness in fighting a friend, a brother. But some people forced me into this fight. They made me do what I didn't want to do.'

But he did it, and he did it with that chilling air of savage detachment which this sport demands from its most accomplished practitioners.

They paid Ali $8 million to take his hiding. It was futile compensation for the vicious hooks and the stiff, sickening jabs which Holmes threw, virtually without reprisal.

After only three rounds, the years started to crowd in on Ali. 'Make him eat jabs, champ,' bawled Richie Giachetti in the Holmes corner. 'Don't be hit, don't be hit!' yelled Bundini Brown from Ali's side of the ring. Holmes responded to the advice. Ali could not achieve even token compliance.

Suddenly, he began to look really old. The black dye in his hair, which had served to disguise the advancing years, slowly trickled away as the corner splashed on water and the grey temples were exposed.

Once or twice, he started to dance. It was no more than a gesture to an age long departed. The beating continued, and occasionally we found ourselves turning away as Ali grunted out the agony of his punishment.

It was the faithful Dundee who ended it. At the end of the ninth round the referee had been persuaded to give Ali one more. After that round Dundee had seen enough. There was an angry scuffle in the corner and Angelo could be heard shouting: 'Stop it. For Christ's sake, that's enough.'

Bundini attempted to pull Dundee away, but Angelo stuck bravely to his stand. Ali played no part in the argument. He simply sat and accepted both his fate and his pain.

Some of his followers, for perhaps eight million reasons, could not accept the pitifully obvious. 'He was two years out of the ring and it took Holmes ten rounds to beat him,' yelled one of the entourage as Ali was led away. 'Next time, we'll take the bastard.'

By then, Ali had disappeared into the frantic crowd. He was halfway to the dressing room when a rocket screamed into the night sky, exploded above Caesar's Palace and sprayed a shower of techni-coloured sparks upon the Strip before spending itself and spluttering to the ground.

'Fighters,' said Larry Holmes, 'they all come . . . and they all go.' The greatest of them all went last night in Las Vegas.

Back to the Marshes

London Evening News, 31 October 1980

THE MANAGER LOOKED A little like Clough, a sturdy, intense figure in early middle age, with a track suit draped around his shoulders and a cap rammed firmly upon his head.

And when the penalty was awarded, in the last few seconds of the match, his team turned to their tutor for instruction.

'Stevie!' he yelled. 'Stevie takes the pens. Go on, me son!'

So up strode Stevie; blond, muddy and ten years old. He wiped the toe of his right boot down the back of his left sock, screwed up his face, took an earnest run . . . and drove the kick a yard above the bar.

The substitute was still chasing the ball across the neighbouring pitch when the whistle screeched an end to the match and Stevie's team had lost 2–1.

Stevie stood and stared at the ground for a long time, then the shoulders of his green and yellow jersey began to jerk and the tears started to trickle down the muddy face.

The manager was with him in an instant, wrapping an arm around the tearful kid.

'Ne'mind, Steve,' he said. '*Everyone* misses penalties. No disgrace, son. You wait till next week. You'll get a hat-trick next week. You wait.'

Stevie rubbed his eyes with his sleeve, smiled through the tears and ran off to join his friends, dreaming about next week when he would be a hero.

It was good to return to the cradle for one brisk October morning; good to stroll across the Hackney Marshes as a thin autumn sun peeped around the high-rise blocks and flooded a hundred seething pitches with warmth and colour.

Up in Solihull, the elders who run the professional game were clustered around its sick-bed, offering patent medicines and brightly belated ideas.

But the patient was old and tired, riddled with cynicism and disillusion. The days of glory were distant memories and survival was the overriding ambition.

It was different on the Marshes. There the game was young and vigorous and untainted; it was the game we fell in love with all those years ago.

There were centre-forwards who battled and sweated and scored; inside-forwards, marvellous little confections of flicks and touches. And wingers who darted and dribbled. You remember *wingers*? You must remember *dribbling*?

There were memorable half-time conferences held at pitch-side. 'Dave, you'd better come off this half, we're bringing Frankie on.' 'But it's not my turn! I came off last week!' 'Did you? Right. Alan, sorry son, but someone's got to come off for Frankie.'

Sometimes there were tears as when poor Stevie squandered his penalty. But more often there were triumphs, minor eruptions on distant pitches with the keeper sprawling in the mud and ecstatic forwards bounding away, quivering with the sheer excitement of it all.

And nobody kicked, nobody cheated, nobody demanded a petulant transfer. You had forgotten what a wonderful game it could be.

Len Spiller hadn't forgotten. A middle-aged man who lives in Wanstead and manages a dress shop in the City, he turns up every Saturday and Sunday to referee for the kids.

Although he does not know it, he is more important to the game than any of the people who gathered at the Solihull summit.

'Smashing game today,' he said as he walked off the pitch through a crowd of small boys who had run across to thank him. 'All ten years old they were, and one or two could play a bit. Lovely to see kids doing the right things naturally – and listening when you try to give them a bit of advice.

'Sometimes they get a bit naughty. They want to argue with you because they've seen it on telly or they've listened to people on the line. But I say to them: "Behave yourself, son. Don't spoil it," and they're as good as gold.

'I don't have too much time for the professional game these days. How can you expect players to behave properly when you're offering them the earth just to win a football match? Winning's the only thing that matters. I think it's very sad.

'Yet I'm not too worried about the game's future. I see so many kids who want to play it properly. They want to enjoy it and they're going to resent people who try to take the enjoyment away from them. It might take a long time, but I reckon their attitude will win in the end.'

His optimism finds a powerful ally in the finest player the Marshes ever produced.

Tommy Harmer served as the patron saint of all those tiny inside forwards who carried the conviction that if they tried hard enough they could get the ball to say a few words.

All his formative football was played upon the Marshes, before Spurs claimed his talents. And while he is the most reticent of men, you sense that he sees the salvation of the game in the attitudes which are bred in that corner of Hackney.

'I watch the pro game sometimes and I find myself looking for wingers like Cliffy Jones or Terry Medwin,' says Tommy. 'To be honest, you don't really see them around, do you?

'I can't really get on with that lark where you stick two players at the front and tell all the rest they're defenders, you know what I mean?

'And yet I seem to meet more people than ever who are mad about the game. Especially the kids. They're potty about it. I know gates are falling and all that, yet a lot of people really seem to love the game. And if they're that fond of it, they'll get round to playing it the right way.

'A lot of people tell you football's dead, but you look at the kids and you know it can't be. It'll come back. If we get enough good kids and we leave them alone and give them the chance to enjoy themselves, it'll come back all right. I mean, it's a smashing game, isn't it?'

You gazed across the Marshes and you saw just what he meant. A hundred matches in progress. Substitutes and fans and dads and brothers on every touchline. More than three thousand people involved, ordinary people who need neither seminar nor summit meeting to enjoy the appeal of the finest of all ball games.

Football's problems are depressingly formidable, yet even in its darkest days it can call upon a vast degree of genuine affection from the people who really matter, and it is that affection which eventually will secure its future.

I only wish we could be here to share that future with you.

1981

A year which yielded a crop of eccentrics, from the Raging Bull of New York to the Cobbolds of Ipswich to the glorious joggers of London to Sir Geoffrey of Yorkshire.

Then, of course, there was the London Marathon. I was sceptical at first, but I came to realise that it was the best idea that British sport has ever had.

The Bull from the Bronx

Evening Standard, 22 January 1981

THE CHAMP MADE A quiet entry, brushing the Second Avenue snow flakes from the sleeves of his sober blue coat and glancing around to see if anyone would recognise him.

He needn't have worried, and he knew it. The restaurant came to a halt, the way restaurants do in all the B-pictures, and a dozen tables squealed a greeting. 'Champ . . . why, hello, champ.' Much embracing and back-slapping. A few kisses and a couple of autographs and the hero doing his best to blush beneath the Florida tan.

He enjoyed it immensely. 'How about that?' he said. 'Champ. I lost the title in 1951 and I won it back 30 years later. Ain't that something?' And you agreed, because the shoulders are still ominously broad and the scar tissue around the eyes insisted that the man had seen some strenuous action. On the whole, people tend to agree with Jake La Motta.

Next month the British public will be able to see Raging Bull, the film of his extraordinary life. It is the cinematic equivalent of a knee in the groin, a pitiless film, awash with explicit brutality and dialogue which rarely extends itself beyond four letters.

The original British distributors took fright, weighing discretion against realism and cancelling the London premiere. But the film has now been picked up by Lord Grade's Classic chain.

La Motta frowned when he heard the news of the controversy. 'They did what?' he said. 'They thought it was too violent?' He chewed at a plump cigar and considered the point. 'The Second World War was pretty violent. Korea was violent. Vietnam. Yeah, that was kinda violent too. Movies didn't ignore them, did they? No, that picture is just the way things were in the forties. It's the truth. I mean, I'm the guy who knows. It was my life.'

'My life.' It is difficult to accept that the man across the restaurant table could lay claim to that kind of history. Born on New

York's Lower East Side, raised in the Bronx . . . and then the fun began.

A conviction for attempted burglary, five marriages, 106 professional fights, world middleweight champion, a morals conviction involving a 14-year-old prostitute at his Miami night club, prison, poverty, a brief career as a stand-up comedian and now success.

Jake La Motta is established as a full-time shop-soiled folk hero of outrageous charm. After 58 years, life has never been 'so kind.'

He tells his tale in that fascinating slurry of cement-mixer Bronx and every so often he reaches across the table and grabs your arm: 'You listenin to me? You makin notes? That's good, I like that.'

It began, as many of his tales begin, in P. J. Clarke's Third Avenue bar which was Jake's home from home. 'Suddenly, I get a phone call from this beautiful guy name of Robert de Niro. Wants to make a movie about me. Would you believe it?

'The guy turns out to be cuckoo, but cuckoo like a genius, not cuckoo period. He wants to learn how to fight, so I teach him. Never saw a guy work like him. For a whole year he trains. "Don't hold back" I tell him. You know what happens? In a year I get four black eyes, a fractured rib, my upper set for which I paid four grand gets broken and I damage my nose, which is a problem because I don't breathe so good. He trained like he was training for the championship.

'And all the time he studies me. Always watching, watching. Every word I say to him goes on tape. Every action he copies. At the end of it, he's more like Jake La Motta than I am. I don't know if he should make a movie or go fight at the Garden. Incredible man.

'Then I see the performance. Well, that was something. Tell him how it was when I saw the movie, Jake.'

Jake Junior, a 30-year-old former teacher, has been drinking in every word. He rarely leaves his father's side these days, prompting when old Jake searches for a phrase, explaining the more arcane passages of Jake's stories.

'You were in a state of shock when you saw the picture, Pop,' he says.

'That's it,' says old Jake. 'State of shock. I went very quiet. I was reliving my whole life. I'm thinking, Was I really that kind of guy? And I was. It was so accurate. As for De Niro's performance, forget about it. Give him the Oscar right now. Call off the contest. I never saw acting like it.' At that moment a bouncy little man with a face like an un-made bed bustles up to the table: 'Didn't you used to be

Jake La Motta?' he says, and Jake grabs his hand.

'I want you to meet my friend,' he says. 'Meet Rocky Graziano. We was at reform school together.' Then he drifts into the stand-up comic routine.

'Rocky and me, we had ethics. When we was kids, we'd only steal things beginning with the letter A – A truck, A car, know what I mean? And I tell people we invented rock and roll. I'd hit 'em with a rock and Graziano would roll 'em.'

Rocky laughs like a man who has heard it a thousand times before. Jake watches him move across the room. 'Some coincidence, eh?' he says. 'We was raised a block apart, we both won the middle-weight title and we both had a movie made of our lives. They got Paul Newman for Graziano. Somebody Up There Likes Me. You ever see it? It was pretty good. Only difference between me and Rocky, he's had one wife, I've had five. Only difference.'

He grossed more than 2,000,000 dollars during his career, and none of it stuck to his fingers. 'Kids today,' he says, 'they have maybe ten, fifteen fights and they're in for the title. With one fight they can make maybe four times as much as I made in my whole career. Is that crazy?

'But I was champ when the middleweights was tops. The best time in the history of boxing and I was in the best division.'

Jake Junior smiles with pride. 'Did you ever see him act?'

Old Jake picks up the cue. 'To be truthful, I was pretty good,' he says. 'Did two years at drama school, went on at Barbizon Plaza with a little show called An Evening With Jake La Motta.

'I did scenes from Mice and Men, Streetcar, Requiem for a Heavyweight. That kind of thing. I had to learn ten thousand words for the part, and me with no education. And I was broke at the time. I lived in an apartment so small, I used the bathmat as wall to wall carpeting.'

'Please, pop, be serious,' pleads Jake Junior. 'Do our London friend a little bit from Shakespeare. Like, just a minute or two.'

Jake obliges with a speech from Julius Caesar. It isn't Gielgud, but at least he's word perfect.

Then I ask for the On The Waterfront soliloquy. He is flattered.

'You'd really like that? I do it pretty good.'

He insists on introducing it. 'Brando and Steiger are in the back of this cab and, like, they're brothers and Steiger has persuaded Brando to throw this fight when he should have been in line for a title shot. Funny, it sounds kinda familiar.

'Listen, you can be Charley.' And he thrusts his face a foot away from mine and thumps the table. And once again the restaurant comes to a halt.

'Why d'ya do it Charley? You was my brother. You shoulda took care of me a l'il bit. You said: "Kid, this ain't your night." I coulda took Wilson apart, but what happens? He gets a title shot outdoors in the ballpark, and I get a one way ticket to Palookaville. I coulda binna contenda . . . instead of a bum.'

For a few moments, there is silence. It was genuinely moving, the familiar lines delivered by a man who might well have written them. Then there is applause and La Motta beams and bows.

Graziano is pulling on a coat and he waves across the restaurant. Jake returns the wave: 'See ya around, Rock,' he calls. Then, after a pause: 'Hey Rock! Somebody up there likes me too.'

Avoiding the Joggers

Evening Standard, 24 March 1981

I T IS APPROPRIATE THAT the London Marathon should be starting in Greenwich Park, since it was there that my misgivings about the fun-running phenomenon first took shape.

An ample-waisted, Adidas-shod man of early middle-age padded past the bandstand at a painful pace. Upon that puce and sweating face there was not only agony but the stubborn conviction that what he was doing was both Right and Good. And upon his scarlet tee-shirt was the simple motto: 'I jog.'

At first I thought it was his name, as in 'I, Claudius' or 'Me, Tarzan'. Wrong. It was merely his statement of faith: 'I Jog, therefore I Am'.

Had his tee-shirt been larger, then surely the message would have been amplified: 'I am not as other men. I am not a slothful, sedentary, smoking, swilling, sluggard. I Jog . . . and, what's more to the point, You Don't.'

I have nothing against them, of course. And certainly nothing against the idea that moderate exercise is better for you than excessive idleness. But there are ominous signs that joggers are destined to replaced golfers as saboteurs of saloon bar conversation.

They are easily spotted, since they are the fellows drinking halves of shandy and walking, almost invariably, with a limp. 'Ran a swift "10" this morning. Quite nippy, too, considering the dodgy ankle. And you?'

'Only managed eight. Same old trouble. Bloody hamstring.'

There is an air of invulnerable self-righteousness about them. Scorn no longer riles them as once it did. For jogging is chic, and the chic have inherited the earth.

They have picked up some powerful allies along the way. For instance, it is now impossible to lie in bed on the Sabbath morning and read the sports pages of the Sunday Times. Guilt, you see. Sunday isn't Sunday without a few fanatical warnings that lying in bed is a major cause of tired blood and tooth decay. Get out and jog, they scream. It's Good For You!

Last Sunday was even worse, since The Observer alternative featured Chris Brasher's advice to the London Marathon Runners. He made it sound like a 10,000-mile service: 'Vaseline all moving parts: toes, ball of foot, heel, groin and where your arm meets your back.'

If all 7500 competitors decide to take Brasher's advice, the start of the marathon will resemble an oil-slick.

If the weather is cold, Brasher himself will be found in a long-sleeved polypropylene vest and long johns, shorts, a tee-shirt, an extra top, old gloves and a hat. I should check that Worzel Gummidge has not submitted a late entry before you offer the race director a cheer.

In fairness to Brasher – who is a marvellous enthusiast as well as a skilled entrepreneur – his marathon has attracted what one might call the super-joggers.

The field may be short of true class, but it is largely composed of people who do not feel the need to reach for oxygen at the very thought of running 26 miles.

No, the ones I worry about are the occasional joggers, the people who have noted the trend and suspect that it might do them some good. Particularly, I worry about the politicians.

Does Roy Jenkins really believe that European haute cuisine can be so easily eroded by an occasional scamper around Belgravia? And Roy Hattersley: what is he trying to prove by his immoderate pounding of fashionable pavements? Then there is Jimmy Carter. Remember Jimmy Carter?

The significant thing they have in common is that none, for the moment, holds a position of power, whereas the people in the top jobs are unlikely to be found rubbing Vaseline into all the moving parts.

And some are simply, well, eccentric; converging upon those pleasant parks where children play and dogs may safely defecate and shattering the serenity with their grunting, gasping search for fitness.

You may judge which category best suits Mr Geoffrey Cannon, a self-styled 'Fun Runner' who delivered a few thoughts to the latest issue of the magazine Running.

He describes a recent excursion with Russell, his 'regular running companion.'

'We found that the best way with dogs is to face them as they charge up, and snarl and bark and shout at them very loudly.

'This disconcerts them. Sometimes, like this morning, the owner takes the counter-attack personally: The next move, I suppose, is to bite the owner's leg.'

As you line the route on Sunday, keep an eye out for Mr Cannon: an amiable fellow, they say, with a gruff bark and extremely sharp teeth. And another thing, leave your dog at home.

'Give Us a Bloody Cheer'

Evening Standard, 30 March 1981

THE CANNON BOOMED across Greenwich at nine o'clock, and five minutes later the first of 6,700 runners arrived at the top of our road. We don't get too many marathons passing by on Sunday mornings, and our reactions were uncertain. To the leaders, as they bounced past, grim and purposeful, we offered fatuous formal nods. The second-ranked athletes seemed slightly discouraged to be met by a smattering of handclaps and the sight of a small boy being violently sick with suppressed excitement.

Then came the first of the scrubbers, the magical mystery tourists, the fellows who were challenging nobody but themselves. And one of them turned to the crowd.

'Give us a cheer,' he pleaded. 'For God's sake give us a bloody cheer.'

And on a suburban Sunday morning, as soft drizzle leaked from a grey and sulking sky we stood three-deep by the roadside and cheered them to an echo, envying their courage and applauding their marvellous ambition.

We cheered the extroverts, the ones who took extravagant bows and waved at passing helicopters, just in case they should contain a camera.

We cheered the freaks, the man with the umbrella hat and the lovely, loony waiter with his bottle and tray. We cheered that extraordinary eccentric Jimmy Saville and cursed ourselves for ever having winced at his television programmes. A man who lightly trots through marathons is a man to respect.

We cheered the stunning girl in the tee-shirt which said simply: 'Just call me Rosie.' Hello, Rosie. We cheered the most famous initials in sport, J.P.R., trundling forward at prop-forward pace, and the plodder who felt frisky enough to chat up one of the more desirable lady competitors and the young man who said to his toiling colleague: 'Wonder if my Mum's got the kettle on?'

We cheered the poor bloody infantry, thousands strong, who stared at the 25 miles which lay ahead and knew that survival would represent success.

And our cheers swelled and swirled around the streets of the capital as the queen of cities roared a welcome to its marathon.

The athletes not only relished those cheers, they came almost to depend upon them. You could sense it at the six-mile mark, as the field started to stretch out and rebellious legs began to buckle under the pace.

'Come on, love,' called an elderly lady. 'Not far to go now' and the sweat-suited dreamer beamed his thanks for the friendly lie, drew back his head and recovered his faltering stride.

Most of all, you could sense it in the later stages, when the stragglers were running into great walls of pain and the crowds screamed them through, hurling them forward with a hurricane of sound.

The BBC television coverage, a masterpiece of sports broadcasting, captured the agony and the ecstasy of the closing stages: rubber-legged runners lurching towards the end of their suffering, Joyce Smith, the leading lady, looking as if she'd been out walking the dog. And Chris Brasher, the man who started it all, padding home with a grin 26 miles wide.

But you needed to be out on the streets, tasting the atmosphere and relishing the magnificent spirit of the day, to realise that the first London Marathon is likely to prove the most impressive, most endearing and easily the most satisfying sports event of the year.

A few days ago, this column poked a little fun at the new breed of joggers, with their puritanical zeal, their self-righteous air and their eternally damaged hamstrings.

Well, yesterday the super-joggers came out on the streets of London to reveal the results of all that preparation, and nobody was going to belittle their efforts.

Instead, by their hundreds of thousands, Londoners discovered the joy, the pain and the overwhelming drama of the finest foot-race man has devised.

On a damp and dismal Sunday morning, the London Marathon was born. The capital wishes it many, many happy returns.

The Cobbolds of Ipswich

Evening Standard, 10 April 1981

'**O**H DEAR!' SAYS Mr John. 'I rather fear I've done it again.' And the passing waitress puts down her tray and pauses to listen. He's always got a story, has Mr John.

'Been greeting the Germans at the hotel,' he says. 'Did it pretty well, too. "Welcome-to-our-town. How-is-your-delightful-city? Haven't-seen-Cologne-since-'46. 'Spect-it's-changed-a-bit, eh?" You know the sort of thing.

'Buggers just stared at me like I was loony. Turned out they weren't Germans at all. Group of Swedes who just happened to be staying there. Oh well . . .'

A moment later there is an explosion of giggles from the kitchen: 'Here, you'll never guess what Mr John's done now.'

He stares into his plate of smoked salmon. 'Sometimes,' he says, 'I think people don't take me altogether seriously.'

A charming man is John Cobbold, and much of his charm springs from the fact that he takes nothing in this world at all seriously.

He is an Old Etonian, a member of the East Anglian brewing family and, by one of those strokes of good fortune which the game scarcely seems to deserve, the vice-chairman of Ipswich Town Football Club.

He used to be chairman before handing the job to his brother, Patrick, a few years ago. Between them they run the happiest, most outrageous and, currently, the most successful football club in the land.

'Well, we sort of run it,' says John. 'I mean, Bobby Robson does a little bit, being the manager and all that. And the players, yes, they come in handy. But we're the chaps who actually take the decisions. Frightful pressure.'

He adopts his 'decisive' air. The effect is wholly unconvincing. 'Do you know,' he says, 'when things are going well, we have to attend two board meetings a year!'

And when things are going less well? 'Oh, we don't have any at all. No point. Only makes us miserable.'

The Cobbolds are the sort of directors that managers dream about. Completely devoid of social or financial ambition, they simply appoint the manager and let him get on with it.

'Leaves us free for important things,' says John. 'Like having parties. That's why we love playing in Europe. Gives us the excuse to have super parties all over the place. The players love it too. They pop along and they don't feel they have to talk about football.'

The players, in fact, have a genuine affection for the Cobbolds. 'We're all great chums,' says John. 'That probably sounds terribly patronising, but it's true. I read the other day that Brian Clough said he'd fine any of his players £25 if he ever caught them talking to directors. Absolutely ridiculous. Our chaps would be broke in a week if we had that system.

'Good God, we even get on rather well with you fellows. Journalists. They're always saying to me: "We love coming here, John, and that's enough tonic, thank you." There's one reporter, a great chum, whose doctor actually banned him from the ground. "You can do what you like," he told him, "but you can't go to Ipswich. Bad for the liver." That's absolutely true.'

At that point, brother Patrick enters the restaurant: A tall, patrician figure in comfortable tweeds. 'Hello Johnny,' he says. 'Been eloquent, have you?'

''Fraid I dropped a clanger this morning,' says John. 'Mixed the Germans up with a load of bloody Swedes.'

'Easily done,' says Patrick, attacking the wine.

The brothers swap a stream of anecdotes about each other, laughing uproariously at every eccentric punch-line, each enjoying the other's company. 'Tell the one about mother,' pleads John. 'Oh, very well,' says Patrick.

'Wembley Cup Final, 1978. Us and the Arsenal. Dear old Ted Croker, secretary of the FA, comes up to mother and says: "Lady Blanche. Would you like me to introduce you to the Prime Minister?"

'Mother not terribly impressed. "Actually," she says, "I'd rather have a gin and tonic." Impeccable priorities, you see.'

The Cobbolds distinguished themselves at that final by accepting just one ticket each, unlike those football directors who leap at the opportunity to take along family, friends and bank managers.

'Only needed one,' says John. 'To get me in, you know. My sister rang and asked if I could get her one. 'Fraid I was frightfully pompous. "My dear," I said, "when you want to go to the cinema, do you ring up Lord Rank?"'

'But that was a wonderful weekend. Do you know, we had a police escort all the way home to Ipswich after the match. Tell him what happened when we got to Chelmsford, Patrick.'

'Well,' says Patrick. 'I was feeling a bit thirsty and so was John. We were approaching the Army and Navy pub where I happen to know the landlord. So I bent the arm, the police outrider got the message and in we all went: players, directors, FA Cup, the lot.

'It suddenly struck me. I've been escorted *out* of pubs by the police a time or two. But never *into* one.'

'What made that final so wonderful was that we were playing the Arsenal,' says John. 'Splendid club. It was their late chairman who gave our father the idea of getting involved with Ipswich Town. Very grateful to them for that.

'And they have such style. I remember being with them in Austria for a match. Had a hectic few days, then we waved goodbye to the Austrians and took off in our charter plane.

'Soon as we were airborne, the Arsenal chairman, old Dennis Hill-Wood, sends for a couple of bottles of champagne.

'"Terribly sorry, sir," says the steward. "Afraid we've left the champagne on the runway." "Then we'd better go back and get it," says dear old Dennis. And we did! I was awfully impressed.'

As you will have gathered, they enjoy their involvement with football. 'You meet a lot of nice people. You make good friends,' says Patrick.

'Of course, it's particularly pleasant when you're successful, as our club has been for the past few years. But you keep it in perspective. Winning is important, but it isn't vital.'

The Rejection of Geoffrey Boycott

Evening Standard, 24 September 1981

L ONG, LONG AGO, IN those distant days when Yorkshire could field a respectable cricket team, Brian Close took aside his young opening batsman and offered a few words of instruction.

Close, at the time, was captain of Yorkshire and as such his instructions carried the force of commandments. The young batsman, eyes wide behind rimless spectacles, devoured the advice which went something like this:

'What I want you to do, young Geoffrey, is to get out to that wicket and stay there. Stay there all day if you can. Be as slow as you like. If we've got 300 on the board by the close, it'll give Trueman and Illingworth something to bowl at. Don't forget, we're relying on you, young Geoffrey.'

The youngster carried out his orders to the letter. He would spend hours, days at the crease, coming in only to nibble at lunch or toy with afternoon tea. And the county acclaimed his concentration, his dedication, his devotion to the cause.

Championship followed championship. Close took his place in the pantheon of Yorkshire skippers and Geoffrey Boycott became a folk hero, simply by obeying the seductive command of his captain: 'Play for yourself. Let the other ten play for the team.'

Yorkshire created Geoffrey Boycott. The county encouraged him, sustained him and defended him in the course of an extraordinary cricket career. And this week, after taking a poll among its players, Yorkshire destroyed him.

Fifteen Yorkshire cricketers announced that they would, in no circumstances, like to see Boycott reappointed as County Captain. And ten of those cricketers declared that they would be highly delighted if he never played for Yorkshire again.

In a sport which customarily conceals criticism with platitudes, a sport in which plain speaking is usually regarded as the mark of the barbarian, no condemnation has ever been more public, more wounding or more conclusive than that which the Yorkshire players hurled at Geoffrey Boycott this week.

They have told the man whose run-making achievements are almost unparalleled in the history of his sport, the man who is still regarded as England's principal batsman and the man who, for several years past, has been operating as the unofficial patron saint of Yorkshire, that they would be far better off without him.

It is the kind of insult which might have sent a normal man to seek, in John Arlott's phrase, 'the solace of a hotel bedroom and six-chamber revolver.'

And yet, by common consent, Boycott is not a normal man. 'Eccentric' is the word most often applied. A man wholly and obsessively absorbed in his own welfare and his own talent.

Over the past two decades there have been repeated attempts to portray him as a stereotype, don't-give-a-damn professional Yorkshireman in the manner of Fred Trueman and Harvey Smith. The attempts have been thoroughly unconvincing. Boycott is too remote, too austere to settle obligingly into a plastic mould.

He carries, one suspects, the conventional Yorkshire chip on his shoulder. He believes, quite plainly, in Establishment conspiracies designed to deprive him of his rights, be it the smooth, Southern MCC Establishment, who denied him the captaincy of his country, or the well-born, well-heeled Yorkshire Establishment who stripped him of the leadership of his county.

But whereas Trueman, in similar circumstances, might have cursed and thundered and Smith might have raised two belligerent fingers to all and sundry, Boycott has usually managed to hold his frustration in check; to seethe and, some would say, to sulk.

The public rejection by his fellow-professionals and the certain knowledge that, for all his ability, precious few counties will be seeking his services, must have struck him a savage blow.

Yet much of the pain will be rooted in the fact that once again the Establishment have beaten him. Desperate to be rid of him, terrified at the inevitable reaction of a public which still worships him, Yorkshire simply handed the matter over to their players.

They did it in the obsequious fashion of men well-practised at slipping the stiletto into the ribcage: 'Whilst the Committee is loath to involve playing members of the club staff, they feel that the views of the contracted players . . . should be known.'

And they achieved the result they were seeking; their hands

unstained, their consciences unsullied.

There is good reason to believe that Boycott views those men with something like hatred, certainly with an emotion which goes far beyond the normal bounds of sporting controversy.

They, after all, were the people who took away his captaincy just three days after the death of his mother. Boycott was very close to his mother. They lived together in the village of Fitzwilliam in a tiny terraced house which belied his affluence.

She was fiercely proud of her son's success, proud of the honour he had brought to the family and to the whole of the local community. He returned that pride, indeed he continues to demonstrate his pride in the village in a tangible way and is frequently to be found in City boardrooms, drumming up investment for the Fitzwilliam area and seeking employment opportunities to help offset the effects of recession.

Yorkshire's timing of the captaincy decision was seen both as an insult to his family and to his birthplace and will never be forgiven. Yet, while the timing was crass, Boycott's own shortcomings made that decision almost inevitable.

Of course, the faintly preposterous Yorkshire Reform Group, a band of Boycott loyalists, continued to tilt at windmills. 'Pressure was put on those players to submit,' said Mr Peter Briggs, one of the Group's leaders. 'Geoffrey Boycott is a giant playing among pygmies.'

But the facts are heavily against him. Yorkshire cricket is in a decline which offers no obvious signs of recovery. And Boycott's attitudes have played their full part in accelerating that decline.

His captaincy was a virtually unqualified disaster. Experienced players were discarded, youth failed to deliver its promise and all the time there existed the barely-spoken conviction among the team that Geoffrey was playing only for Geoffrey.

Boycott's inability to communicate with his colleagues only exacerbated the situation. Cricketers are gregarious people, yet Geoffrey preferred the company of epic novels, working remorselessly through them both on England tours and on the county circuit.

He was also rarely seen at the bar, the cricketers' parliament. 'A bit of a careful fellow, our Geoffrey,' a fellow-tourist told me. 'Sometimes you'd see him with a small Guinness, but usually he avoided the riotous rounds.

'The only time I can remember him going out of his way to buy drinks was in the West Indies when Botham looked like being sacked from the England captaincy.'

The term 'selfish' was frequently applied, yet it was the kind of selfishness which did not discriminate against colleagues; rather, it failed to recognise their existence.

Trevor Bailey, one of the game's most perceptive observers, explains it very carefully: 'I don't wish to be detrimental to Boycott, but the fact is that he doesn't always give a thought to the others on his side,' he said.

'You see it so often when he's batting. He plays the ball and works out perfectly logically that he can get in at the other end. What doesn't always occur to him is that his partner might not share that view. The result is that he's run out an awful lot of batsmen over the years.

'Unlike, say, Denis Compton, whose running was a disaster, Boycott doesn't run himself out. He's a very good judge of his own run. I've often thought that Boycott running with Boycott would never ever be run out. But, unfortunately, the game doesn't work that way.'

Bailey offered his view without malice, yet in that view you could almost detect the epitaph for a professional cricket career.

As long as records are published Boycott will be revered as one of the genuinely great players of his generation. But reputations do not rest solely on statistics. When cricketers gather together and pints are produced and stories are told, they do not discuss figures and averages.

They speak of the great ones and how they played, and how much pleasure they gave, and how they inspired lesser men to reach out beyond the bounds of their talent. These are the criteria by which they arrive at their verdicts.

The cricketers of Yorkshire applied those criteria to Geoffrey Boycott this week. And history will record that they reached a devastating verdict.

1982

And in the blue corner . . . Steve Ovett. The press plundered the comic books to find appropriate labels. Thus Coe was Wilson of the Wizard while Ovett, his eternal rival, was Alf Tupper, the Tough of the Track. Simplistic, of course, since they had more in common than either would admit. But they obeyed their popular images; Wilson granting regular interviews and Tupper maintaining media silence.

This was one of Ovett's rare excursions into print, an interview conducted in conditions of the deepest secrecy in an Italian restaurant on the Sidcup by-pass. As Ovett walked in, a waiter thought he recognised a famous face. 'Welcome to our restaurant, Mr Coe,' he said. Ovett giggled. 'Don't you dare write that,' he warned me. And I didn't. Until now.

Ovett – Going Through Hell

Evening Standard, 11 February 1982

A FEW DAYS AGO, an old gentleman was sweeping pebbles from the Brighton promenade when he saw a tall, track-suited figure striding towards the pier. The old fellow paused, leaned on his broom and shouted: 'Steve! For God's sake take care of that leg.'

And the man in the tracksuit turned and smiled and slowed down to a jogger's pace. 'The leg's all right,' he said. 'It's the rest of me that's cracking up.'

Steve Ovett chuckled as he told the story. 'The fellow thought I was kidding,' he said. 'If only he'd known. I think he could have beaten me to the pier.'

Yet the chuckle was encouraging. Ovett had just put his damaged leg to the test for the first time. A severe muscle injury, sustained when he crashed into some railings, had erased his winter training programme. A complicated operation had sentenced him to months of idleness.

But now he had taken the first steps which hopefully will lead him to three mid-summer meetings with Sebastian Coe, to the European championships in Athens and the Commonwealth Games in Brisbane, perhaps even to new and still more improbable world records.

He was a little heavy, a little stiff and the leg was throbbing a muted protest. But he was relieved as he sat down to dinner. Depression was yielding to a touch of qualified optimism.

'I hope people are patient with me,' he said. 'I hope they realise that you just can't throw away an entire winter and bounce back as good as new. Sometimes, though, I feel sure that they don't understand me at all. With the public image I've picked up, you couldn't really blame anyone for thinking I must be a very strange bloke.'

The public image: It is a subject which concerns him, yet he does little or nothing to amend it. He distrusts the media to such a degree that an Ovett interview is as rare as a Coe cuss-word, and those of us who find him one of the most engaging and interesting personalities in contemporary sport have learned to accept our place among the eccentric minority.

He outlined his image in a sentence: 'I represent the brutal, animalistic side of the sport – Seb stands for the educated, articulate side. To most people, it's as simple as that.'

Rachel, the stunning model who became Mrs Ovett a few months ago, giggled across the restaurant table. 'I still get amazed at the way people react when they meet Steve for the first time,' she said. 'They sort of stare at him and they say: "Good gracious, you're really human, aren't you?" I shudder to think what they imagined he was before he spoke to them.'

Steve shook his head. 'Maybe I should try to get across to people,' he said, 'but there's a purist streak in me that won't let me compromise. By and large, most media people are looking for quick, easy comments: "I felt great . . . it's marvellous to get the record back from Seb." If I was prepared to flip out a few clichés like that, I suppose I'd be a lovely chap.

'But I won't go along with that. It takes me a long time to form a useful opinion. I tend to consider everything; the effect it might have on Rachel, on my family, on the sport itself. Rather than risk offending any of those, I don't say anything. So people form their own views.'

Yet for a man who shuns the media, he is strangely aware of their attention. 'True,' he said, 'I suppose it's because they seem to turn up all the time. Do you know, when I came round after my operation, I opened my eyes and the first people I saw were two journalists. God knows how they got in there. I thought I must have died on the table! Decent blokes, too. The man from the Guardian said: "How are you, Steve?" and the guy from the Daily Star said: "Now about these races with Seb . . ." Honestly!'

'Seb': the word infiltrates his conversation at regular intervals. The stroke of fate by which one generation has produced the two finest middle distance runners of all time has thrown them together in a fashion which neither can really comprehend. In fact they have more in common than either will admit.

Yet they are condemned to perpetual rivalry through that peculiarly British desire to discover which is the better. As Ovett puts it: 'People are desperate to find an outright winner. Perhaps they're even more anxious to find a loser.

'Everywhere I go, people come up to me and say: "What about Seb? Do you hate him? What's he really like?" Ridiculous. How do I know what he's like? He lives in Sheffield and I live in Hove and we only meet a couple of times a year.

'I tried to discuss things with him once. It was in Moscow, just before the 1500 metres final. The whole thing had been built up for months: Coe against Ovett, the Big One. I'd already won the 800 metres, so I was pretty relaxed.

'Anyway, it suddenly hit me that everything was being blown out of proportion and I looked across the dressing room and said to him: "All this is for nothing, isn't it? We're just being used." But then I saw how he was, how his whole life at that moment depended on winning the 1500, and he gave me a look that said: "What the bloody hell are you on about?" So I shut up. It wasn't the time to talk things over.

'But he knows what I mean, and I dare say he'd agree with me. We were just two ordinary guys going through hell, even though we knew, deep down, that it was only a sport.

'Obviously, things would have been easier for me if Seb had never existed. But I've never resented him in any way. I knew he would become a great athlete; you didn't have to be a genius to realise that. And it was necessary for the sport that he should emerge. In a way, he provided the factor which balanced the equation.

'Of course, he finds it easier than I do to handle the public-figure bit. He seems to go to loads of dinners and things and he performs pretty well when he has to speak. I get embarrassed. I really don't think of myself as a superstar. I can't get over the fact that people actually want to invite me. Why me? But Rachel says: "Go. They want to see you. Be yourself."

'Then I have to work on a speech because I couldn't do the same pat chat all the time.

'I tend to feel very deeply about things. Seb and I getting the MBE for instance. It's a tremendous honour, of course, and I wouldn't dream of refusing it.

'But I got very upset when I realised that Daley Thompson and Allan Wells were getting nothing. It's obviously a hangover from the Moscow Olympics row, but I thought it was rather scandalous. When you think of the season Allan had last year, he deserves it for that alone. I think somebody's made a mistake. In fact, I reckon somebody's been pretty callous.'

For all the pressures, all the sacrifices, Ovett, at 26, still loves his sport to distraction. 'When I look back, there were so many great moments,' he said. 'And not necessarily the obvious ones. I remember winning my first English Schools title and how proud I felt when I went home to my parents. Fantastic.

'And that night in Milan last year when I almost touched the world 1500 metres record and I wasn't even breathing heavily. With a bit more self-belief, I could have taken five seconds off the record that night. It frightened me how well I felt.'

The whole of British sport will hope and pray that he can somehow rediscover that feeling in the months ahead. But our expectations will remain impertinently high. As midnight approached and we rose from the restaurant table, a businessman who had dined too well called for the manager. 'Do you know who that was?' he said. 'That was Steve Ovett. I hope you've collected his bill, because you'll never catch him.'

Steve smiled and looked down at his injured leg. 'I don't know,' he said. 'I think he's got a bit of a chance . . .'

Gerry Cooney: Great White Hope

Mail on Sunday, 23 May 1982

L AYDEEZ 'N' GENNELMEN, will you welcome the co-managers of the next heavyweight champion of the world. Let's hear it for Mr Dennis Rappaport and Mr Mike Jones!

And in a small gymnasium up in the Catskills, New York's rag traders interrupt their Spring vacation to applaud a pair of unlikely heroes.

Mr Rappaport leans against a No Smoking sign, lights up a menthol cigarette and offers the photographers his very best profile. Three diamond rings flash upon his fingers as he steadies himself upon built-up heels and throws a carefully careless wave to the crowd.

Across the makeshift boxing ring, Mr Jones is working hard for his share of the ovation. A smile splits his plump face, the jowls wobble and the hard eyes take on a touch of benevolence as he raises his arms and reveals two dark rings of sweat spreading across his chest.

They have come a long way. Once upon a time they sold real estate on Long Island. Superior real estate, by all accounts. V Des Res's with stacks of receps and drm ktchns and the occasional jacuzzi. Life was lucrative, but life was dull. And then they discovered Gerry Cooney.

Now as he stands 6ft 6in and weighs something over 16 stone, you might think he was difficult to miss. But they found him, signed him and sold him to a public which had been crying out for such a man.

And so, in less than three weeks, they will be calculating their own percentages of the 50 million dollars which the title fight between Cooney and Larry Holmes will generate. Real estate, even on Long Island, was never like this.

Their rhetoric is both predictable and word-perfect. 'I am seriously worried,' says Jones, looking less than seriously worried. 'Holmes will get hurt so bad, the world cannot comprehend.' His partner matches him all the way. 'Gerry is gonna be so big, it is truly awesome,' says Rappaport. 'He'll have the most recognised face in the world, know what I mean?'

Even Gerry's mother, Mrs Eileen Cooney, has learned her lines. A large, pleasant lady with a strong Irish face, she sits at ringside and assures you: 'I don't worry about my Gerry. I worry about the boys he fights.'

Their confidence is almost overwhelming, but if you ignore the hyperbole and concentrate on the evidence, you can detect doubts. And those doubts are echoing ominously across the world of boxing.

The sport, quite simply, is in a mess. The postponement of five major American fights within the past few months has promoted an unprecedented degree of public apathy and cynicism, and the probable retirement of Sugar Ray Leonard has deprived the noble art of its most attractive figure.

In Britain, the disease is still more dangerously advanced. The last two shows at Wembley have been watched by the kind of gates which bring Fourth Division football clubs to the bankruptcy court, and one hears that BBC television executives are less than ecstatic at the fights they are being asked to subsidise.

There is not, it seems, an urgent public desire to follow the fortunes of people like Neville Meade, Roy Collins, Ray Cattouse, John Feeney and Roy Gumbes: each of them a British champion, not one of them a household name in his own household.

All of which places a terrible responsibility on the shoulders of Gerry Cooney. He is young, he is new, he is huge and – as Rappaport conceded in a rare moment of candour – 'it don't hurt none that he's white.'

It is a crass and uncivilised factor, but it remains a major consideration. Most of the fight's 50 million dollars will be contributed by white Americans, who will swill their Budweiser, munch their Big Macs and root for their first genuine contender since Marciano abdicated 26 years ago.

Should Cooney win, they'll come back for more. If Holmes should endorse both logic and expectation, they might just turn back to baseball.

At times, the big man looks a novice; awkward and stiff-legged and perilously easy to hit. But his sheer power is impressive, and so is his manner: gentle and artless and curiously vulnerable for so massive a man.

'I sure wanna thank everyone for coming here, and watching me work so hard,' he says. 'It's nice you're all interested in me. And I'm feeling so good. I just wanna fight. Some people, like, said I was afraid to fight. I'm tired of all that nonsense.

'Sure I fought some bums. Louis, Marciano, they fought bums too. You think I'm unique? Sure I never fought 15 rounds. I never had to. I haven't had to take a punch, either. Boxing's self-defence, ain't that right? Maybe I should have let Ken Norton mess me around for a while. But I didn't. I beat him in 54 seconds. Terrible thing, huh?

'So I'm getting ten million dollars for this fight. I don't think about it. I don't know what ten million dollars is. All the money in the world won't matter if I'm not right for the fight. I'm the guy who's got to live with himself.'

His deficiencies are all too obvious. His style is crude, almost primitive, he has never been under serious fire and those murderous 54 seconds against the ageing Norton represent the sum total of his ring experience in the past 19 months. Holmes observes, somewhat pointedly: 'That sucker ain't even paid his dues,' and even the faithful Rappaport concedes: 'There's been some inactivity.'

But he can punch, with fierce and frightening power, and that is an imposing credential to carry into a fight for the heavyweight title.

And if he seeks encouragement, as he makes his final preparations in Las Vegas for the fight on June 11, he may find it draped across the narrow chest of his co-manager. 'The American Dream Coming True,' shrieks the slogan on Rappaport's tee-shirt.

For Dennis Rappaport, certainly. And for Mike Jones. And for the hordes of hustlers who have secured a slice of what might prove to be one of the final spasms of big-time boxing.

But for gentle Gerry Cooney? He may have to wade through a lot of blood before that dream is delivered. And, sadly, much of it is likely to be his own.

'Can You Believe That?'

Mail on Sunday, 31 October 1982

JOE BUGNER'S TROUBLE, I suspect, is that he has never really relished the idea of hitting people.

While this may be a perfectly admirable trait in a postman, say, or a nuclear physicist, it does carry certain disadvantages for a professional boxer.

Bugner tries to play the part. How he tries! He pulls the most ferocious faces and strikes some thoroughly aggressive poses and every so often he releases the kind of right hand which won him an undistinguished little scuffle in Bloomsbury on Thursday evening.

But still the impression is of a man speaking lines which were written by a passing stranger.

His heart isn't in it. He has been exhumed at the age of 32 simply because British boxing is in roughly the same shape as the British economy.

Somebody brought him a bottle of champagne after his victory over Winston Allen, a man who was outweighed by 2½ stone, who had not fought for a year, and who now boasts precisely 12 successes in his 22 fights. Bugner had the grace to look embarrassed.

Indeed, he was far more concerned about the angry red weal which had appeared on his neck.

'He bit me, can you believe that?' said Joe. 'Bit him, could you believe it?' said Marlene Bugner from across the hotel suite. 'A deliberate bite,' said Joe. 'Deliberate,' said Marlene. 'Can you believe it?' said Joe. And he really couldn't.

For all his 60 and more fights, for all his years at this brutal trade, Joe Bugner will never really understand a game in which people bite and gouge and butt, a game which requires that he hit them very hard and very often in order to discourage their baser instincts.

For such a game, Joe's own instincts have never been sufficiently base.

1983

More eccentrics. The duke who had devoted the bloodiest part of eight decades to the slaughter of dumb animals. The discreetly cursing clerical gentlemen and the large London dentist who was, I learned much later, not best pleased by this irreverent account of his forward prowess.

His Master's Voice

Mail on Sunday, 10 April 1983

THE 10TH DUKE OF Beaufort, Henry Hugh Arthur Fitzroy Somerset, stood on a hill in Gloucestershire, waved a blue spotted handkerchief and bellowed across the misty valley.

In this sleepy corner of the West Country, people tend to move rather briskly when the Duke murmurs. When he bellows, they break into a gallop. And so it was with the horseman; three fields, two streams and a busy little B-road away.

Gathering a dozen hounds about him, he bounded up the slope, arriving breathless and blustering to receive congratulations and a slug of cherry brandy from the hefty old gentleman in the hacking jacket.

'Most kind, Master, most kind,' said the horseman doffing his cap. 'Not at all, my dear chap. A fine day's sport,' said the Duke. And a handsome chestnut hunter sealed the convivial moment by passing water in a gushing, deafening torrent, flooding the footpath and halting half a dozen conversations.

The Duke seemed not to notice, but then he had other things on his mind. Eighty-three years old last Monday, patron and Joint Master of the Hunt which bears his name, he has hunted all his life. Yet he and his fellow sportsmen have suddenly become an endangered species, threatened by the Labour Party's recent commitment to abolish hunting.

Outwardly, he maintains a rigid upper lip. 'Sad,' he says. 'A little worrying. Nothing will come of it though. Politicians like votes, d'you see. No votes in this for them, none at all.'

His companions, few of whom had actively planned to award Labour their votes, are less sanguine. Bucolic farmers glowering beneath bowlers; side-saddle ladies with dark veils and cut-glass vowels; dashing gels with deep voices and broad bottoms; they speak of fighting funds and personal liberty and quote great chunks of pompous tosh from a leading article in Horse and Hound. 'Truth and Justice are on our side,' etc, etc . . .

Yet their sincerity is not in question, their argument not without merit, and they had presented an undeniably stirring spectacle that morning as they assembled in the field next to the sewage farm beneath the village of Avening and trotted off through the woods of Princess Anne's Gatcombe Park estate.

They were pursued, along public roads and ill-trodden tracks, by a small army of foot-followers, a cavalcade of cars and – in a mud-spattered Land Rover – by the joint masters, the Duke of Beaufort and Major Gerald Gundry.

The Major is tall, bluff and utterly committed. At 72, he still curses the frequent falls which caused him to retire from the saddle. He had spent the previous evening writing a letter to Michael Foot.

'I asked him why he was so anti-hunting,' he explained. 'Can't understand the fellow's mentality. Clever chap, you know. Very good brain. In a way, rather like Enoch, who's a good friend of mine. But there's a very fine line between brilliance and insanity.' And he peers over his half-moon spectacles to check that his message has been received.

'Look,' he says, 'we've been hunting round here since 1760. Used to hunt the red deer, but it got short, so we turned to the fox. Been hunting him ever since. Proper thing, too.

'Town people don't understand. It's not a question of killing. In fact, if he's a good fox you rather hope you won't kill him . . . 'cos you can hunt him another day. The important thing is the sport, the riding, using the countryside.'

Even the Major concedes that fox hunting embraces certain customs which could be misunderstood. He shuffles a little when you mention 'blooding,' the practice of smearing young members of the Hunt with the blood of the slaughtered fox.

'Blooding. Yes. Bit archaic, really,' he says. 'We still do it, though we wouldn't do it in the middle of the main road with everyone looking. But it's harmless. Like a christening. Me? Oh Lord, yes. I was blooded. They told me not to wash it off for a week, and I didn't.'

The Major offers courteous assistance to the novice observer as the Hunt performs its mysterious rituals beneath young trees dappled with soft spring sunshine.

The horsemanship is bold and brave, and if the hedges are friendly and the walls of Cotswold stone less than daunting, you can still recognise the antecedents of Becher's and Valentine's.

By 2.30, three hours into the hunt, the rain is gusting in from the west and the trumpeting horn has taken on a soggy tone. We have spotted one scurrying fox, breaking across open ground, and escaping over a main road. It is not the one the pack is hunting.

'Wrong scent,' asserts the Major. 'As Mr Jorrocks said: "There's nothing so queer as scent . . . except women".'

By three, hailstones are falling in great white globules. By 3.30 they have called it a day. The Duke is on his hilltop, the fox – to my ill-concealed delight – has escaped and the huntsmen are shaking puddles from the brims of their bowlers. Nobody seems to mind.

'The thing is, there's always another day,' says the Major. 'This season's nearly over, but there's always next season. Four days a week. Splendid. How do we find the time? How do people find the time to go shooting? Same thing.' And he shakes his head at a damn fool question.

The Duke packs up the remains of the hamper and climbs into the Land Rover. 'A good day,' he says. 'A very good day. Nothing better.'

And a footsore foot-follower, a middle-aged lady in a dripping anorak, trudges off to prepare the evening meal. 'Once a week I follow the Hunt,' she says. 'I just love listening to those hounds. It's tradition, isn't it. Hundreds of years they've been doing it. I like hunting the way some people like to walk miles after a golf ball.'

Incautiously, I point out that very few golfers tear the ball to ribbons when they catch it. She gives me a long look. 'You're from the town, aren't you?' she says. 'Town people don't understand hunting. I don't think they ever will.'

The Daily Round . . .

Mail on Sunday, 3 July 1983

N A SMALL ROOM AT the rear of the clubhouse, a young curate stared at the results board and murmured a litany: 'Ely, Exeter, St Albans, Bath and Wells, Effing and Blinding . . .'

He spun around when he heard the visitor splutter. 'Just our little joke,' he said. 'One of our chaps tends to let rip from time to time. Only slipped out once today, though. Bunker at the 16th, poor wedge shot, sand all over the place, and he, um, fell by the wayside. Poor old Effing and Blinding.'

And he strolled off to relay the tale to his chums, who could be seen chuckling over the halves of ginger beer shandy at the club bar.

The Inter-Diocesan Golf Tournament is not popularly regarded as one of the landmarks of our sporting summer. Essentially, it is a large group of clergymen, blessed with more enthusiasm than skill, swishing their way around Frilford Heath for the unofficial championship of the Church of England.

But, after enduring the chaos, the crassness and the rampant commercialism of Wimbledon, it was a joy to discover in a glowing green corner of Oxfordshire that sport can still be civilised fun.

Modesty was the overwhelming emotion among the contestants. Nobody would admit to having played well.

John Prior, a retired clergyman from Guildford and brother of the Northern Ireland Secretary, expressed the mood. 'You know that hymn about "The daily round, the common task". Someone once said that clerical golfers were people who paid more attention to their daily rounds than their common tasks. Myself, I played pretty appallingly today.'

By and large, this modesty extended to their dress. They do not subscribe to the myth that it is necessary to dress like Nicklaus in order to break three figures. They favoured faded flannels and Viyella shirts buttoned at the wrist, and some wore the kind of caps which are usually seen on the heads of elderly county umpires.

Their humour was distinctly clerical in tone. Tony Gardner, the Rural Dean of Leamington, gazed down the fairway from the second tee and was commanded by his partner to 'Keep to the straight and narrow'. Excellent advice, which went unheeded.

Tim Watson, from Bath, watched his partner stub a short iron from the rough, then yelped as the ball scuttled to within six feet of the pin. 'Proof!' he said. 'The ends can justify the means.'

I offered them the tale of Lee Trevino, who was struck by lightning on a championship course. As the doctors reached him, Trevino explained: 'When He wants to play through, you gotta make way.'

'I say, old chap,' said a West Country vicar. 'Would you mind if I used that on Sunday?'

Excellent men and excellent company. They replaced every divot, raked every bunker, applauded every good shot and stared at the skies in faint reproach when a belligerent drive failed to clear the tee.

Then, as the shadow of the flagstick crept across the 18th green, they retired to the clubhouse for genial gossip: 'I hear the Bishop of Exeter sponsored his team for £25. What does that do to their amateur status? . . .' 'Chap was telling me that the Rector of Nailsea arrived yesterday and played a practice round.'

The said rector, John Simons, stood smug and silent. He finished second, won three golf balls and divulged no secrets.

But when the points were finally collected, Leicester Diocese had finished top of the heap. Much applause.

An announcement that next year's tournament would be held on June 28, 'the eve of St Peter'. More applause. The Ecclesiastical Insurance Office promises to sponsor the event for another five years. Still more applause.

On the far side of the bar, a couple of crusty members blinked across at the cheering clergymen. 'Who's that lot then?' asked one. 'No idea,' said his friend. 'But they're a noisy lot of buggers, whoever they are.'

I slipped away by the side door. The light was fading and Wimbledon was at least a million miles away.

Fun, Beer and Eskimo Nell

Mail on Sunday, 16 October 1983

A T TEN MINUTES TO three, the man at the bar stared through the clubhouse window and sniggered as a bunch of forwards ran out into the cold Kentish rain. 'Daft buggers,' he said. 'You wouldn't get me out there today if you paid me.'

He was in the process of ordering a third pint of Mr Truman's finest when hands were laid upon him. There was shouting and scuffling, even a curse or two, and at three o'clock he reappeared in shirt and shorts. The fist which clutched a pint now held a whistle, and the match between Park House A and King's College Hospital Seconds had found its referee.

'I only came in for a drink,' he said, but nobody listened as they led him out into the rain with strong arms and promises of good behaviour.

Certainly, he was never going to get any trouble from Ken Hymas in the King's second row. An affable character, Ken, mountainously tall and prematurely balding, with a walrus moustache clinging to a sad face and eighteen and a half stones hanging indiscriminately from a sturdy frame.

And Ken was in a world of his own, shuffling from scrum to ruck to line-out, seemingly praying that his next breath would not prove his last. In 80 minutes, I never saw him actually touch the ball, but he never stopped trying, though his colour changed from tombstone grey to perilous pink.

He was not encouraged by the gaggle of elders on the line, who compared hangovers, replayed their days of glory and poured ceaseless scorn upon the efforts of 30 men and the conscript referee.

Even the touch judge was without pity: 'See that chap who just kicked our prop? He's a doctor, they say. Hope he never operates on me.'

Eventually, it was over, Park House A had won by 12–9, and the teams trudged to the bath, that steaming democracy of sweaty bodies, where players sit and lie about their performances and a party-going winger shampoos his hair while the forward next to him uses the lather to wash his boots.

Ken Hymas was the last to leave the bath, still pink but no longer perilous. An elderly 27 year old; massive, yet with the kindly air which must reassure patients at his dental practice in Croydon.

He sank a preliminary pint without thinking, accepted another from the bottomless Park House jug, and blushed at the suggestion that he and his kind might represent the timeless, unchanging face of Rugby Union.

'Do you think so?' he said. 'Well, I suppose there's something in that. I mean, you can't get much more grass roots than King's Seconds. Unless it's King's Thirds. Actually, I usually play for them.'

He has heard of the threat to the amateur game, heard that an Australian named David Lord is trawling for recruits to his circus, heard that sums of £90,000 are being tossed about. And he is unimpressed.

'Can't see that sort of thing appealing to our chaps,' he said. 'It's a different world down here. Sure, we've got a bit of sympathy for the top players. They're under a lot of pressure and they have to take time off work and maybe the Rugby Union should be more generous. Perhaps they should pay their wages when they're on a long tour, that sort of thing.

'But we don't go for the idea of professional rugby. If people want that, they've always got Rugby League, haven't they?' He lit his pipe and pondered. The very thought of taking money for playing the game which God invented was faintly appalling.

'You see,' he said, 'the essence of this sport is fun; fun and beer. That's what it was made for. Oh, we go to the internationals at Twickenham and we're amazed that the backs catch nearly every pass and the forwards are always up with the play. But we don't even think about reaching that sort of level.

'I mean, I'm ambitious. I'd love to play at No. 8 and get hold of the ball in the open and have the odd run or two. I dream about playing No. 8, but they won't let me. They say I'd be no bloody good. And they're probably right.

'I don't train often enough. I don't have the time. In a way, I suppose I'm not really dedicated. But that doesn't stop me loving the game. I don't know what I'd do without rugby on Saturdays. It's the centre of my week.'

By now, he was almost rhapsodising. 'Fifteen people, all battling together, then going off and socialising together. You feel you belong to something worth while,' he said.

'Take tonight. Park House is a smashing club, really hospitable. We'll buy a few jugs, they'll buy a few, and our lot will all leave together and stop at, maybe, three or four pubs.

'We'll be back in our pavilion at King's by ten, and we'll sing a few songs' – even in 1983, grass roots rugby men retain an extraordinary capacity to be surprised at the antics of Eskimo Nell – 'then we'll go across to the hospital bar and when that closes we'll move on to a party. Fantastic night.'

It is an attitude and a programme which sober sportsmen might consider a shade cavalier. Yet, while Ken worries about his physical fitness – 'I really try to lose weight, but nothing seems to happen' – those worries have not restricted his social life.

He cares far less about personal achievement. 'Do you know, I can't remember when I last scored a try,' he said. 'It must be years and years. I'd love to score just one and, sort of, run back with the ball in my hands. But there's no sign of that. Just as well nobody expects too much of me.'

A nice man of modest ambition and fixed values. 'Fun and beer,' he had said. And when I left him he was organising another beer kitty.

On one side of him stood a colleague with his arm in a sling, flaunting the X-ray plates of his newly-broken collar-bone. On the other stood a gentleman with a blood-sodden bandage around his head.

Across the bar, the referee was accepting drinks from men who had twisted his arm at ten to three. 'A good game,' he said, like one passing judgment on a presumptuous little Burgundy. 'Not a great game, but a good one.'

His words from the early afternoon came drifting back: 'Daft buggers. You wouldn't get me out there today if you paid me'. It is a pithy slogan. Perhaps David Lord might care to adopt it . . .

The Sneer of Roberto Duran

Mail on Sunday, 13 November 1983

THERE WERE RED WEALS around his ribs where the body punches had bitten. Faint bruises were blushing above his eyes and his lips seemed puffed and swollen, but it was hard to tell because they were twisted in a sneer.

Roberto Duran has worn that sneer through sixteen years, sixteen title fights and 530 rounds of professional combat. Even in the throes of painful defeat, it was never likely to desert him.

As Marvin Hagler was being borne away to his dressing room 'the winner and still champion,' Duran's sneer followed him across the parking lot of Caesar's Palace.

A few seats from the ringside an old fighter studied Duran's reactions with unqualified approval. 'Willya look at that son of a bitch,' grunted Jake La Motta. 'The guy got beat, but he's never gonna believe it. He's an animal. I love him.'

The Raging Bull, who once held the very title which Duran had fought so hard to secure, was recognising a kindred spirit. That he was beaten, and beaten emphatically, is beyond dispute.

A few romantics, seduced by his courage and his gutter expertise, insisted that his dream had been delivered. Indeed, the three judges came dangerously close to joining them in this delusion; especially the Japanese official who gave it to Hagler by a single point and scored six rounds even.

Such arcane arithmetic earned the derision of one American observer. 'Crazy Jap,' he said. 'He's the kind of guy who would have scored World War II at a draw.'

But this conflict transcended such quibbles. The sight of Hagler, an exceptional champion, being taken to his very limits by a man fighting beyond both his weight and conventional expectations, generated a rare fascination.

Naturally, this incomparably tawdry town did not deserve such commitment. The high rollers, calling a temporary truce with the tables, sat in $600 seats and boomed out macho yells for the benefit of their plastic ladies. A millionaire pornographer was cheered all the way to the ringside. Bo Derek looked pretty and bewildered. Paul Anka did not look pretty.

Only an extraordinary will could impose itself upon such trivia. But Duran possesses such a will. All those tricks learned in the slums of Panama City and polished in various American fistic academies came flooding back to him. He used thumbs, elbows, and head. He has traditionally regarded the belt as a basis for negotiation and constantly he strayed beneath it.

And always there was that sneer, even when Hagler's punches were most murderously accurate, even through that sixth round when the champion's assault would have laid lesser men to rest.

The only time the sneer faded was when his own punches were finding their mark. Then his face lit up. This, he suggested, is what it was really about. Not the fame, not even the $8 million fortune, which was rewarding his efforts. Just the sheer pleasure of hitting and hurting.

He knew many such satisfying moments the other evening, yet they were plainly insufficient to land him the verdict. Although he was under heavy fire, he seemed genuinely to resent the final bell.

He screamed at Hagler: 'You couldn't knock me out. You're a lucky champion.' But since the insult was delivered in Spanish, a language which did not feature highly on Hagler's ghetto school syllabus, the big man was unmoved.

Despairing of Hagler, Duran looked across to his old foe, Sugar Ray Leonard, and gave him a conspiratorial wink. Leonard beamed and bowed in a gesture of respect. He knew what Duran had suffered and he knew what he had achieved.

Hagler also knew his man. There were no illusions. 'I betcha if he'd beat me he wouldn't have shook my hand,' said Marvin. 'Wouldn't have gave me no kinda credit.'

Absolutely true, of course, but it was the cry of a man who feels that even now his gifts are not properly appreciated. 'C'm on,' he pleaded. 'I beat a guy who won three world titles. This man's a legend.'

That kind of talk usually fuels the prospect of a rematch. But this is unlikely. Hagler's plans will probably be to accommodate the crude Argentine Juan Roldan, while Duran, though insisting he will not retire, may decide that at 32 life has other attractions.

It was impossible to guess what was in his mind when he went off to console his wife Felicidad, clad in white fur and weeping. Hard to know how he felt when he looked in on his four children in their suite at Caesar's Palace to tell them that Daddy was home from the war.

He took a call from the President of Panama and was told that the citizens were dancing in the streets. He dunked his swollen right hand in iced water for two hours: 'No good for fighting, only for counting money.'

He laughed like a sewer at Hagler's charges of butting and thumbing and he celebrated modestly enough to emerge clear-eyed in the morning.

But the normal public face was maintained when he offered a few typically generous observations on his conqueror.

'I didn't learn anything from Hagler,' he said. 'He's nothing special. I should have beaten him, but I just got tired.'

And away he shuffled, spitting in the dust, intimidating back-slappers with that terrible sneer. As La Motta said, an animal. A basic, primitive fighting man.

He will not change. One day he'll sneer at the undertaker. And you may be sure that he'll never, never accept the decision.

1984

They showed us the spot by the river where Franz Ferdinand was shot, and they told of how his assassination lit the flames of the First World War. But they never spoke of ethnic tensions or the possibility of appalling conflict. That kind of thing wasn't mentioned back in '84. In Sarajevo.

And then there was Los Angeles. Another Olympics damaged by boycott, yet one made thoroughly memorable by the quality of its performers, the beauty of its setting and the raging enthusiasm of its public.

'We Bought the Olympics'

Mail on Sunday, 19 February 1984

I N THE ZETRA ICE rink in Sarajevo, an American TV crew stood in front of Princess Anne and thrust a camera into her face.

Her personal detective, alarmed by this breach of protocol, asked them to move aside. He was immediately advised by a large crew member to perform an act which was not only obscene but physically impossible.

'Remember, buddy,' went on the charmless American, 'we're ABC Television. We bought the Olympics. And we do what the hell we like.'

In the foothills to the east of town, a bobsled raced down the run at Trebevic under the eye of an attentive camera. Suddenly, a young man raised a placard at the side of the course. The camera paused, unwisely. Domino's Pizzas Delivers, said the sign, and the slogan yelled its message across 50 states.

'Son of a bitch,' cursed an ABC executive. 'The guy just ripped off 100,000 dollars of prime time.'

Over at the ice hockey stadium, a group of U.S. Marines brought in banners bearing the national colours. As they waved them, they unfolded an exhortation to Drink Miller Beer.

They were chased off by an executive of the Coca-Cola company. He was not a naive man. 'We invested three million dollars and four-teen million fluid ounces of Coca-Cola in these Games,' he said. 'Millers are owned by the Philip Morris company which has a sub-sidiary called 7-Up which is a competitor of Coca-Cola. And nobody gets the drop on Coca-Cola.'

A few nights later, Coke struck back. Jayne Torvill and Christopher Dean came off the ice after their perfect exhibition. Somebody thrust a can of Coke at them . . . and they smiled and thanked and drank as the cameras stared on.

'Beautiful job,' said a marketing man. 'Bee-autiful job.' And he was not talking about Torvill and Dean.

The most important people here at the XIV Winter Olympics wear neither skates nor skis. Instead, they favour Brooks Brothers suits and Jermyn Street shirts and they work their influence across discreet restaurant tables in the Old Town or in private suites at the Holiday Inn.

Most of them are employed by ABC, some by Coca-Cola, Mitsubishi or one of the host of sponsors paying expensive homage to the god of 'brand awareness'.

The athletes are bit players, the International Olympic Committee a garrulous gerontocracy which exchanges platitudes for presents and benevolence for hospitality.

For the Olympic Games have been sold, body and soul. For 92 million dollars. And the man from ABC who said, 'We do what the hell we like' was speaking nothing but the truth.

Over the past few weeks, this city has been occupied by 900 men and women in blue anoraks which bear the ABC logo.

Most are utterly professional, many are extremely engaging and all are aware that these Winter Olympics are being run by the men who pay their salaries.

They occupy four hotels and an apartment block. They summon competitors at will and drop them at whim. They have brought with them the gastronomic delights of hot dogs, popcorn and hamburgers so that they can go abroad without actually travelling and their tipping has left Sarajevo's taxi drivers wearing the smiles of pools winners.

They are imbued with a gung-ho spirit that baffles the Yugoslavs and makes the small corps of Britons shudder politely.

'Let's do it for America,' you hear. 'Let's go get 'em this time.' But it's not the racing they're talking about. Typically, they didn't stage rehearsals for Sarajevo, they held 'War Games', with 10 million dollars worth of equipment.

And when work is done, they bustle off to their hotels where they lift weights, thrash table tennis balls and attack endless video games – all provided courtesy of ABC.

'Their whole attitude is about three hundred miles over the top,' said a BBC man. 'They even put out a programme which told everyone how well they were covering these Games. Extraordinary!

'But it's *their* Olympics, all right. We just can't compete with that kind of money and we'll never be able to.'

That money has procured their power. Great green mountains of dollars have ensured that ABC will have the last word in any Olympic arguments.

In addition to the 92 million dollars for the Sarajevo Games, they have paid 225 million dollars for this summer's Olympics in Los Angeles.

'People say we're mad,' said Tom Mackin, an ABC executive with an amiable smile and a shimmering silver toupee. 'But they said that when we paid 12 million dollars for the Munich Olympics. We have never yet failed to show a profit on an Olympic Games.'

This is not wholly surprising when you consider their advertising rates. They are charging 260,000 dollars for 30 seconds of prime time and they have contracts for more than 600 million dollars of advertising revenue from Sarajevo and Los Angeles.

Even after paying a total fee of 317 million dollars for the 1984 Olympics, along with monstrous overheads, they will still retain something to cheer their stockholders at the end of the day.

Tom Mackin insists that there is more to Olympic business than mere money. 'Prestige,' he says, and the word rolls off his tongue. 'We have a slogan, "The Olympic tradition continues at ABC". That means a lot to us.

'You see, if you don't have the Olympics then you're not Number One network. And we've got the Olympics. It is just immensely prestigious.'

There was a time in these Games, towards the end of the first week, when ABC began to lose faith in their prestigious investment. The American ice hockey team had met an early demise, interest had sagged, ratings had tumbled and 92 million dollars suddenly seemed an absurd amount of money.

But on Thursday afternoon, a Californian named Bill Johnson pulled on his candy-striped ski pants, flew down a mountain and won the downhill race, the most glamorous event in the Games.

The ABC studios on the Proleterskih Brigada erupted with joy and relief. Engineers danced, secretaries squealed and one middle-aged enthusiast clambered forward to plant a kiss on Johnson's face as it beamed from a television monitor.

'Ya did it, Bill!' he shouted. 'Ya did it for us.'

The whole of America was watching the victory over breakfast – watching on ABC. The ratings were sensational. There was scarcely a dry American eye in the house.

But one Yugoslav interpreter, whose father had fought with the partisans in the mountains of Sarajevo, was unmoved by the sight of grown men beating the chests of their ABC-issue anoraks.

'On the whole,' she remarked, 'I think I prefer the Germans.'

She was disregarded. All the confidence had returned, more deafeningly buoyant than ever. Back came that invincible air of self-satisfaction, exemplified in the words of one Julius Baranthan, President of Broadcast Operations: 'To bring the best athletic competition in the world back to the United States and at the same time receive high ratings – nothing could be greater.'

Yet along with this high-minded saccharine goes a splendid capacity for street-smart trickery.

Over the past two weeks, bus-loads of fans and employees have been pushed off to events by courtesy of ABC. Advertising is banned in Olympic arenas, but somehow the ABC crowd shots manage to pick up hand-written banners bearing thought-provoking messages like Hi Minnesota! or Hello Detroit, U.S.A. All bear, with great prominence, the ABC logo. And all were written by ABC hands.

Inevitably, when others employ the same cynical methods to force themselves upon the ABC stage, the reaction is splutteringly indignant. The man pushing pizza is a 'son of a bitch'. The Miller Beer Marines are not playing the game. The skiers who reach the finish of the downhill, rip off their skis and push the brand names at innocent cameras are quite reprehensible.

'I know they all have contracts with the manufacturers,' said Tom Mackin. 'But I wish they wouldn't do that kind of thing.'

Harsh words were spoken last week about the man with multicoloured hair who turns up at major sports events the world over with a banner which says: John 3: 16 (God loved the world so much that He gave His only son . . .).

'The guy ain't so innocent,' I was told at ABC. 'We used to avoid him real easy. Now he carries a portable television and leaps out of the bushes when he knows the cameras are coming. Is that fair, for Chrissakes?'

But these are minor irritations, for ABC are way ahead of the game, making the pace and re-writing the rules.

They will have 2,500 people working at the Los Angeles Olympics and already they have succeeded in extending the 1988 Winter Games in Calgary so as to cram in three weekends of prime time viewing.

There was opposition to the move – indeed the Olympic Charter was cited. But the arguments were ended with an ABC bid of 309 million dollars, applied with all the subtlety of a wet sandbag.

Their delight in this newly-won power is undisguised and almost contagious. You could see it most clearly at the Press village in the early hours of Friday morning, when two portly men in mandatory blue anoraks were celebrating the downhill victory.

They were walking away from several bottles of heavy red wine and leaning clumsily upon each other.

'Some year, 84,' said the first man. 'We got the lot. Winter Olympics, Summer Olympics, two conventions and a Presidential election. We got the lot. Ain't that right, Al?'

Al grunted and turned a lighter shade of pale. His companion ignored him. 'No question, Al, ABC is a class act.'

Al tried to mutter agreement, but instead threw up in the wayside snowdrift. His friend walked on, oblivious. 'Yeah, a class act . . .'

Just two soldiers in a large army. Nice, ordinary men doing a good job for people who are exercising unprecedented power over sport.

Quite possibly, they have never heard those words of Lord Killanin, who sounded a warning a decade ago.

'I appeal to every single sportsman not to come to the Olympic Games for political purposes or commercial exploitation,' said the last president of the IOC. 'If this is not accomplished, then the Olympic movement and all sport is doomed. We shall retreat into barbarism.'

Some would toss aside that warning as weary idealism.

Others, less kindly, might suggest that the barbarians are now at the gate. Wearing wide smiles and blue anoraks. And throwing up in snowdrifts.

'You Can't Compete with Gold'

Mail on Sunday, 12 August 1984

MIKE MCLEOD ARRIVED breathless from the track, sank into a chair and started to tell 23 British reporters just how he had won the bronze medal he wore around his neck.

Suddenly, a shout from the next room announced that Tessa Sanderson had arrived with her gold medal. McLeod's audience disappeared. Some ran, some walked quickly and a few had the grace to blush . . . but they went just the same.

McLeod simply smiled and shrugged. A fine athlete, he has been around a long time and he never really expected to be famous. But it would have been pleasant if fame had lingered for more than 30 seconds.

Still, he understood. 'You can't compete with a gold medal,' he said, and he walked out clutching his consolation prize.

He is 32 years old, and he has served his purpose.

For the past week, we have revelled in the deeds of some of the finest track and field athletes on this planet. Yet even as the cheers rumble around the Coliseum, you can sense a vague unease in many a mind. It is over all too quickly. All the pain, the suffering and the self-denial, all consummated in the space of a single afternoon.

Soon they must get on with the rest of their lives, and a medal of bronze may prove slim shield against a forgetful world.

Brendan Foster understands, although he has shaped his own future. He is an accomplished commentator with BBC TV and a successful executive with the Nike sportswear company but he remains at heart an athlete with a knowledge of the athlete's fears.

'People don't really care about you, and you have to accept that,' he says. 'It's fine when you're on top. The public, the officials and the media: They're all delighted to come along for the ride.'

And when you finish? 'It's as if you're dead. Somebody else arrives on the scene and they're all climbing on his train.

'The athlete is used. I let myself be used because I always wanted to think that there was a twelve-year-old kid in Glasgow or somewhere who'd listen to what I had to say and think to himself: "One day, I'd like to be an athlete like that".' He added: 'I was lucky that I had things to turn to, things I'd throw my energies in to. But it wasn't easy to come to terms with not being an athlete.

'In East Germany, they have detraining programmes for sportsmen. I just stopped. It was two years before I could join in a fun-run without people expecting me to win automatically. Nobody wants to get old, but for an athlete it can be terrifying.'

Foster has his Olympic bronze from Montreal, Alan Pascoe won his Olympic silver in Munich. Like Foster, Pascoe has established himself both in television and commerce. But he experienced the same withdrawal symptoms.

'It was bad for me, but it's probably worse for people who have actually lived on athletics,' he says. 'Take a man who has been existing on a few under-the-counter payments, some odd grants and the dole. He's never had to work, and suddenly, he's thrown into the real world. It must be shattering.

'People will go along to hear Sinatra sing, even if his voice is fading. They'll just sit there and remember the way he was. But they won't go out to watch a couple of middle-aged fellows trudging round a track. It would be embarrassing.

'Athletics is for young people, and the athlete counts off the passing months and wonders how long he can survive. You've got to use whatever fame you've found as an athlete as an investment in your future.

'And to do that, you've got to remain at the top for a long, long time. Only an athlete would understand the unbelievable sacrifices and pressures involved in doing that.'

Those pressures are the products of an age which sees the sportsman as a willing victim: a commodity who can be used to sell a political system or a packet of soap flakes. Wheel him on, make him smile for the cameras, then forget him.

It was not always thus. Robert Tisdall, who won the 400 metres hurdles gold medal for Ireland at the Los Angeles Games of 1932, has spent the past few weeks as a feted guest of the organising committee.

He never considered that his triumph was terribly important. 'In my day we won it and forgot about it,' he says. 'I forgot about it for more than forty years. People didn't know and I didn't think it worth mentioning.

'I feel so sorry for the lads today. It's so essential that they win and cash in. I really don't think I could have coped with that sort of stress.'

Gentle days, but they have gone forever. Some fifteen years ago, Lillian Board told me of her fear of living out her days as an ex-athlete. 'Mustn't it be awful to spend the rest of your life talking about what you did at twenty-one?' she said.

Poor Lillian was never allowed to grow old, but she understood that fame is fleeting and sporting fame most fleeting of all.

Mike McLeod stumbled across that truth the other evening, when he smiled and shrugged as a crowded conference turned into an empty room.

1985

Bradford: the year was dominated by that single word. For decades we had complained that our football grounds were spartan, inadequate and potentially dangerous. And then, on a bright Saturday in spring, all our nightmares became terrifying reality. In time, the grounds would be transformed by infusions of money and energy. But Bradford was a monstrous price to pay for that transformation.

In simple sporting terms, it was the year of Barry McGuigan. All pretence of neutrality was abandoned on that summer evening at Loftus Road, when we stood and screamed for the little man until his title was won. I have suffered many a misgiving about the legitimacy of boxing and the morality of allowing men to inflict brain damage in the name of sport. And yet, if asked to list the half-dozen most compelling sporting occasions I have known, then McGuigan v Pedroza would take its place close to the summit.

Bradford: Coping with a Crisis

Mail on Sunday, 19 May 1985

H E HAD COME STRAIGHT from work and his overalls were streaked with grease. A big, awkward man, unsure of his reception as he approached the young policeman at the barrier.

'Be all right if I, like, pay respects?' he mumbled. And as the officer stepped aside, he walked across the forecourt of Valley Parade, Bradford.

For a few minutes he stood alone, taking it all in: the jumble of charred planks, the twisted turnstiles, the alley deep in ashes where dozens had died, the scorched football field, the wreaths and crosses bearing their simple messages and the stench of lingering smoke.

Then his shoulders started to heave and he moved quickly away. And the policeman stared at the ground, not caring to look into his face.

Over in the broken shadow of the stand, Chief Inspector Jack Acton watched the man retreat. 'It's just sinking in,' he said. 'This city's been in shock for a week. Now it's feeling the pain.'

Jack Acton's men could feel the pain. Like him, they had rushed in from garden and shopping centres when the first news came through from Valley Parade. Some of them, officers well used to disturbing sights, retched and vomited amid the carnage. But nobody stopped.

Now they are finding it difficult to sleep. They turn up at the station at odd hours, searching for company. Anything to avoid being alone and remembering.

'People reckon policemen are automatons,' said the Chief Inspector. 'It might look like that. When you're flat out, you can't afford emotion. It's technique that gets you through. Later, when you think about it, that's when the tears come.'

Yet even through the tears, you could discern a city behaving with extraordinary grace and dignity in the depths of its crisis.

The days when the world came to Bradford for its wool are largely past. Yet shreds of that late Victorian assurance have survived first depression and now disaster. You can see it in the faces of the people, and you can sense it in the aura of City Hall, a plump, confident edifice frowning down on Sixties Legoland.

On Thursday afternoon, a newspaper placard leaned against the side door of City Hall: 'Blaze Disaster: Names of the Dead,' it shrieked and the queues formed to study the bleak lists on the front page of the Telegraph and Argus.

Evocative Yorkshire names: Ackroyd, Crabtree, Hindle, Hutton, all running deep down the columns. Seventy years before, similar queues read similar lists when the men of the West Yorkshires were cut down on the Somme.

But these lists were heavy with young children, teenage girls and frail, elderly people consumed by a fire which had moved faster than they could run.

'There's no point in looking, really,' said a man on Market Street. 'I see the same faces every week at the football ground. I only know them by their faces. I won't know who's gone till next season when the faces are missing.'

Those faces were vivid in the minds of the hundreds who had flocked to the service at the city's Anglican Cathedral and to the Requiem Mass at St Patrick's, close by the Bradford City ground.

Other, more worldly towns might have reached for the whisky bottle or the medicine chest. Bradford, instinctively, had turned to its churches to seek some meaning from the catastrophe.

'Religious roots go very deep in this city,' said Father Brendan Lilly, the priest at St Anthony's on Bradford Road. 'Everybody was affected.

'At evening Mass on Sunday, I saw a gang of young lads at the back of the church. Complete strangers.

'That usually means they're chasing girls or out for a lark. But they just stood there, quiet and prayerful. They wanted to think things over. A terrible happening like this, somehow it's brought the whole community together.'

The whole community embraces the Indians and Pakistanis who live in the mean little terraces surrounding the Bradford City ground. They had come out in force on Saturday with tea and blankets and tearful sympathy for the survivors. All through the week, relatives and friends have been calling at those houses to offer token presents and grateful thanks.

Even in its deepest grief, the town retained a decent desire to do the right thing. As John Helm was relaying his graphic and sensitive description of the disaster for Yorkshire Television, his commentary position was attacked by a group of young men.

'Turn those cameras off!' they screamed, and they hurled stones and coins at the gantry.

Helm, a Bradford man, was deeply upset until he took a telephone call at home two days later. 'I was one of those lads,' said the caller. 'And I'm sorry. It was right to show the pictures. People ought to know.'

That feeling is widespread and genuine. Bradford believes that the world should be told in detail about the kind of tragedy which saw a widow identify her husband's body by the shreds of his shirt cuff and a mother learn of her lost son by the cold evidence of dental records.

Which is why the journalists and television crews swarming across the city have been astounded at the tolerance they have discovered.

Old ladies call them 'luv', the man in the pub strikes up conversation with the ease of an old friend. Nobody says: 'Get the hell out of here and leave us alone.' People ought to know.

And, so far, there has been little evidence of recrimination. Stories of warning letters, belatedly discovered, may fill newspaper columns, yet they are being swept aside as an irksome irrelevance. There is a real measure of sympathy for Stafford Heginbotham, the Bradford City chairman, who wanders across the scene like one of Priestley's minor characters, shattered and bewildered by the scale of events.

All this may change and attitudes may harden, but for the moment there is a real intention to do something positive for the afflicted. No fund-raising idea is too trivial. Hairdressers are donating all their tips to the Appeal Fund, sponsored pram-pushers are out in force, a hypnotist has emerged to deliver charity performances of his skill and auctions are everywhere.

Everything will help, yet ultimately Bradford must come to terms with the pain of its loss.

John Crook, the Director of Social Services, has no illusions. 'Sometimes, we're not good with our grief,' he said. 'It's not quite manly to show emotion. There's a terrible feeling of guilt about people who were at the back. "Why did I get out? Perhaps I could have gone back one more time?"

'People have to learn that grief is normal, that these feelings are expected. It will take months and years, in some cases for ever. But we can help them through it. It's not just social workers, it's neighbours, friends, clergy, voluntary organisations. Everybody.

'We've had no shortage of offers, the whole city wants to play a part. There's got to be sharing and understanding, and it's only just beginning.'

Just beginning for the relatives and friends, yet it ended suddenly and brutally, for 52 people on a sunny Saturday afternoon.

A day to celebrate their team's championship, a day when grandfathers were taken along to see the tide turn after years of failure and children were sat in the stand and ordered to remember every detail. All devoured, indiscriminately, by the smoke and the flames.

Up at Valley Parade, the young constable took a small posy from a woman who could not face the walk across the forecourt. He strode to the seat of the fire and gently laid the flowers alongside the other tributes.

As he returned to his post, he looked back at the skeleton of the grandstand. 'How do you explain it?' he said. 'Lovely day, happy crowd, everyone full of life. And now nothing. Just dust.'

You do not explain it. You endure the consequences and reach out to the future. Over this past, appalling week, the city of Bradford has taken the first few brave steps in that distant direction.

Last Stand of the Little Men

Mail on Sunday, 9 June 1985

G REY OF HAIR AND grey of mind, they sat and they nodded, like a Home Guard platoon awaiting inspiration from Captain Mainwaring.

Jack Dunnett did not fail them. 'We shan't jump into action,' declaimed the President of the Football League. 'When we have enough information, we shall, if necessary, er, call a meeting.'

As clarion calls go, it did not rank with the eve of Agincourt. But then, Jack has never seen himself as Henry V. He gave his audience what they wanted: Don't jump, take your time and then, if they really pin you to the wall, call a meeting.

The delegates to the Football League Annual General Meeting continued to nod and passed on to their next business, the election of a vice-President. One candidate. Tough decision.

Outside the Royal Lancaster Hotel, the newspaper placards told passing Londoners of FIFA's admirable decision to confine English fans to their own battle grounds. A week earlier, those same placards had carried a simpler, starker message:

'*Brussels Riot – 38 Dead*'.

Now some sensitive souls might have believed that the national game was facing the tiniest crisis; shunned, isolated, blood-stained and, as a consequence of the Bradford disaster, confronted with the need to find huge sums for ground safety measures.

But if you expected the game's most influential forum to discuss those kind of trivialities, you were quite wrong.

They presented a long-service award. They mused upon the virtues of two substitutes instead of one. They lingered an age on relations with the Gola League and finally, with a show of boldness, they decided that linesmen could in future carry flags of whichever colour they chose.

The real world, the world in which people die heaving for breath on devastated terraces, that nasty world was never allowed to raise its voice.

There was no sense of shame or urgency, no feeling that the game has exhausted its credit with the public, no realisation of the revulsion which football's excesses has evoked among decent, ordinary people. Just a group of little men gathered together to exchange gentle platitudes.

In years gone by we would drift along to their annual meeting to enjoy their eccentricities: the arcane points of order, the procedural wrangles, the verbal dexterity of a former President who once boasted that his club's new stand was 'constructed with non-ferocious metals'.

Their habit of greeting every problem with minds and eyes tightly closed had seemed harmless in those days. In the year of Bradford and Brussels, such indulgence has lost its charm.

The little men have been overwhelmed by sombre and sinister events, quite beyond their comprehension or control. Impotence has made them uncomfortable, and occasionally they attempt to conceal it behind a veneer of truculence.

Even before the League meeting began, secretary Graham Kelly could be seen ejecting a camera crew. 'Out . . . shift it . . . you've got ten seconds . . . you're trespassing,' he snapped. They yawned, smiled and languidly complied. But they seemed not the least bit terrified.

Dunnett himself was doing a little chest-puffing to prepare for his meeting with Mrs Thatcher. Now some of her own solutions to football's problems may be hasty and half-baked, but I suspect that she is losing little sleep at the prospect of confronting President Dunnett. For his part, he sounded strangely like a man who is planning to mug Marvin Hagler.

'Some of us are seeing the Prime Minister next Wednesday,' announced Dunnett. 'The PM would like us to spend all our money on the various matters she has in mind.' He paused before dealing his trump card: 'Unfortunately,' he said, 'as I shall tell her on Wednesday, we haven't got any money.'

Twaddle; trivial, mind-numbing twaddle. And there they sat, drinking it in, as if vivid revelations had been made.

They actually found the nerve to demand more money from the television companies, hiking the price of a shoddy product to moguls who are increasingly unwilling to purchase it.

Even Robert Maxwell, who presides over the affairs of Oxford

United when not publishing newspapers, succumbed to the illusion that television is football's pot of gold. But he did, to his credit, attempt to incite a discussion of the crisis facing the game. Dunnett, astoundingly, ruled him out of order.

Maxwell, who is not the most reticent of men, responded by summoning his own press conference in the lobby, and splendid headline stuff it was.

'Anyone from the Mirror here?' he boomed. 'Yes, sir', came the cry. Away he went: 'Ramshackle organisation . . . failure to grasp the enormity of the problem . . . Margaret will not stand for this . . . Management Committee held in contempt by ministers . . . football has failed itself and the country.'

All true, every word, and delivered in Churchillian vibrato by one who is highly unlikely ever to ascend to the Presidency of the Football League.

Inside the conference room President Dunnett and Secretary Kelly awaited the return of the Press; Dunnett fidgeting, Kelly glaring out of a face like a municipal cemetery. Each of them failing utterly to grasp the nature of the crisis.

'Talk about Brussels or the FIFA ban? You don't understand,' said Dunnett. 'We shan't know the facts until we see the official reports. Anyway, the AGM is simply a meeting at which we alter regulations.' Kelly nodded: 'You don't understand,' he echoed.

And that was when you could have cried for their insularity, their insensitivity, their refusal to recognise that a meeting of the most powerful men in this tarnished game would have offered the ideal opportunity for a few hours of soul-searching. Instead, they had seen it as an exercise in book-keeping.

Dunnett, an intelligent man floundering beyond his depth, was now ready to go under for the third time. A despairing journalist suggested that the game was no longer saleable, that violence and disaster had irredeemably reduced its appeal to television and its public.

Dunnett first turned necessity into a virtue: 'Nonsense, it's much more saleable now because fewer people are going to grounds. They'd much rather watch the game in the safety of their own home.'

Then his head sank beneath the waters, with the most fatuous and damaging remark I have ever heard uttered by a sports administrator . . .

'I don't watch television myself,' he said. 'But my family do and they tell me that the most popular programmes are the ones which are full of violence. On that basis, football ought to do rather well.'

Maxwell stood at a distance, a huge figure in a summer suit, shaking his head. 'The public will never forgive them for this,' he muttered. 'Never.'

Dunnett continued to twitter. 'Come on,' he demanded. 'More questions. You must have more questions. Only intelligent ones, though.'

And, in the mind's memory, you could hear the Yorkshire vowels of the Fulham chairman Ernie Clay, asking a question which remained unanswered. "Oo's taking the urine out of 'oom? That's what I'd like to know,' he had boomed.

But by this time, we already knew.

'Unanimous Decision . . . Barry McGuigan!'

Mail on Sunday, 9 June 1985

O N ONE OF THE wildest and most memorable nights in the history of British boxing, Barry McGuigan turned a daring dream into staggering reality.

Driven by a raging will and the passionate support of thousands of his countrymen, McGuigan overcame Eusebio Pedroza to take the world featherweight title home to Clones, County Monaghan.

Pedroza had come to the Queen's Park Rangers football stadium with a daunting sequence of nineteen successful title defences. He returns home to Panama City with a purse of some £900,000 as his glittering compensation for a points defeat.

Pedroza took the first round behind a long, stiff jab, reaching McGuigan with disturbing frequency. Barry looked tight and tense as if the passion of the crowd was temporarily freezing his natural movement.

But in the second he began to demonstrate why he earned the chance to fight for this title. Still he had to accept more than his share of that discouraging jab, but he fought his way in, throwing strong right hands over the lead and raising the pace to a still more intolerable level.

By the third, McGuigan was beginning to ensure that the fight was conducted on his own terms.

He seemed careless about the damage he was having to absorb as he fought his way in, stood toe to toe with the Panamanian, and calculatedly flung an extra punch after the bell to remind the man that he, too, had come to do some serious business.

Came the sixth and we were aware that this was a fight which would stay in the memory. McGuigan was finding the time and the confidence to throw his favourite punch, that lacerating left hook which thudded into Pedroza's ribs.

Again it was his round but you began to worry at the pace he had established.

All his conditioning, all his work was now looking for its dividends. Yet the man from Clones was performing with a confidence which this vastly capable, vastly experienced champion can seldom have encountered.

It seemed that he would need all of that confidence for the first two minutes of the seventh when, for the first time, Pedroza seemed to have solved the puzzle in front of him with a whipping left jab and occasional shuddering right crosses.

But the remarkable Irishman bullocked his man against the ropes, tossed a straight right and suddenly the place was celebrating the sight of the champion toppling slowly to the canvas.

He rose with a mute shrug, took his mandatory eight count but weathered the storm.

How McGuigan managed to maintain the murderous pace was a mystery. The niceties had long since been dispensed with. Elbows flew, heads lunged, anything was accepted as currency in this most bitter of world title fights.

While the fans were willing McGuigan on to still greater efforts in the 13th, Pedroza would not fade. From here on it was to be a matter of will.

Then McGuigan found the disconnecting punch once again. A vicious right detonated on Pedroza's chin with less than a minute of the 13th left, but once again the bell saved him.

McGuigan poured his soul into the last round, but Pedroza poured his talent and a fusillade of jabs.

As the referee leapt between them at the end, they fell briefly into each other's arms awaiting the verdict.

And then it came. 'By a unanimous decision Barry McGuigan is the new featherweight champion of the world.'

Taking Charlton Out of Charlton

Mail on Sunday, 22 September 1985

Charlton 2 Stoke 0

THEY KILLED OFF OUR club yesterday. They didn't put it quite like that, of course. In fact the people who take decisions talked of the future, the First Division and the great days to come.

But just before five o'clock, 66 years of tradition had been swept aside, the Valley was just another open space and Charlton Athletic were dead.

The businessmen of the Charlton board will offer persuasive reasons why the abrupt move to Crystal Palace was inevitable.

They do not begin to understand. Take Liverpool from Anfield, United from Old Trafford, or Charlton from the Valley and you are stealing the soul of a football club.

The red and white wreaths which appeared on the centre spot moments before yesterday's game with Stoke was more than a melodramatic gesture. It was recognition that something valuable in the life of a community was disappearing.

Chris Lewis, a university lecturer from Bexley, understands. After 30 years on the Valley's terraces he was entitled to speak for the fans.

'They should have closed the whole thing down. That would have been kinder,' he said. 'Suddenly you're told you've got to go to Selhurst Park to watch them. I won't, and I don't know who will.'

But if the club is without a future, it retains a marvellous past and yesterday the ghosts of the men who created that past were swimming across the Valley.

The names came tumbling: Leary and Hewie, Hurst and Summers, Tees and Treacy, perky Benny Fenton and busy little Ron White.

And Sam, the incomparable Bartram, who served 22 years between the sticks; carrot hair, roll neck sweater and a grin as wide as the Valley. Dear Sam: How he would have hated yesterday.

The one consolation was that they departed with a victory, Stoke surviving until the 78th minute, when young Mark Stuart took a header from a couple of yards. Five minutes later Robert Lee ran through for the last League goal at the Valley.

But now it's over. Charlton have lost their ground, their identity and their public.

As one who had turned up at the Valley for the past three decades, through the days of hope, the months of failure and the odd, glorious interval of success, I shall also call it a day.

For me, the lad sitting in front of the main stand held the banner with the most relevant slogan. 'There's no place like Home,' it said.

I hope the people who took Charlton out of Charlton read it. But I doubt that they understood the message.

1986

Another World Cup in Latin America. Some will remember the sight of Diego Maradona at the peak of his powers. The English will recall the darker side of his nature, and in particular the outrageous piece of cheating by which the Hand of God defeated the hands of Peter Shilton. I shall remember the shanty by the Aztec and the people who were so kind to their uninvited guest.

And McGuigan again, pale skin burning in 110 degrees of desert heat as he lost the title he had fought so hard to acquire. I yield to nobody in my loathing of Las Vegas, but I never hated it quite so much as I did on that dreadful night.

Sell-Out on 74th Street

Mail on Sunday, 19 January 1986

E IGHT O'CLOCK ON THE coldest night of the Brooklyn winter, and a foot-stamping, arm-flapping queue stretches down 74th Street.

At the door of Our Lady of Angels school hall, a little old man barks at the crowd: 'The Monsignor says if you don't have tickets, forget it. This is a sell-out.'

A few of them offer token protests, a racial cocktail pleading a common cause. But the old man is immovable, so they shrug and move away. This is the Golden Gloves. Why wouldn't it be a sell-out?

Over the past 60 years, the Golden Gloves has become a New York City institution, an orgy of amateur boxing spread across 38 promotions, offering ghetto kids a target and a dream.

'Bigger than the Olympics,' says the man from the Daily News, its faithful sponsor. And it is a genuine boast.

A few will reach Madison Square Garden for the mid-March finals. Others will work and train, sweat and bleed and eventually fall by the wayside in Queens or Manhattan, the Bronx, Brooklyn or similarly perilous points of call. And all will take to their graves the boast that they fought in the Golden Gloves.

Inside the hall, the opening night audience watches a Puerto Rican named Cristobel Ramos abort the ambitions of a Mexican called Luis Ricardo, after a hundred seconds of active service.

The fans are a volatile mixture, black and Hispanic as well as the occasional camel-coated Italian and rows of Irishmen with faces bearing the contours of Kerry.

Yet they watch and nod, clap and cheer and agree through mouthfuls of McDonalds: 'Yeah, the kid can fight. Jeez, he could go the route.'

In the Ramos corner, a sawn-off shotgun of a man with gold at his neck and wrists readily agrees. Juan Laporte was once world featherweight champion. Last year, he lost to Barry McGuigan in a memorable title eliminator in Belfast. He knows about fighters.

'My father, he sent Ramos to me from Puerto Rico,' says Laporte. 'The kid lives in my house, he wants to make something of himself. I say to him, "You must go for the Golden Gloves." And here he is.'

In another corner lurks another world champion. Emile Griffith won the Golden Gloves in 1958 and went on to win the world middleweight title. He is a bald, chubby caricature of his youth, but tonight he is animated, swinging and swaying with every punch.

'I love it,' he says, 'just love it. Good kids, good boxing, and folks who appreciate what they're seeing. For a whole evening, you forget all the problems.'

Jose Torres cannot forget the problems. As the former world light-heavyweight champion, he has a reputation. As boxing commissioner for New York State, he has a responsibility.

'I treasure my pair of Gloves more than any other prize I earned in boxing,' he says. 'But you have to live in the real world.

'Most of these kids don't have many options. There are great temptations: hard drugs, heavy crime . . . or the gymnasium. Boxing gives them the gymnasium option, the Golden Gloves gives them a goal.'

Around the fringes of the ring, the monsignor with a firm line on ticket sales presses the flesh: 'Hi, Jose . . . How are ya, Juan? . . . Emile, good to see ya!'

Jimmy Cavanagh is an ebullient priest with that sense of optimism engendered by bleak urban poverty. 'Ain't this something?' he says. 'All these people enjoying themselves. Great night.'

He is, you think, the kind of priest who should have been played by Cagney. The man from the Daily News chuckles: 'Jimmy Cagney did good for the Gloves.

'You remember his movie City for Conquest, the one where he's trying to make money so's his brother can be a musician? And they tell the champion, "Go easy, this kid's a novice – but he did fight in the Golden Gloves." Cagney knocks the champ out. Terrific film. Did great for our image.'

At the back of the hall, a trio of Brooklyn's finest settle precinct bets: 'Hank took 20 dollars on the first . . . pay Eddie 15 bucks on the third fight.'

When action resumes after the interval, a silky black mover named Leonard Lee digs murderous hooks into the body of a yielding novice called Steve Lamberti. It is all over within 58 seconds of the second round.

Lee later reveals himself as a sociology graduate of St John's University, an academic haven in the ominous borough of Queens.

'No job, not yet,' he says. 'I just work out every day in the gym in Times Square. I've only ever had five fights, but just five more and I'll be the winner of the Golden Gloves. I'll keep working.'

The crowd moves away, content with the performances. 'They worked hard, the fighters,' says a huge Irish longshoreman. 'You gotta remember, kids who can fight three rounds don't run around with needles in their arms. They're making something of themselves.'

Suddenly it's all over and Monsignor Cavanagh sends them on their way: 'Great, lads. Ya did us proud.'

Leonard Lee gathers his tiny entourage and heads for the Fourth Avenue subway. 'Hey, that was some night,' he says. 'Now I gotta keep in shape. Five more fights. Gimme them Golden Gloves, baby.'

It was midnight and the wind was screeching down from the Arctic. But nobody cared. For, perversely, a warm breeze was springing up on 74th Street . . . and it drifted across the whole of New York City.

Beardsley – A Secret Desire

Mail on Sunday, 18 May 1986

THERE IS A WIDESPREAD impression that footballers are not excessively bright. Indeed, some would say that the higher they rise in their profession, the more firmly their brains remain lodged in their feet.

This is a vile calumny, and in evidence I present Mr Peter Beardsley of Newcastle United, who is currently lending his effort and intellect to England's World Cup preparations.

He recently appeared in a fan magazine to answer a series of searching questions. Now this inquisition usually yields a stream of predictable responses; the actor whom Mel Sterland most admires is one 'Dirty Den'; the person Viv Anderson would most like to meet is Hilda Ogden and Ray Stewart's favourite possession is his wife.

But Beardsley chose to unburden his soul. 'What would you do,' he was asked, 'if you could be invisible for a day?' He replied: 'Stand at a pelican crossing and keep pressing the button.'

Brains in their feet, indeed! With minds of such originality at work in Mexico, England's World Cup chances have acquired a new and hopeful glow.

The Neighbour of Graciela Arroyo

Mail on Sunday, 1 June 1986

THE HOME OF Graciela Arroyo stands upon a pile of rocks. It is a tiny, creaking shack with slender walls and a strip of asbestos for a roof.

Senora Arroyo cooks her family's food on an altar of charred bricks by the side of the road. She draws her water from an open storage drum, chattering with her three children and cursing a stray mongrel as it snaps at her heels.

She is a sturdy woman, and although her face is tired and strained, her smile comes easily. 'Life is hard,' she concedes. 'But life is hard for many people. And, anyway, I do have a fine neighbour.'

Yesterday, her neighbour launched a party which will rattle on through the month of June. Flags flew, bands played, 110,000 people cheered and sang. And the sound of that celebration in the Aztec Stadium could be clearly heard 150 metres away, in the home of Graciela Arroyo.

The European conscience is offended by such brutal contrasts. Inside the stadium sat people who had paid ticket touts some £800 for their grandstand seat.

They have rented apartments for £1,000 a week during the World Cup, hiring servants and chauffeurs for a handful of pesos. And, with a flourish of credit cards, they have settled restaurant bills at prices which would have fed the Arroyo family for a month.

True, there is some Mexican resentment of this affluence. On the very walls of the Aztec Stadium, a radical hand has smeared a string of aerosol slogans: 'No to the World Cup . . . Give us Land and Liberty . . . This stadium is a symbol of inequality.'

Yet the people of Mexico City seem generally indifferent to such notions. As the lady in the shack said, life is hard. What is one glaring symbol among so many?

And, anyway, this city has much to forget; deep pockets of savage poverty, bleak economic depression, last September's earthquakes which killed at least 10,000 people and rendered almost as many homeless.

Perhaps the Mundial, the World Cup, can help them forget for the moment?

Certainly, the Mexican government believes so. Ignoring their foreign debt of around £8 billion, they have met a security bill of £5 million and provided 30,000 police to ensure tranquillity.

Inspired by the media mogul, Emilio Azcarraga, whom many believe to be the most powerful man in Mexico, they stepped in when penniless Colombia withdrew three years ago.

With skilful lobbying, they convinced FIFA (whose president, Joao Havelange, is a business partner of Senor Azcarraga) that the ideal venue to start and finish a World Cup is a city which is a mile and a half high, is notoriously prone to earthquakes, and chokes daily beneath a blanket of smog.

Commercial interests agreed with the Government. The television networks snaffled broadcasting rights for a trifling £18 million, around £192 million less than America's NBC had agreed to pay for the 1988 Olympics in Seoul.

Twelve multi-national companies have secured sponsorship rights, and, for the privilege of flaunting four advertisement hoardings at each match, the Coca Cola, Philips and Canon corporations are each understood to be paying around £6 million.

With almost 25 per cent of the population of this planet expected to watch the final on television, the executives of the sponsoring firms are congratulating themselves on their eye for a bargain.

Quite naturally, these extraordinary figures hold little meaning for you or me or for the eighteen million people of Mexico City.

There is no great air of excitement, few outward signs that a festival has begun and little expectation of great deeds from a Mexican team which was beaten so soundly, so recently by England.

There have been indications during this week that the Mundial administration is in danger of premature collapse; the process of ticket distribution, for instance, has evoked images of Fawlty's Manuel attempting to organise the London Marathon.

Yet, even the malfunctions have been conducted with beguiling grace and charm. 'Believe me, gentlemen, I'm on your side. I really am,' a stunning hostess assured a queue of tetchy journalists, and they blushed like guilty children. 'No problem,' they said. 'What's another four hours anyway?'

The mood of the city was succinctly captured by a restaurant owner in the fashionable Chapultepec district who had obligingly re-written his price list to honour the World Cup.

'What harm can the Mundial do?' he asked. 'Can it make the traffic worse? Impossible. Can it make the poor poorer? I don't think so. The people who want it, let them enjoy it. That's what I say.'

And that, in her own way, is what Senora Arroyo says. She stood in the doorway of her pitiful shack, as a little girl with huge eyes and a ragged dress tugged at her skirt. She cuddled the child. 'We hope you all have a good time,' she said. 'Everybody loves the football. But I think that maybe some things are more important than football, eh?'

Across the road and beyond the empty car park, the Aztec Stadium was glowing in the thin evening sun, but Graciela Arroyo ignored the spectacle as she ushered her children down the rocks to fetch more water.

We left them and returned to the more congenial area of this admirable city, where elegant ladies served cocktails and a string quartet played discreet airs. We discussed Robson's shoulder, Lineker's wrist and other important things.

It was almost time for dinner, and poverty seemed such a distant pain.

'That's All I Need: Circuses!'

Mail on Sunday, 29 June 1986

MID-MORNING IN CAESAR'S PALACE, and the little boy skips across the lurid carpet in front of the Spanish Steps Sea Food House.

He dances past a line of dull-eyed croupiers. He sings a little song and hears it drowned amid the clamour of slot machines fed by fat ladies from Wisconsin. And he never gives the whole sordid scene a passing glance.

For young Blain is clutching his father's hand and smiling up into his father's battered face. After five weeks of separation, he has his dad all to himself. And only those of us with three-year-old sons can imagine their feelings.

'He wants to go to the circus,' says Barry McGuigan. 'Jeez, that's all I need; circuses! And me, supposed to be resting.' And he throws back his head and roars as the child pulls him past a contraption which promises eternal prosperity for 25 cents.

By now, the fight is receding into painful memory. Microphones, notebooks and a world title had disappeared two days earlier and now he is confronted by a face full of purple bruises and the kind of career decisions which once seemed inconceivable.

Steve Cruz has departed for Fort Worth, Texas, to the prestige of a featherweight title, the comfort of a 15-year-old wife and the approval of his colleagues at the Rivera Plumbing Company, which pays him £170 a week for his expertise with leaking taps.

And Barry can now look back on defeat with the cold appraisal of an historian.

'I knew from the start that things weren't right,' he says. 'I knew it when I could only throw two-punch combinations instead of the clusters I usually let go.

'I panicked. By halfway I was praying: "Please let me nail him quickly. Please God. Quickly." The corner was chaotic. The Nevada inspector kept getting in the way, asking if I was all right. Mr Eastwood kept pushing him away, but our routine went out the window.

'And all the time I was feeling worse. The heat had got to me. It was like trying to drive a car in traffic without first or second gear. I felt so slow and sluggish. My legs felt like I was wading through gallons of warm water. And he kept on catching me. I was just desperate.'

At the ringside, you could sense his desperation. In a trifling way, you could even share it. England's footballers might, with some justification, complain of the heat in Mexico City or Monterrey. Squads of absurdly over-rewarded tennis players are currently yelping about the pressures of playing before the squealing suburbanites of Wimbledon.

But nothing remotely compares with the agony of performing in 110 degrees of desert heat, being punched and gouged and punished by a young Texan who was stronger and more able than any of us had dreamed.

They say it was an epic battle, a featherweight classic, but we really wouldn't know. When McGuigan is in action, he engages your emotions. You roll and flinch with every punch. You abandon phoney neutrality and scream when he attacks, cower when he comes under fire.

You believe him without question when he says: 'He would have had to kill me to finish me. I'd never have stopped. I'd have died in that ring.'

And that is the most disturbing aspect of all. Anybody who watched the fifteenth round, when the American got through with the short left hook which provoked the collapse, knew that he really would have perished rather than quit. He was facing an inferior fighter – 'There's no way he would have gone the distance in Belfast,' declared McGuigan – but a fighter who showed that a man from Fort Worth copes with scalding heat rather better than a pale-skinned warrior from Clones.

Steve Cruz, and the way he fought, has forced McGuigan to stare at his future. At a post-fight Press conference, he agreed that his mother, back home in Co. Monaghan, wants him to retire.

'She never wanted him to be a fighter in the first place,' grunted the London promoter, Mickey Duff, who clearly knows a great deal about the fight game but very little about Irish mothers.

Barney Eastwood, his manager, behaved with intelligent sensitivity. 'I could probably get him a return with Cruz, but I'm not sure that Barry honestly wants one,' he said. 'What he really needs is a good long rest. And if, after that, he wants to talk about boxing, he knows where to find me. If he decides to retire, that's fine by me.

'I've taken a lot of stick these past few days, but Barry's a wee lad from the country who's become a millionaire. I'm glad to have been involved. If it's all over now, well, we've had a grand old time, haven't we?'

Eastwood's son, Brian, was less philosophical. He had not shared the foresight of the anonymous gambler who brought the odds tumbling with a $170,000 bet on Cruz. Instead, he had endured the same financial misfortune as the masses of Irish punters who crammed this terrible city to support their man. 'Don't talk to me,' said Brian. 'If I'd bought a duck the bloody thing would sink.'

But, inevitably, the most relevant reaction belongs to McGuigan. In all his conversations, the word 'retirement' comes frequently to his lips. 'I'm only twenty-five. I'm not past me peak yet,' he insists. 'But whether I want to go on with all that training and the build up again, that's another thing.

'In the next few months, I want to see if I can earn my living without using my fists. I want another career which will give me a choice.

'I'll decide finally then, not in two or three years when I might be past it. I'll talk a lot with my family, then I'll make up my mind.'

It is a huge decision, and you pray that he gets it right. But the random thoughts of some of his closest connections might sway his judgment. 'He's been sliding away ever since he fought Juan Laporte,' you hear. 'He wasn't at his best when he won the title against Bernard Taylor, worse still against Cabrera. Now this. Maybe he's burned out. Maybe the best days are behind him.'

And they may well be right. The heat played its obvious part, but McGuigan's performance was still a caricature of his finest form. This man was the best of his breed. He combined the instinct of a great fighter with the grace of a Corinthian.

He endowed a grim and savage game with a kind of nobility and he wore his title with decent dignity. You sense that he could never settle for being ordinary.

Yet he will always retain that knack of triggering the emotions. He grips your hand in that dreadful casino. 'Thanks very much for coming all this way,' he says. 'The trouble you've gone to and I bugger it up. Jesus, I'm so sorry for letting you all down.'

The remark is so monstrous that only later do you realise that he actually means it.

He has a way with him, has Barry McGuigan; a way that can leave a grown man sniffling into his handkerchief while the croupiers stand and stare and a thousand infernal machines clatter out their messages to the losers of Las Vegas.

1987

The football authorities were as complacent as ever. Hooliganism, we were assured, was a thing of the past; a problem long since solved. But people living in the cities were telling a different tale. They spoke of disrupted train schedules, diverted traffic schemes and shopping centres brought to a standstill on match days.

So I sought my information from Scotland Yard rather than Lancaster Gate. And I spent an anxiously revealing evening in East London.

Charlton at Wembley – Again!

Mail on Sunday, 29 March 1987

W E WOULDN'T WANT TO sound blasé, but we should like it known that Charlton are at Wembley again today. We were there in 1946 and '47, now we're making the old, familiar journey in '87.

True, it is only the final of the Full Members Cup, whatever that may be, but Wembley is Wembley and we're glad to be back. Again.

They tell us that nothing has changed. The trams will be as crowded as ever, and we'll have to arrive early if we want a decent spot at the half-crown end.

But, all being well, we'll be safely inside the Empire Stadium when the teams are presented to Mr Attlee and what a noise we'll make when the King hands over the Cup.

The opposition, by the way, is Blackburn Rovers. Nothing to worry us there. They played all their best Cup Finals at the Kennington Oval, and any side which can lose to the Old Etonians is not a serious test for Charlton Athletic.

So we shall pack our spam sandwiches, pick up our sweet coupons and take ourselves off to Wembley once again.

In a way, it's our second home. And as we haven't played at home since they turfed us out of The Valley 18 months ago, we are duly grateful.

'It's All About Potting Balls'

Mail on Sunday, 3 May 1987

NEAL FOULDS SAT IN a corner of the hotel bar and stared at his mirror image on a portable television. He fidgeted with his drink, ran his hand through his blow-dried hair and silently mimed the responses which the image was offering to the benign questions of David Vine.

When the interview was over, he sank back in his chair. 'Was I all right?' he asked, and the small, protective group of handlers answered as one. 'Great, son. You done great. Lovely words.' And he smiled a doubtful smile.

An hour or two earlier, Foulds had earned himself a minimum of £24,000 from his efforts on the green baize table down the road. But that was simply money, a cup of water to be tossed into Niagara. This was An Issue, the Great Beta Blocker Controversy of '87.

Now the fact that young Foulds apparently takes the beta blocker drug to slow down a rapid heartbeat would seem to concern nobody outside the patient and his doctor. But over the past two, interminable weeks, snooker has good reason to be grateful for this spurious fracas.

An MP, with his marginal seat in mind, has yelped a transparent protest, and the rules of the International Olympic Committee, no less, have been invoked. Snooker has been made to seem important.

There are those, of course, who cling to the view that the whole thing stands or falls by what happens on the tables.

Whispering Ted Lowe, who has himself received a rare tabloid hammering this week, spoke for that school when he remarked: 'The game of snooker, to my mind, is all about potting balls.'

It was the voice of a man who plays the piano in a brothel. For snooker's appeal is essentially roguish. The heroes, ideally, should be hustlers, creatures with nicotine-stained fingers and pallid complexions.

We draw the line, perhaps, when they butt the tournament director or urinate into the sponsor's plant pots, a la Alex Higgins, but we don't really mind beta blockers, neither do we mind if they play cards all night while consuming fifteen pints of Old Peculiar. So long as they are interesting.

Sadly, the really interesting people in Sheffield are the players' 'connections'. They roam the bars and lobby of the Grosvenor House Hotel, glaring at passing reporters who may have scandals up their sleeves.

They shout into telephones when they are certain of an audience: 'I'm talking five per cent over three years, for Christ's sake! Do we have a deal?'

Some of them wear custom-tailored suits with shiny grey shoes. Others possess the kind of faces which only a benevolent jury could acquit. All are riding the snooker fad for every penny, fearful that it will disappear as quickly as it arrived.

Naturally, they bend a collective knee to Barry Hearn, the entrepreneur who controls three of the four semi-finalists and is destined to be one of the biggest winners at The Crucible this week.

'We've got the keys to the chocolate factory,' he says, with the air of a man who has swallowed the coffee creme.

Yet even Hearn may experience the odd, small pang of anxiety when he looks at the way his game is developing. Joe Johnson, who is not managed by Hearn, is a recognisable human being; nonchalant, jovial, and still bemused by the fate which made him world champion. Jimmy White possesses the brash and roguish traits of the hustler. But most of the others are starting to talk like footballers.

Steve 'Interesting' Davis, of course, has forged a career from amiable platitudes and this week he reassured us that he still possesses that familiar wooden touch.

Taking his seat beneath the line in the sponsor's advertisement which read: 'Cigarettes can seriously damage your health', he rolled out the verbal wallpaper. 'I'm pleased I've got so far . . . Joe's done tremendous . . . with all respect to the other players . . . yeah, I'm pretty happy with my game.' And so on.

Unfortunately, the younger ones have, so to speak, picked up his cue in the way that Chris Evert's tennis success bred a grey cluster of earnest base-liners with double-fisted backhands.

So Foulds, whose expression suggests that he is permanently wrestling with a quadratic equation, felt obliged to say: 'I'm very pleased to have got to the semi-finals . . . I haven't actually played well yet, taking nothing away from anyone . . . this is new territory for me and I'm, well, pleased.'

While Mike Hallett, who had earned a pitiful £12,000 reward for losing to Foulds, was 'very disappointed,' he intends to come back next year and believes, without fear of contradiction, that 'it doesn't matter who you're playing, you've just got to go out and win.'

They look, sound and dress like that breed of young City trader for whom the Big Bang has bought a Porsche, an ulcer and a manor house in Essex. And, sad to say, they are equally dull.

I cannot imagine that the public will stand for much more of this. Snooker was not meant to be taken too seriously.

We need more abuses of plant pots, more scandals and many more indiscretions to hold our attention. They got away with beta blockers this year, but they will have to do much better next time.

If they fail to deliver, the fad will fade. David Vine will fall silent and snooker, once more, will be 'all about potting balls'. It is a grim prospect.

Smiling Over the Sandown Card

Mail on Sunday, 17 May 1987

THE FOOTBALL HEADLINES were dripping with money.

Breathtaking contracts were being thrust upon wide-eyed young men, the Cup Final bonuses were ready for the record books and ordinary players were changing hands for fees like long-distance dialling codes.

Stan Bowles glanced at the stories and smiled. Then he turned the page and searched for the Sandown card. Over the past decade he has lost two wives, a small fortune and an army of fair-weather friends. But he has retained his precarious sense of priorities.

They held a testimonial match for him at Brentford the other evening, because he was the kind of player that people like to remember. A well-known bookmaker chipped in £250 and everybody sniggered and said it wasn't so much a donation, more a short-term loan.

Stan smiled at that, too. He smiles a lot these days; largely, you sense, because he is too embarrassed to cry. Yet the futility of his existence came crowding in on him three weeks ago in a ward of the West Middlesex Hospital.

'My second wife had walked out and everything kind of got to me,' he said. 'I started drinking non-stop, all day long for seven weeks. I couldn't stop smoking, either. Eighty fags a day, one after the other. Then I find myself in this bed in hospital.

'There's one bloke who's had a stroke and keeps talking in French to me. There's a fella in the next bed who thinks my name is Eric. He wakes me up at half past three in the morning: "Come on, Eric," he says. "We've got a train to catch in ten minutes."

'I called the nurse. I said "Nurse, this place is full of bleeding nutters." And she gave me one of them laughs, like she was saying "What d'you think you're doing then, sunshine?" Frightened the life out of me, that did.'

It frightened him to the extent that he forswore the dreaded vodka in favour of halves of lager and he took to smoking small cigars as cigarette substitute. But he knows that the changes are merely cosmetic.

'People like me don't really change, do we?' he said. 'We duck and dive, we live from day to day and we're happy just to wake up in the morning. Of course, it should have been different, but I'm thirty-eight years of age. It's not going to get too different now, is it?'

Bowles was one of those players who was only at ease with the world when he walked on to a football pitch. Outrageously gifted, he stood in that line of seventies footballers whose genius was flawed by spectacular indiscipline.

For Bowles you could read Alan Hudson, Peter Osgood or George Best, and inevitably they are the players he most admires. 'We might have been a bit wild, but we could play, couldn't we?' he says.

'I look at some of the people around today and I bloody weep. That Mark Hateley; they're talking about spending millions on him and the poor bloke can't play the game. Couldn't trap a dead rat, yet he's made a fortune.

'Then I listen to those people on the telly who tell us what the game's about. That Emlyn Hughes, for instance. Drives me mad, he does; a very average one-paced player who was lucky enough to play for a good team, and he comes on like he was Besty. Bleeding liberty. Me, I won't go to a game these days; not unless Glenn Hoddle's playing. He seems to be the only one who knows what he's doing.'

Bowles speaks with the authority of a man who won five England caps when his talent should have brought him 50. Of course, the caps are gone now: 'Jim Gregory of Queen's Park Rangers, he's got one. And I think I sold the others.'

He treated his career as lightly as his international mementoes. Starting at Manchester City in the great days of Lee, Bell and Summerbee, he moved to Bury where he was sacked over an unpaid taxi bill.

He laid the foundations of a reputation at Crewe, which was managed by an affable milkman named Ernie Tagg. 'Great man, Ernie. He once got so involved in a darts match at his local that he forgot to send a team to a reserve match. They fined him for that. I loved him for it.'

It was Tagg who said of Bowles: 'If he could pass a betting shop like he passes a football, he'd have no problems.' They discovered the truth of that observation at Carlisle.

Stan didn't like Carlisle. 'You ever been skint in Carlisle in the winter?' he asks. 'Terrible. Cold like you wouldn't believe, sheep in your back garden and nobody willing to lend you two bob. That's Carlisle.'

The great years were at QPR, where he played with Rodney Marsh, Gerry Francis and the rest, almost won a championship for Dave Sexton and enjoyed a love affair with a doting crowd.

After that, it was slowly down hill. 'I could have gone to Hamburg before Kevin Keegan. Six of them came over to sign me, but Jim Gregory said: "Tell them to stuff it." So I did. I wasn't sad, really. I don't like Germans, anyway.'

He had ten predictably miserable months at Forest under Brian Clough: 'Stone mad, he was. Wouldn't talk to me. We communicated by rumour.' He left after refusing to travel to the European Cup Final and suffering a lengthy suspension.

The League career ran out at Brentford and his football finished amid glorious farce at non-League Epping.

'We were short one day, so the chairman had to play. He got in a row with two of the other team, knocked one out and chased the other geezer through the woods. They chucked us out of the League. Goodbye Epping, goodbye Stan.'

His troubles came in clusters after that; the gambling, the drinking, the break-up of his marriage, the dole and, finally, that frightening ward at the West Middlesex. The hair is now streaked with grey, the drinking has piled pounds upon that slender frame and there is a worried anxiety behind the ready smile.

But he insists there are no regrets. 'The money's gone and I don't reckon the bookies will give it back. The booze; that was my choice, I suppose. And the family, yeah, that was hard to take, but these things happen.

'But I don't want people feeling sorry for me. I enjoyed it all, well, most of it. And I'm grateful to the game in a way. You know, if it hadn't been for football, I could really have got myself into trouble.'

The thought amuses him and he is still chuckling as he orders another half of lager and buries his head in the Sandown card.

Quiet Night in Green Street

Mail on Sunday, 15 November 1987

T HE TRAIN ARRIVED AT Upton Park station at ten minutes past seven, and the chant of a thousand voices was rumbling down Green Street before the last passenger had cleared the platform.

'Mill-wall, Mill-wall,' they boomed, and the sound bounced off the walls of the terraced houses, drowning the din of police sirens, the clatter of police horses and the distant drone of a police helicopter.

Two hundred yards along the street, close by the windows of a funeral parlour, a young constable fingered his truncheon and tried to keep the fright from his face. 'Here we go, then,' he said. 'This is it.' And he walked towards the station to meet the visitors.

The occasion was the first round of a mundane competition called the Simod Cup. West Ham were playing Millwall, East London versus South London.

And the cost of containing this threat to public order involved the use of 729 policemen, 32 horses, 17 dogs, one helicopter and around £100,000 of public money.

At a time when persuasive voices are insisting that the problems of football violence have been largely overcome and that our clubs are once again fit to play in Europe, the experience of Tuesday evening in East London offered an appalling contradiction.

For several weeks, intelligence sources had been informing the Public Order Branch at Scotland Yard that this match held the potential for serious violence. Although circumstances had prevented their meeting for several seasons, there was long-standing antagonism between both sets of supporters.

After a series of planning meetings involving Operational Commanders and Yard experts, the Metropolitan Police decided to meet the threat with a show of unprecedented numbers.

Days-off were cancelled, police leave was rearranged, reinforcements were drafted in from all over London and parts of Kent. And at nine o'clock on the morning of the match, the plan was put into action.

Millwall supporters, meeting at various points in South London, found their movements monitored by uniformed police. 'We followed them everywhere, street to street, pub to pub,' said Chief Inspector Mick Hoskins of the Public Order Branch. 'And we let them know we were following them.'

The result of this surveillance was that around half of the 5,000 Millwall fans planning to cross the river decided that the odds were too great and turned back. Some of the others, desperate for confrontation, tried to make other arrangements.

Their leaders, who are not merely football hooligans but vicious and violent criminals, contacted their prospective opponents at West Ham. They told them that Upton Park would be a difficult site for the intended battle and suggested that Liverpool Street Station would provide a suitable venue for conflict.

Millwall arrived there en masse in the late afternoon. The ranks of West Ham thugs were armed and waiting. But before the carnage could begin, amid home-going commuters and mothers taking children on Christmas shopping trips, the City of London Police arrived in large numbers. Once again, intelligence had paid off. But Upton Park lay ahead. It was the hooligans' last chance for the fight they were determined to enjoy. The police were about to be put to the ultimate test.

As the chanting fans paraded down Green Street, they were met by a force of eight inspectors, 28 sergeants and 194 constables, including 32 mounted officers and 17 dog-handlers.

The police established themselves between the long file of Millwall fans and the hundreds of West Ham supporters who had infiltrated the side-roads off Green Street in the hope of springing an ambush. Police reserves were packing these side-roads. The ambush was forestalled.

As the fans approached the entrance gates and prepared to pass through the metal detectors, they started to jettison weapons; CS gas canisters, flares and knives were later picked up in the streets around the ground.

The major worry was the Stanley knife, which has become the hooligan's standard tool. Some attempted to smuggle this fearsome weapon into the ground concealed in a kebab. Others hid them about their body. Several were detected.

Inside Upton Park, the police presence numbered 159 officers, who were later supplemented by most of the outside force. In the event, they needed every man and woman.

Millwall were penned into a section which covered one quarter of the South Terrace. For a while, they screeched abuse at the ranks of police, spitting at them and hurling coins from the anonymity of the terrace.

They implored the distant West Ham fans to come over and fight. 'You'll get the same as Luton,' they yelled, remembering the ground they virtually destroyed two seasons ago.

Then they tried to burst out of their pen, almost overwhelming the police who struggled to hold the gates. 'On the pitch! On the pitch,' they chanted, and for a time it seemed they would succeed.

The game went on, virtually unremarked by terrace or grandstand as the struggle between police and fans continued.

The chants grew more obscene, the frenzy more fierce and when West Ham scored early in the second half, it seemed that sheer force of numbers would deliver the promised invasion.

But the police line held and suddenly a strange salvation was at hand when Millwall scored an equalising goal, then took the goal which proved to be the winner.

The fans were in no doubt about the significance of their team's success. 'You should be happy we won this,' they chanted to the lines of police, and their meaning was unmistakeable.

When it was over, they continued to taunt the departing hordes of West Ham supporters: 'We thought you was hard, we was wrong, we was wrong.' And 25 minutes after the final whistle, they were released, under escort, to Green Street.

The windows of the little houses were dark. Nobody showed their face to the malevolent mob on the street. Every station along the District Line was manned by police support vans, just in case the thugs should escape from their special train. There were police vans on London Bridge, nine miles from Upton Park, to see home the last of the stragglers.

All over London, the thin blue line had been dangerously stretched by the need to control the first round of the Simod Cup. A total of 729 policemen had been required to attend a crowd of 11,337, only 260 officers fewer than attended the last FA Cup Final with its 98,000 crowd.

Green Street had been temporarily closed to traffic and to innocent pedestrians. Four policemen had been slightly injured. 53

arrests had been made, largely for possession of offensive weapons, drugs, drink and public order offences.

The financial cost had been huge, as it always is. Last year the Metropolitan Police spent some £8m on policing football. Less than £1m of that money was recovered from the clubs.

Chief Inspector Hoskins was relieved that the evening had passed off without major disturbances, saddened by the necessity for such drastic measures.

'They're not kids, like some people imagine,' he said. 'The average age of those we arrested was 23–24. I don't know why they do it. All we can do is plan and analyse and try to get it right. This time we did. Next time . . .'

As they cleared up the mess in Green Street, another policeman, his coat streaked with spittle, was offering a similar sentiment.

'Bloody madness, isn't it,' he said. 'I was hoping to get a quiet pint before closing. No chance. Sometimes I hate this job, dealing with idiots who can't tell the difference between football and war. When's it all going to end, eh? When?'

And he never really expected an answer.

1988

It began with a wheel turning full circle; Holmes, who had punished Ali eight years earlier, was himself battered by Tyson. It finished with a gentle English farce played out at Old Trafford. But these were mere diversions, for this was Ben Johnson's year. Nobody else came close.

On a Saturday evening, we were celebrating history's most extraordinary 100 metres. Came the early hours of Tuesday morning, and we realised we had witnessed a sham. It is possible that the censorious tone of my second piece on Johnson had nothing to do with my having been so comprehensively deceived. But I cannot be sure.

'We Don't Want No Tragedies'

Mail on Sunday, 24 January 1988

A
S THE OLD FIGHTER LAY on his back and stared into the searing arclights in the roof of the Convention Hall, he heard the soft, Hispanic tones of Joe Cortez pronounce his professional obituary.

'It's over, Larry,' said the kindly referee. 'We don't want no tragedies, do we? It's all over.' And in that brief, bewildering moment, reality came crowding in on Larry Holmes.

For the past several months, Holmes has lived with the delusion that a 38-year-old grandfather could somehow gather together the shreds of a talent which once had made him heavyweight champion of the world.

Now, as his handlers pulled him to his feet, the shrieks of the crowd assailed his senses. In the front row of the privileged seats, the aristocracy of American popular culture, Streisand and DiMaggio, Mailer and McEnroe, peered at his predicament.

And across the ring, punching the innocent air and smiling a smile of pure malice, Holmes could see the man who had consigned him to history.

Before this brutal night in Atlantic City, there were those who believed that Mike Tyson's reputation exceeded his ability; that hard selling and soft opposition had falsified his true merit.

Like Jeffries, Louis and Ali before him, Holmes was charged with the task of restoring the old order. And, like each of those three great champions, his ultimate failure was both painful and pathetic.

Ali, to his immense credit, turned his face away from the wretched spectacle. A portly, confused figure, he had hovered over the event like a dire warning.

Eight years ago, in a converted parking lot in Las Vegas, he suffered a hideous beating at the hands of the young Holmes. Now he was ushered in to give Larry a swift hug and a word of encouragement before the opening bell.

The gesture offered slim insulation against the murderous assault of Tyson, and Ali was left to sit and stare at the ground, shaking his head.

'I knew it would happen,' he mumbled. 'I always knew it would happen.'

In truth, even those of us who do not possess the instinctive awareness of Muhammad Ali might freely have forecast the passage of events. Holmes had prepared meticulously. He had shed 30lb and honed his body to a state of impressive hardness. But he was fighting out of his era, his last contest was buried 21 months in the past and, crucially, he was giving away seventeen years.

'The Tyson kid's getting better. Larry's just getting older,' declared one sage. And so it proved.

For the first two rounds, Holmes rummaged through an old pro's repertoire: sliding away from bullish assaults, tying up the flailing arms and frustrating Tyson's urgent ambition with experience gleaned from two crowded decades.

He walked away from the second round with an extravagant stage wink at the champion, and in the third actually raised some improbable hopes among his following by setting himself, flat-footed, for some solid right-hand reprisals.

But that qualified success was to prove ominously expensive. He entered round four on dancing feet, flicking out half-a-dozen chastising jabs and shuffling in the manner of the great man at the ringside.

Tyson accepted the jabs, relaxed and awaited his chance. When it emerged he seized it with a predator's relish. A long clattering left hook early in the round set Holmes back on his heels. The final barrage was being prepared.

It began with a scything right cross, thrown through the parted gloves like a pace bowler searching for his quicker ball. Holmes took it on the side of the jaw, numbed by the blow which sent him bouncing to the boards.

Amazingly, he was up at the count of five, but the credits were starting to roll. A malevolent combination of punches concluded with a scuffing right, high on the head, which sent the challenger down for another five seconds, and he arose to face the inevitable.

By now, he was almost impossible to miss. Short, wicked shots crashed into head and body as Tyson sought the conclusive blow, and he discovered it with five seconds of the round remaining.

The final punch of Larry Holmes' glittering career was a champion's right hand thrown with a vicious turn of shoulders and hips which reached inside his defences and almost tore his head from his body.

In his mercy, referee Cortez declined to count, ending the affair with an abrupt wave of the hands and a few compassionate words for a man who seemed to have aged 10 years in 12 minutes.

Tyson reappeared an hour later, wearing that terrible smile and a grey, hooded cap, sodden with sweat. He lisped his reflections with an assurance which many find chilling in one so young.

'I knew his style, I studied it for years,' he said. 'Even when he was champion, he held his left hand low. I knew he could be hit with a fast right. I thought maybe the crowd got him souped up in the fourth. He let his ego get involved. I just said to myself: "He's gonna get it".

'Holmes is a courageous fighter, but he's had his time. His reign is completely over. I just wanted him to know that. I believe I'm the best fighter in the world right now. I'm the champ. I'll take on all comers.'

Whereupon, with the sensitive timing which only the best American fight managers possess, Mr Butch Lewis – in full evening dress, black and white bow tie and bare chest – suddenly produced Michael Spinks, Tyson's only plausible challenger.

Tyson simply sneered and ignored the interruption. 'Will I fight Spinks?' he asked. 'Sure. Any time. Winner take all.'

Mr Lewis performed a rapid calculation involving some 40 million dollars and retreated at speed. Like the rest of us, he sensed that the champion actually meant what he said.

As for Larry Holmes, he was bravely trying to face defeat in a sensible perspective.

'Tyson is better than I thought. A lot better,' he said. 'People can talk about Spinks all they want; Tyson is the true champion. This fight was just something I wanted to do. I wanted to prove a point. And it kinda hurt the way things worked out. But, hey, I earned three million dollars tonight. That's what I fight for. I'm a professional. If they'd said: "Do it for free", I wouldn't have showed up. I got nothing to be ashamed of. I'm gonna have a party tonight. And another one tomorrow night. Things ain't so bad.'

Then, almost as an after-thought, he said something which in its self-revealing fashion told the story of the whole affair. 'We all get old,' he said. 'Somewhere along the way, somebody has to get us.'

Your mind travelled back to that distant evening in Las Vegas when another old fighter went in search of his youth and discovered only pain and suffering.

Larry Holmes chose to ignore the lesson of Muhammad Ali. And even three million dollars may not represent adequate compensation for the disastrous oversight.

'I Hope He'll Be All Right'

Mail on Sunday, 12 June 1988

T HE WIND CAME SCUDDING off the Irish Sea, throwing its drizzle against the guest-house windows and carrying the scent of frying bacon along the length of the Central Promenade.

It was an enticing smell on a raw morning, but John Weedon rejected the temptation. 'I never have breakfast on race days,' he said. 'It's not a good idea to have food inside you. Just in case anything happens out there.'

The other residents of the Shaftesbury Hotel had no such qualms. They worked their way through eggs and rashers and focused bleary eyes on Motor Cycle News. A few of them waved to John as he gathered up his red leathers and left the hotel, but he was preoccupied. He kissed his wife Sandra and his five-year-old son Jon and set off up the hill. Sandra looked at the rain and worried quietly. 'He won't like this weather,' she said. 'None of them do. I just hope he'll be all right.'

Little Jon scampered around the hotel steps, hands clutching imaginary handlebars. Other children jumped out of his way as he swept past them, roaring like a motor cycle.

That roar is the sound which pervades the Isle of Man during its Tourist Trophy festival.

That roar carried Brian Warburton into eternity when he took the wrong line at Appledene and perished against a low stone wall. He was 57 years old, but had falsified his age for the thrill of one more TT race.

The roar marked the passing of Ricky Dumbell, whose sidecar struck a lamp-post at the bottom of Bray Hill during practice. And the roar was the last sound that Kenny Harmer heard on this earth when his neck was broken at Waterworks Corner. His machine came to rest high in a tree, and they brought in a crane to retrieve it. The Coroner decreed that all three deaths were the result of mis-

129

adventure, the verdict which has attended most of the 146 fatalities in the 81 years of TT history.

There are those who insist that the entire event is a protracted misadventure. The contestants are required to negotiate a 37 and three-quarter mile circuit containing 200 bends at speeds which can touch 160mph. Since the races are staged on public roads, safety measures are minimal and escape alleys non-existent. As one rider put it: 'If you get in trouble, there's nowhere to go. You can hit anything; walls, trees, road-signs, even horses. You don't get a choice.'

In fact, as any non-combatant could have told him, there is a fairly obvious choice, but it is not one which commends itself to the likes of John Weedon from Leicestershire. 'I do it because I enjoy it, simple as that,' he said. 'I'm 37 now and I only race once a year, but this is the place to do it. I've had friends killed here, good friends, but death doesn't cross my mind. Even Sandra and young Jon being here doesn't affect me. Maybe it should, but it doesn't.

'Sure there's some fear, there's got to be. But it's controlled fear. Perhaps that's the appeal. All I know is, mile for mile, the TT's the safest place in the world to race. It's kerb to kerb, very fast, keep the nerve and don't get in trouble. That's all it is.'

This casual assessment is not shared by the bikers who make the pilgrimage, for they have come to watch gifted men enact their own dangerous dreams. They seem an intimidating bunch, with their matted hair, lurid tattoos and ability to make 250cc sound like Armageddon.

Yet their conduct confounds preconceptions. They form orderly queues for Bingo, for the Miss Wet TT Shirt contest and for the current attraction at the Gaiety Theatre, The Tart and the Vicar's Wife. They drink deeply and hold their liquor commendably.

As the rain cleared and the field screamed away on 150 miles of the Junior TT, you could begin to understand what had drawn them to the island. Those of us who are paid to watch grown men play children's games have fixed ideas about courage in sport. For us, courage is the 90-metre ski jump, or carelessly taunting Mike Tyson or hooking Malcolm Marshall.

No more. From here on, courage is that compromise between technique and insanity made by men who steer through the bends at Glen Vine at 140mph, with six inches of clearance on one side of the road and large trees on the other to penalise miscalculation.

Flitting around the course with a camera crew, we picked up Roger Hurst, whose bike had expired midway through the TT. 'I don't like watching it,' he said. 'I worry about the lads when I see them go that fast. You have to come here, of course, but you're always glad when it's over.' He began his race on a Kawasaki 600. We returned him in an elderly Ford Escort.

Meanwhile, John Weedon was having his own problems. After two laps he was lying 14th and averaging 108mph. Then, up in the hills at Bungalow, his Yamaha 350 betrayed him. 'Never mind,' he said. 'I'm still walking. That's the great thing, isn't it?'

You do not doubt their sincerity, neither could you question the right of such men to risk their lives in the way they choose. Yet as the riders gathered in the bar later, you watched the supporting cast of loyal wives and adoring children and you wondered about their deep and private feelings.

Perhaps the inquest into the death of Ricky Dumbell offered a clue. A police constable testified that Mr Dumbell appeared to be unconscious when he reached him after the accident. When his crash helmet was removed, however, he opened his eyes and said: 'Jesus Christ, I should have listened to the wife.'

Those were his last words. They do not invalidate the enormous pleasure which the TT brings to thousands of people. But they may have sounded a tragic and timely note of caution, a note which is often difficult to discern amid the thunderous roar of the racing engines.

'No Riot Today. Maybe Tomorrow'

Mail on Sunday, 18 September 1988

WHEN THE GAMES OF THE XXIVth Olympiad were awarded to Seoul, some of us drew a scurrilous conclusion. Beirut and Belfast, we decided, must have declined the honour.

Now if it is possible to compose an abject apology whilst holding your breath, then rest assured we shall do our best.

The ingredients for disaster are still alarmingly apparent. North Korea's brooding resentment may yet take appalling shape, and one of a dozen terrorist groups may yet secure its place on the teeming Olympic stage.

But for the moment, Seoul is gripped by nothing more sinister than a warm and beguiling sense of pride. Never was a city so patently happy to host the Olympic Games . . . and never was a city so determined to justify that precarious privilege.

Over the past few months, the government of South Korea has been exhorting its people to smile at their visitors. The chief of police, shepherd to a notoriously robust flock, was a touch dubious. 'I'm not sure my men know *how* to smile,' he said. 'But they will try.'

And try they have, exercising restrained authority while adding their diligent grins to a sea of ten million beaming faces.

Yet you know that things were not always thus and you sense they may change when the Olympic circus moves on. That suspicion is emphatically endorsed by the students of Yonsei University, who find the concept of a laughing policeman strangely difficult to absorb.

But, inevitably, the arrival of the world's media has reduced even radical protest to the status of street theatre.

Early last week, the students mounted a form of designer-demo; four o'clock kick-off, a few petrol bombs, a ritual burning of the American flag and home sharp at five, gleefully aware that the police would not dare employ their usual methods with the world watching.

The coverage exceeded their wildest dreams. And so, through discreet channels, they informed the media of a repeat performance: same place, same cast and, if enough people were interested, perhaps a bus could be laid on.

The bus was unnecessary, indeed, the mildly curious were accommodated in three taxis for the hour's drive across the city.

When we arrived on campus, a forlorn figure in a baseball tee shirt approached, shaking his head. 'It's off,' he said. 'No riot today. Next riot, maybe tomorrow, maybe next day.'

'Thanks,' said an American reporter. 'We really had a ball.' But irony was clearly wasted upon a man capable of burning stars and stripes while wearing the uniform of the Chicago Cubs.

The students now realise that they need a truly dramatic gesture to recapture their place on the network news, and the form of that gesture may well determine the success or failure of these Olympics.

Yet the citizens of Seoul are apparently unconcerned by the prospect. They wrestle magnificently with the English language. They hold the British in embarrassing esteem. 'All British true gentlemen,' they say, with the wonderful innocence of people who have yet to be visited by English football teams.

They whisk you across their fascinating city, they flaunt their superb stadia, they thank you for travelling so far to visit their Games. And they smile. Constantly they smile.

And you find yourself hoping and praying that nothing will happen in these next fifteen days to steal the smiles from all those shining faces.

Ben Johnson at the Peak

Mail on Sunday, 25 September 1988

IT WASN'T THE RECORD AND it wasn't the title. As Ben Johnson confessed after winning the fastest race in history; it was personal.

'The most important thing was to beat Carl Lewis,' said the new Olympic 100 metres champion. 'I don't care about the gold medal and all that stuff. I had to beat Lewis.'

For the past months and years, Johnson has insisted that the Olympic final was just another race, Lewis just another opponent. Now, in his moment of victory, this brooding, complex athlete was telling the truth.

Johnson is not an eloquent man. He has a slight stutter and he does not easily assemble his thoughts. Elements in the Lewis camp have lampooned him as a robotic character, devoid of wit and charm.

But in the space of 9.79 seconds, the robot had won the ultimate battle. And he was behaving just as Sonny Liston might have behaved had his arguments with young Cassius Clay worked out differently: unsmiling, yet unmistakeably gleeful.

He described the defeat of Lewis with a delight which approached sadism. 'I concentrated on the race for about 30 metres,' said Johnson. 'After that, I didn't see anyone. But all the time I was thinking: "Lewis. Where is he? He must be coming".' But at that murderous, unprecedented pace, Lewis was never going to arrive. And Johnson knew it. The first man to break the 9.90 barrier at 100 metres had now ventured into unthinkable territory. Not merely the best sprinter in the world, but surely the best the world has ever seen. And he had flourished the proof in an Olympic arena.

Those of us who believed Lewis would become the first man to retain an Olympic 100 metres title saw our view reinforced by the heats and semi-finals in which Lewis flew while Johnson toiled. We did not know, nor could we believe, that he was withholding a critical edge of pace.

Even when Johnson detonated that controlled explosion from the blocks, we awaited the surge which Lewis has been producing to order this week. But this time the pace was maintained and increased. And after 70 metres, the rest of the field was competing for minor medals, with Lewis eventually relieved to steal the silver from Linford Christie as they careered through the line.

The statistics were dazzling: Johnson 9.79 seconds, Lewis 9.92, Christie 9.97 for a new European record and Calvin Smith, condemned to run 9.99 and finish outside the medals.

'Didn't surprise me,' said Johnson, with the air of one who habitually strips four-hundredths of a second from a world record. 'I guessed it might be pretty fast.'

Lewis accepted defeat with dignified grace: 'I ran a good race, but he ran a great one. I didn't see him until around 70 metres, and by then it was too late. But this is the Olympics; the best people come, they run their best and someone wins. That's how it is.'

That is precisely how it was in Seoul's Olympic Stadium yesterday when we were given an athletic performance which was a treasure to commit to memory.

Lewis will go on to seek consolation in three other events, and his form suggests he will find it. But Johnson now assumes a position on Mount Olympus with the greats of his events – Owens, Hayes, Borzov and the rest.

And when history places this performance in sober perspective, it just might decide that Ben Johnson has earned a place at the peak.

The Man in Room 1728

Mail on Sunday, 2 October 1988

TODAY, IN SEOUL's Olympic Stadium, the Games of the XXIVth Olympiad will be consigned to history. There will be songs and speeches and a deal of self-congratulation.

If all goes well, it should be quite a party here. Yet it will be marked by the absence of a significant guest.

But while Ben Johnson is out of sight, he can never be out of mind. When historians come to demonstrate how international sport declined into chaos and corruption, his contribution to the Seoul Olympics will provide a pivotal chapter.

Johnson faced a preposterous gamble: the looming possibility of liver and kidney failure, along with various forms of cancer, in exchange for the chance of honour, glory and $10 million.

All he had to do was undergo a course of the steroid Stanozolol. He did, and at 3.30 am on Tuesday, officials arrived at Room 1728 of the Seoul Hilton to inform Johnson that his gamble had failed.

Perhaps only another Olympic athlete could understand his motives.

A recent poll posed Olympians an apparently insane question: 'If you were offered an undetectable drug which could guarantee a gold medal but would also kill you within five years, would you take it?' Of those asked, 52 per cent replied Yes. Death was an acceptable reward for success in a boyish game.

Now a grown man who excelled at boyish games had been revealed as a cheat, and the world quivered with indignation.

The scale of that indignation reflects the grotesque importance which the modern Olympics have acquired. Within 12 hours of the Johnson revelation, a tourist approached me at the entrance to the Olympic Village. 'I just want to apologise for being Canadian,' he said. 'The people of Canada will never live this down.'

After all, if a nation can be elevated by Olympic success, then that same nation must necessarily be mortified by shameful failure.

Those alarming illusions have been communicated to athletes, the hapless standard bearers of national prestige. The message is simple and direct: 'Do it for us and we'll do it for you.'

The Russians are offering around £8,500 for a gold medal, the French £20,000, the West Germans and Malaysians £18,000.

Even Britain, whose investment in sport remains pathetically parsimonious, retains a stock of OBEs and civic receptions for successful Olympians.

Ben Johnson was naturally prey to such pressures. As his muscles and talent expanded, he acquired a flamboyantly ambitious coach, a dubious personal physician, and a business manager who made him acutely aware of the riches in store.

Only success could guarantee those riches and only drugs could guarantee success. He knew the dangers, but a sporting career is short and $10 million is a powerful incentive. So he took the decision which destroyed him, and that business manager was reduced to hawking Ben's story in pursuit of his final percentage.

The reaction of Johnson's peers was almost as disturbing as his offence. In public, they offered expressions of outrage tempered with compassion. Privately, they marvelled at his stupidity. 'How did he do a dumb thing like that?' asked one American sprinter. 'He knows how the thing works. How did he get it so wrong?'

This cynicism has contaminated the Games. Even as you watch the staggering performances, you wonder about the chemical contribution to such excellence. Minor improvements are scrutinised, dramatic advances are derided. Linford Christie's achievements in Seoul deserve our unqualified praise, yet the split decision to acquit him of a drugs transgression will sow doubts in many a mind. In the current climate, accusation has become almost tantamount to proof.

When such suspicions take root, the whole future of the Olympic Games is called into question.

There are those who believe that Johnson's downfall will serve as an ominous warning to others.

But many of us here are not encouraged by the words of Ed Moses, a double gold medallist and perhaps the most respected Olympic athlete.

Moses insists that the discovery of Johnson's transgression was no more than a happy accident, born of the Canadian's desperation. 'Athletes know they can get away with it because they know how the testing procedures work,' he says. 'It's very unlikely that an athlete will be caught, because they are way ahead of the testing people.'

Those 'testing people' would dispute the claim. Professor Robert Dugal, a member of the Olympic Medical Commission, is paternally proud of the £5 million testing centre here.

'Our equipment could spot a spoonful of sugar in an Olympic-size swimming pool,' he says. But when the untutored eye stares across the Olympic track, it seems to discern an unacceptable amount of sugar.

Yet drugs are merely a symptom of the deeper problem which threatens international sport.

The final bill for the Games will come in at around £1.8 billion – and if peace should prevail until the Olympic flame is extinguished, then South Korea will account it money well spent in terms of international status.

The whole affair is a shameless display of giganticism, top-heavy with expensive fripperies, like that exercise in group drowning known as synchronised swimming.

But the stars of the show – the track and field athletes, swimmers and gymnasts – realise that theirs is a central role in a billion-pound entertainment, and, naturally, they exact their price in hard cash or national prestige. In exchange, they are prepared to pay an obscene price to secure their rewards.

So the girl gymnasts reach for puberty-suppressing drugs to retain litheness of movement, the swimmers reach for anything which will help them go faster – and Ben Johnson reached for Stanozolol.

Their obsessive determination to succeed is increased by the gargantuan scale and tone of television coverage. At a cost of £179 million, America's NBC network has funded the Olympics. They call the shots, set the agenda and generally reduce the most important sporting occasion on Earth to the level of an Idaho State Fair.

Their attitude was summed up last week by an NBC executive. 'I have one criterion,' he said. 'Will it play in Pittsburgh? If not, forget it.'

As an Olympic motto, it seemed distinctly inferior to Citius, Altius, Fortius, but it served his parochial purpose.

Television also creates the illusion that this corner of Asia is currently the centre of the universe.

Liver and kidney failure as well as cancer could seem small risks for a man who could dominate such a setting.

One man who took that gamble paid an expensive penalty. Others may have been saner, shrewder or more fortunate. But they did it in the insane belief that sport carries an importance which transcends the honourable pursuit of excellence.

As John Arlott observed many years ago: 'We take sport too seriously and life too lightly.'

It doesn't have to be like that, and there were times here last week when the world seemed to have discovered a civilised focus.

At the heart of the Olympic Village athletes sat in sprawling groups across an artificial lawn, laughing and gossiping in a dozen languages. In a brave attempt at an alien language, the Village newspaper's front-page headline declared: 'What A Nice If World Is Just Like Village.'

But when you listened, you discovered that the athletes of the world were discussing the dominant topic of the Games.

They were speaking of the man who surrendered his gold medal in Room 1728, the fugitive who will miss today's farewell party.

Yet those athletes are precisely the people who will decide the direction of the Olympics when the circus moves on to Barcelona in 1992. Despite disastrous ratings, American television coverage will not become cheaper or less crass. And the International Olympic Committee will still insist upon making its elephantine event more grandiose and unwieldy.

The only hope lies with the athletes. Beginning with Barcelona, they have the power to create a safer, cleaner Olympics. Sadly, they also have the power to dig a pauper's grave for the most expensive show on Earth.

High Noon in Great Court

Mail on Sunday, 30 October 1988

A THIN AUTUMN SUN glinted off the Bell Tower of Trinity, a cheering crowd democratically trampled the lawns of Great Court and a Prince clapped his hands and stamped his suede shoes.

Steve Cram, still panting from his noon-day exertions, surveyed the scene and made a prophesy. 'Now,' he said, 'something really corny is going to happen.'

He was right. Within seconds, the synthesised twang of the Chariots of Fire theme filled the ancient Cambridge quad and Cram and his conqueror, Sebastian Coe, were swept into a lap of honour.

'Bloody hell,' said Cram. 'They're really laying it on thick, aren't they?'

Indeed they were. With a silver-plated trowel, in fact. But on such a day, nobody minded in the least.

The attempt by Coe and Cram to run the circumference of Great Court within the noon chimes of the clock was attended by 1,500 people, covered by the television cameras of 15 nations, watched by untold millions and raised more than £50,000 for Great Ormond Street Hospital for Sick Children.

It was, as Coe remarked, the sort of event which could only happen in England. Others, more darkly, observed that the National Health Service was once run without recourse to charity.

But times have changed, fund-raising is not only worthy but essential. And yesterday, Coe applied himself with all the spirited diligence of an aspiring Conservative politician. Officially, the feat had been achieved only once – by the late Lord Burghley, who did it in 1927 in 45.75 secs. Burghley was the inspiration for the fictional Lord Lindsey who, in the film Chariots of Fire, raced Olympic athlete Harold Abrahams around the quad.

In real life Abrahams never ran the courtyard, but the race has been attempted by generation after generation of Cambridge undergraduates awash with high ambition and strong drink.

The most recent attempt was made a week ago by 300 students fresh from the Matriculation Dinner. 'I don't know if anybody succeeded,' confessed one of the participants yesterday. 'You see, the buggers turned off the chimes. They're like that here.'

He, like many of his colleagues, was amazed that the college authorities had agreed to yesterday's escapade. They had, after all, refused facilities for the makers of Chariots of Fire, who were forced to transport the scene to Eton.

'They didn't like film-makers,' said the screenwriter Colin Welland yesterday. 'Bloody carpet-baggers, we were. But it's amazing what you can bring off when you've got royalty involved.'

Prince Edward, in truth, may well have worked the trick. And he seemed to have enjoyed himself hugely, bringing the runners to their marks and lecturing them briefly with the air of a Head Prefect determined to ensure that Speech Day goes off jolly well.

Neither Cram nor Coe, it should be said, was treating the event with quite the *gravitas* they might have brought to an Olympic final.

Cram warmed up in an adjoining courtyard with sweat barely staining his yellow Jarrow vest, while Coe's preparation consisted of signing copies of his latest book at the local bookshop before pulling on a pair of long, baggy Twenties running shorts.

But, once away, they flew around the 367 metres of flag-stones and cobbles, checking almost to a stop at the right-angled corners, then sprinting smoothly down the straights.

Past the Master's Lodge they ran; past the Great Hall and Queen's Gate; past the rooms where Sir Isaac Newton once worked and where William Makepeace Thackeray and Lord Macauley lived; past the Great Gate and the Chapel and finally, with the booming chimes drowned by cheers, across a white line in front of the Trinity Clock.

Coe had taken a lead within five strides and on such a course it was never to be surrendered. Cram was a couple of strides behind at the finish. But had they done it, had they emulated the venerable feat of Burghley? The loud cheering at the finish ensured only that no-one could be sure.

All eyes turned to a calculating machine in a double-breasted blazer, and Norris McWhirter announced the glad tidings: both men had succeeded, Coe in a winning time of 45.52 secs. A kind of history had been created.

Coe and Cram went off to lunch with the Prince, while Trinity breathed a sigh of deep relief as it ushered its visitors from the premises and checked to see if the cameras had damaged the fabric of their ancient Court.

'Bloody marvellous, isn't it?' said Colin Welland. 'You sit in a little room and dream up a scene for a film. Then suddenly the whole world's taking it seriously. Bloody marvellous.'

Great Court was now empty apart from a few wandering students. Bowler-hatted porters were flitting about the lawns and covering the evidence of intrusion. A few million people had been pleasantly amused and a children's hospital had raised a great deal of money.

Bloody marvellous indeed.

Male Members, Behaving Badly

Mail on Sunday, 11 December 1988

THE GENTLEMEN OF Lancashire County Cricket Club strolled out into the lunchtime drizzle at Old Trafford yesterday, blissfully content with their morning's work.

By their soberly considered vote a few moments earlier, they had reaffirmed Victorian values, rejected the twentieth century and put women firmly in their place.

It had been widely expected that Lancashire, in its 125th year as a cricketing county, would finally admit women to their membership. The satisfaction on the florid faces of the lunchtime strollers told a quite different story.

The packed meeting in Old Trafford's Tyldesley Suite actually supported the cause of 'the ladies' by 1,296 to 841. But that support fell short of the two-thirds majority required for change.

The opposition had been led by one Ken Dean: club-tied, horn-rimmed and carrying the wonderfully misplaced self-confidence of the poor club comedian.

'You know me, Mr Chairman,' he bubbled. 'Probably one or two people saw me yesterday on various parts of the media.'

Basking in his new-found celebrity status, he announced that one radio station had referred to him as 'pig' and that a local newspaper had held him up to ridicule.

But his most telling message was reserved for what he will forgive me calling his 'climax'. 'Once you've let them in, you can't undo it. When they passed votes for women in 1918, they couldn't undo it.'

The members were much impressed by his command of history and logic, and equally taken by the observation of a sage from Southport who observed that: 'Male members should hold on to what they've got.'

Why, they even cheered the liberal instincts of a little old chap from Timperley who conceded: 'I would let them in, provided they kept to Tuesday afternoons and didn't bring a dog with them.'

But they growled and grunted at the gentleman member who wanted to attend matches in the company of his wife and family. Strange chap, that one.

And they heckled and jeered when John Brewer, on behalf of the club committee, attempted to put his civilised case.

'What would be said of us if we were to reject somebody because of his religion or the colour of his skin, or even because he was a Yorkshireman?' he inquired. 'The same can be said of ladies. We are in serious danger of being held up to ridicule by the world outside.'

They were not impressed. 'Roobish!' they shouted. And: 'Sit down, you soft booger.' So much for the world outside.

You found yourself idly wondering about the dark and Freudian forces which inform such hilarious chauvinism. You wondered if one or two of the tweed jackets and regimental ties might actually have voted for a woman prime minister.

Above all, you wondered why any intelligent woman would want to become part of such an assembly.

But Lancashire are not alone in their prejudice. Only nearly so. Middlesex, because of their tangled ties with MCC, are the only other first-class county who do not admit women to membership.

Their attitude would be readily understood by many of our major golf clubs. Muirfield, Royal St Georges, Troon, Prestwick and the Royal and Ancient remain exclusively male: beyond hope, beyond parody.

The Royal Yacht Squadron has 450 members and admits nobody who admits to being female. The Royal Thames Yacht Club, marginally more tolerant, now allows women to share their hitherto men-only staircase.

While the Henley Regatta retains an admirably consistent policy towards women: they cannot wear trousers or skirts above their knees. And, it goes without saying, they cannot row.

Lancashire CCC (Patron HM The Queen) may be aware of this wider discrimination which taints so much of British sport, but plainly they are unconcerned. As one member expressed it yesterday: 'It's our club and we'll run it our way.'

But as the waitresses did women's work and cleared away empty glasses after the meeting, your eyes were drawn to the tinselled decorations overhanging the platform.

'Merry Christmas,' announced the banner. It did not add: 'And goodwill to all Men.' But it might have done.

1989

A strange evening in Genoa with Seb, and a wild night in Las Vegas with Bruno and Tyson. They were still printing newspapers at breakfast time in London, such was the interest in the title fight. Unfortunately, the miracle refused to materialise and the tale made sombre reading over the cornflakes.

Mo Johnston made his blue-shirted debut later in the year as he began an historic, if sadly brief, relationship with Glasgow Rangers. And Mike Gatting, who didn't know much about apartheid, undertook an unwise expedition and rendered himself a figure of fun.

A Reason to Quit

Mail on Sunday, 5 February 1989

RICARDO CHACON LEANED against a washbasin and offered his forearm to the needle.

He winced and cursed softly as his countryman pressed the syringe. The vein, swollen by a white ligature, presented a throbbing target between elbow and palm. The needle found its mark.

Thirty minutes later, Ricardo Chacon competed for Cuba in an international athletics meeting.

That incident took place in a public toilet at the Palasport, Genoa, shortly before eight o'clock on Wednesday evening.

It lasted for only a few moments and it may well be easily explained on innocent medical grounds. On the other hand I may have witnessed a brazen example of the drug abuse which is threatening to destroy the sport of track and field.

I had travelled to Genoa to watch Sebastian Coe run an 800 metres race. It was a low-key meeting which featured a sprinkling of Americans and a small Cuban team. There was no drug-testing.

Coe arrived early and attempted to jog away the effects of a calf injury. Peter Coe, Seb's father and coach, fretted as the injury failed to respond. Eventually, he walked off to consider a decision.

He returned, agitated, a few moments later and grabbed my arm. 'Quick!' he said. 'Through that door over there. Bloody disgrace. You won't believe it.'

Inside the white-tiled toilet, I found Chacon receiving his injection from a Cuban official. I stood there watching for several moments and they ignored me. Two young Italians came in and stared at the scene. They, too, were ignored.

When the Cubans emerged, our photographer Keith Waldegrave approached Chacon. The 25-year-old athlete shook his head and put his hand over his face. He began some exercises, but buried his head in his lap when he saw the camera. Then he trotted away.

Peter Coe was genuinely shocked. 'Mustn't jump to conclusions,' he said, 'but I've never seen anything like that. I mean, what are we supposed to make of it?

'I think of all the work, all the agony that Seb's gone through over 20 years. Then I think of people who try to take short cuts by using a needle. It makes me bloody furious.'

His son was equally contemptuous. 'They're just laughing at people,' he said. 'There's no attempt to hide anything.

'If it's that important to win a race at a meaningless meeting in February, can you imagine what kind of State medical technology must be involved in something like the Olympics? Madness.'

By now, Coe had decided against competing. The aching calf was a bad risk. But Ricardo Chacon was exploding from his blocks in the 60-metre sprint and qualifying for the final.

Cuban athletes were to take the first two places in that final, but Chacon finished only fifth.

Seb sat and signed autographs, declining to watch the race. But later, picking at a midnight supper, he assembled his thoughts.

'Whenever I talk about drugs, some people say I'm scare-mongering,' he said. 'They think I should be emphasising the wholesome face of a sport that families can come and enjoy in safety.

'Of course that side's still there, thank goodness. But there's another side. We have people who stick needles in their arms to improve their performances. If we ignore that, then athletics doesn't have a chance.'

As Peter Coe had said, we should not jump to conclusions. Ricardo Chacon could have had reason for his actions.

He might, for instance, have been receiving some kind of pain-killing injection. Perhaps he was a diabetic, dependent upon insulin? There are any number of innocent medications which an athlete may take without fear of penalty.

Next morning, I approached a Cuban official at the team hotel to seek an explanation. He was not anxious to talk, instead he shrugged his shoulders, muttered a few words of Spanish and hurried away.

It appeared that he had used the word 'vitamins'. A vitamin injection would have been a distinctly curious but legal procedure, and a drug test on Chacon would have revealed the truth. But no test was taken.

Ron Pickering, the BBC commentator who is an authority on drugs in sport, was at the Genoa meeting. His reaction to the Chacon incident was one of 'stark horror.'

Said Pickering: 'When kids can walk into a toilet and see an athlete being injected, then our sport's in a sorry state.

'I discount any pain-killer theory because of the way the injection was given. And to get an advantage from Vitamin B12, which may be legal but is bloody unsavoury, he would have had to take it on the morning of the race. Not within an hour of competing. And not in a public toilet, for God's sake.

'They have dressing rooms and a perfectly good medical centre at the Palasport. No, the whole thing is quite disgraceful. We can't just let it go.'

Pickering intends to raise the matter with Alberto Juantorena, a double Olympic champion who is Cuba's representative on the International Olympic Committee.

Certainly, the Cuban must be given the opportunity to provide a full explanation and the Italian Federation must insist that such an explanation is forthcoming. Meanwhile, the sport's crisis deepens.

I had asked Seb Coe if the drugs situation had played a part in his decision to retire at the end of the year. He thought for a while, then he looked out on the arena where Ricardo Chacon was preparing himself for competition.

'I don't know,' said Coe. 'But I hate the things that are happening. If I were looking for a reason to quit, that would be as good as any.'

Bravest Loser in Las Vegas

Mail on Sunday, 26 February 1989

O N A LAS VEGAS EVENING of violent drama and staggering courage, Frank Bruno assured himself an eternal place in the hearts of a doubting nation.

His dream of becoming heavyweight champion of the world perished after two minutes, 55 seconds of the fifth round.

Yet Bruno delivered the most memorable fight of his life and those of us who suffered along with him at that clamorous ringside will forever tell of how close he came to glorious success.

Bruno had spent the past few weeks attempting to convince himself and the world that he carried the equipment to overcome the young champion.

Against a man who was intimidating, undefeated and seemingly invincible, Bruno performed with a resolution and courage which was a credit to his cause.

For a few seconds at the end of an extraordinary opening round, we could almost believe that the most incredible gamble in heavyweight history was about to pay off as a careless Tyson was caught by a concussive Bruno left hook and forced to scramble in order to survive.

Tyson's crisis passed, survival was achieved and eventually his most damaging form was discovered.

Yet Bruno confounded those who had dismissed his challenge. He had fought the fight of his life and the welcome which lies in wait for him when he returns to London is one which he has done everything to deserve.

The opening round had produced one of the most hectic and dramatic starts in modern heavyweight history. And at the end of it, improbably, it was Bruno who was dictating terms.

Tyson had shown his challenger no respect, walking forwards with bar room swings from the opening bell.

His arrogance was rewarded within ten seconds when a series of short punches sent Bruno to the floor for a short, bewildered count.

But Bruno kept his composure, clubbed Tyson to head and body with his heavy right hand and attempted to box behind a jab.

And then within the last minute of that round Tyson's carelessness almost betrayed him. Leaving himself perilously exposed to the hooks of the Briton, he took a left hand high on the head and, for the first time in memory, he was forced to hang on grimly in order to survive the onslaught.

By now the British fans were screaming still louder, urging their man on in search of his miracle.

But those cheers were quelled midway through round two when Tyson tightened his approach, picked his weapons and sent Bruno against the ropes with a heavy combination to the jaw.

Bruno had been warned for punching at the back of Tyson's head during that opening round but the champion's head had cleared ominously in the third as he began to use that stunning right hand to devastating effect, driving his punches through Bruno's tangled guard and slipping the occasional heavy shots to Bruno's muscular midriff.

Tyson's onslaught continued through the fourth when Bruno was forced to accept heavy body punishment with scarcely a retaliatory blow.

To his enormous credit, he was withstanding the heaviest shots that the champion could unload, but there were signs of weariness as Bruno returned to his corner and contemplated what round five might bring.

In the event it brought him the vicious, remorseless punishment we had feared the man might suffer. Tyson began his work with a short, benevolent left hook which was the prelude to an ugly, protracted attack.

He threw hooks which rattled the body, vicious uppercuts which clattered the head and searing combinations which saw Bruno exposed and hopeless.

With courage far beyond the call of duty, Bruno attempted a punishing left uppercut of his own, but he was waving at a whirlwind. Tyson drove him across the ring, hammering punches with awesome effect.

Bruno's gumshield began to slip from his mouth. Bruno's blood began to spatter Tyson's shoulders. It had become an execution.

Terry Lawless leapt from his corner seat, towel at the ready, and began to move along the ropes to signal surrender. But referee

Richard Steele had seen enough and he leapt in, wrapped his arms around Frank Bruno and signalled that the punishment and the suffering was over.

The man was beaten, yet he departs with his courage confirmed and his dignity proudly intact.

The instant verdict of the American ringsiders was that Tyson had fought with the misplaced arrogance which has marked his behaviour these past many months. A man ominously equipped to inflict damage at minimal cost to himself had performed with the recklessness of a Rocky movie.

Yet Bruno's challenge and the authority of his work met with unqualified admiration. He did not freeze in fear as so many had done before him, and even when that opening knockdown seemed to preface instant catastrophe, he kept his head and remembered his craft.

Above all, his courage had been brutally examined and had emerged as his most significant virtue. A chin derided as pure glass had absorbed most of the heaviest shots of boxing's heaviest puncher.

Our man had blinked, winced and occasionally wobbled. Yet his instincts were admirable and, until the fight turned into a flood-tide of ferocious punishment, he had remained in there with a puncher's chance.

The Tyson corner had grown alarmed at this wholly unexpected resistance; demanding, cajoling, cursing and screaming at their patron as they urged him to blow away the target before him.

But the target would not yield until punishment became actual bodily harm.

The British, we are repeatedly told in this town, love a loser. On this wild and memorable evening in Las Vegas, we unashamedly cherished the bravest loser of all.

Charlton Return to the Valley

Mail on Sunday, 26 March 1989

THE QUEUE SPILLED DOWN the town hall steps and stretched along the side'street, where the stragglers turned up their collars against the evening rain.

By the time the meeting began, they had abandoned hope of joining the fortunate 700, packed inside. But they stood and waited for one reassuring signal.

They were not disappointed. Three minutes into his speech, the chairman delivered the line he had been savouring.

'To Charlton supporters everywhere,' he said. 'We're going home!'

The 700 rose and cheered. The chairman blushed, the directors beamed. And, moments later, an answering roar rushed in from the hundreds outside. After three and a half years of exile, Charlton are returning to the Valley.

Now some will say that the domestic arrangements of a largely unsuccessful football club are of small relevance to today's game.

Times, you see, have changed, and English football has embraced profit and propriety with the zeal of a convert.

Grounds which once rang with raucous passion are slowly becoming genteel tax havens where sponsors in glass-fronted boxes may safely entertain.

Major matches, which once began with the blast of a whistle, are now set in train by the nod of a television director.

Ordinary fans are increasingly reduced to the status of studio extras. Soon they will be required to carry ID cards. In time, they may have to furnish a character reference.

Yet the move to re-shape the national game as a sanitised exercise in corporate hospitality is meeting some splendid resistance. And the Charlton Affair is the latest straw in the wind.

At ten o'clock next Sunday morning, hundreds of volunteers will assemble at a derelict football ground, armed with buckets, brooms and spades. They will clear the terraces, sweep the stands and hack away at the jungle of a pitch. And new life will return to The Valley.

Not a ball has been kicked on that pitch since September 21, 1985, when Charlton defeated Stoke City then scuttled around the South Circular Road to share a ground with Crystal Palace.

The following months and years have seen a parade of protests, petitions and public meetings. They have seen the birth of an excellent 'alternative' magazine, dedicated to a return to the Valley. And they have seen a highly effective boycott of the alien Selhurst Park.

Such fervent attachment to a sports stadium would not be understood outside these shores. New Yorkers may have been incensed all those years ago when the Brooklyn Dodgers decamped to Los Angeles, but today the law of the franchise prevails.

Here, loyalties run deeper. The ground is the club and the club the embodiment of the community.

The evidence is littered about the land. Where is Accrington without its Stanley? What lies in store for Newport now County is no more? And how would Wolverhampton have survived the loss of Wanderers?

Without a football club to confer identity, Middlesbrough and Derby would become blobs on a road map. Without a football club, Luton would virtually cease to exist. And without a football club, Charlton would become an unremarkable suburb in South-East London.

Even manager Lennie Lawrence was amazed at the tenacity of the fans. 'To go on and on, the way they did. Amazing,' he said. 'They deserved a result.'

Indeed they did. And a mixture of local pride and a respect for tradition by people who never saw Sam Bartram play nor watched the FA Cup being brought home to the Valley ensured that the result would be delivered.

'Strange how a football ground can catch hold of you,' said Charlton's chairman Roger Alwen. 'I came past the Valley tonight and I found myself staring at it. All those memories! We had to go back, didn't we.'

This wasn't the cold, accountants' jargon which is turning our grounds into theme parks for tired executives. It was the language of one who understands the emotions which have sustained the game.

The men who stood outside the town hall, waiting in the rain; they knew what he meant.

After all, he was speaking their own language.

Pope in Brawl at Ibrox

Mail on Sunday, 16 April 1989

W HEN THE POLICE ANNOUNCED a ban on inflatables at Arsenal football ground, innocent folk chuckled. 'You can't start a riot with inflatables,' they said.

I have news for them.

Last Saturday, a Motherwell fan purchased by mail order a large, life-size inflatable. He took it to the match, bought it a seat and inflated it.

Which explains how His Holiness Pope John Paul II came to be watching Glasgow Rangers play Motherwell from the main stand at Ibrox Park.

As Rangers' fans jeered, the stewards decreed deflation or explosion. The heroic fan acceded – and replaced the Pontiff with an alligator.

Was the Ibrox mob placated? It was not. The alligator, you see, was green. And even its orange eyes were not sufficient to gain it reprieve.

Incidentally, Rangers won 1–0. The Pope, I understand, was not best pleased. And the alligator was as sick as . . . well, you know.

Eeny, Meeny, Miney . . . and Jimmy

Mail on Sunday, 30 July 1989

O N A COOL, BRIGHT afternoon in the West of Scotland, a Roman Catholic named Maurice 'Mo' Johnston played football for Glasgow Rangers.

And, against many predictions, the skies did not descend, the mountains did not sink into the sea and not a single thunderbolt struck the humble Airdrie ground.

Instead, bigotry receded in bewildered retreat and an ancient club took a tentative step towards the 20th century. From where I was sitting, it all seemed to go pretty well. Johnston, of course, is the slim, straw-haired forward who is destined to be remembered for the religion of his birth rather than the talent with which he was born.

And when he ran out in the sacred blue jersey yesterday, his chest tastefully decorated with the logo of McEwan's Lager, he became the first Catholic of modern times to play for the Rangers.

Now Johnston is not the ideal candidate for such distinction. For one thing, he is the typical modern footballer, already the subject of a lurid biography. For another, he used to play for Glasgow Celtic, and was in the habit of making an extravagant Sign of the Cross when he scored against Rangers.

To those of Protestant persuasion, it represented a calculated provocation. To those of his own faith, it was a crass and deeply embarrassing piece of nonsense which held all the spiritual significance of a two-fingered gesture.

Rangers fans do not forget such things. Indeed, as men who still talk about 1690 and the Battle of the Boyne as if it were yesterday, they forget very little. How, we wondered, would they react to their new ecumenical striker?

The past three weeks have not been encouraging, marked as they were by a good deal of scarf-burning, hate mail and a sign proclaiming 'Traitor's Gate' at the entrance to Ibrox.

But, swathed in royal blue and loud with strong drink, they

emerged from the Orange Lodge in the centre of Airdrie and gathered beneath that tiny stand, where they sang about the sash their fathers wore and the joys of being 'up to our knees in Fenian blood'. And they waited for Mo.

The moment arrived, and the moment passed. Johnston ran across the pitch, looking anxiously at that stand. For a few moments there was silence, then somebody began a chant of 'Super Mo'. Gradually, the entire bank of blue took it up. Johnston waved, the fans waved back.

On the Broomfield ground in Airdrie, two minutes before the start of a meaningless pre-season friendly match, an historic barrier had fallen.

But, even as we celebrate its passing, it is important to realise the size of that barrier. The Rangers ban on Catholics has remained unspoken and unbroken down the decades.

Wilfully and wickedly, they cut themselves off from much of football's finest talent by their unswerving bigotry. Had players like Maradona, Di Stefano, Jennings or Brady offered Rangers their services for free, they would have been refused.

Had the greatest of them all turned up, he too would have been rejected. 'Pele, eh? Like the name, son. But what school did ye go to?' And now they have Mo Johnston.

On yesterday's slim evidence, he will do them a fine job. He is sharp and resourceful and he applied a deft touch in the prelude to two of Rangers' goals in their 3–1 victory.

The one slightly awkward moment of the day came 10 minutes from the end, when the Rangers choir was into 'If you're proud to be a Proddy, clap your hands.' Johnston clapped; but since he was merely encouraging his new team, it held no significance.

We must hope that this new atmosphere of sweetness and light will continue. But there are those who will never forgive the young man for turning away from his Celtic allegiance and joining the old enemy.

Indeed, they tell in Glasgow of the Catholic mother who last week gave birth to quads. She called them Eeny, Meeny, Miney . . . and Jimmy.

It is easy to smile at the story, more difficult to confront the bitterness that underlies it. Bigotry is not confined to the blue shirts and certainly Rangers took one small step for decency yesterday. But while people can come together in 1989 to sing of Prods and Papes and battles buried beneath the centuries, all the giant leaps have still to be taken.

PC Dixon Goes to Johannesburg

Mail on Sunday, 6 August 1989

THERE WERE THREE arc lights, four television cameras, a dozen photographers and a small forest of note-books awaiting Michael William Gatting when he arrived.

He blinked a couple of times, flicked a dribble of sweat from his brow and said: 'Evenin', gentlemen.'

Then he proceeded to explain why he is precipitating a revolution in English cricket by selling himself to South Africa.

In truth, Gatting is a most unlikely revolutionary. The wobbling stomach, the brush of grey beard, the club blazer, the pedantic phrasing; they all speak of a suburban police sergeant, recovering from a day of lost dogs and petty crime, eager to put his feet up with a mug of cocoa and a cheese and pickle sandwich.

Even when he admitted that he didn't know much about apartheid, you half-expected him to add: 'We don't get a lot of it on our patch.' Definitely more George Dixon than Che Guevara.

Yet we have to take him seriously, because this week Gatting and his 15 fellow rebels embarked upon an immensely serious course of action.

The likely effect upon English cricket is the most trifling consequence of their decision. True, the pace bowlers have departed almost en masse, nor shall we ever know whether the likes of Paul Jarvis and Matthew Maynard were mere pretenders or the genuine articles. But, by and large, the deserters have merely hastened the inevitable transfusion of fresh blood.

Yet the harm they have done to the moral standing of British sport is infinitely more damaging.

In their eagerness to acquire substantial riches for two short winter trips, they have confirmed what the wider world has always believed; that when apartheid requires a public relations officer, then the English cricketer is your man. To hell with the likely damage to the Commonwealth Games. To hell with the Gleneagles Agreement.

To hell with the deep offence given to the majority, disenfranchised, black community. To hell with the respectability which their presence confers on a repulsive regime.

With eyes closed and palms outstretched, it's off to the Cape we go.

South African motives are exposed by the scale of the money on offer. The fees involved make mockery of market values, from £120,000 for the troops to a reported £200,000 plus for their leader. This is not the currency of cricketing salaries; it is the price of an advertising campaign.

But the excuses have been as nauseating as they are unconvincing. Gatting, the man who doesn't know very much about apartheid, insists that the South African Cricket Union is trying to break it down.

Moreover, he adds: 'They seem to be the only people who are trying to do it.' Which may come as something of a shock to Archbishop Tutu and his friends.

He even exhumes cliches we haven't heard for a decade: 'There shouldn't be any politics in sport . . . I should be allowed to play cricket anywhere in the world without any come-back.' Blessed are the truly naive, for they shall go to Johannesburg. Jarvis was one rebel who seemed to be opting for truth. 'I'm going for the money,' he said on Wednesday. But 24 hours later, he was erecting avarice into principle. Now he was doing it for his family, for his new-born son.

In fact, he was: 'Helping South Africa out of the apartheid mess it is in.' How we had misjudged him!

From Roland Butcher, we heard nothing. As a 36-year-old batsman who played his three Test matches nine years ago and averaged 14.2 runs, he must know that his presence owes little to ability, everything to his black skin. Better, perhaps, that he should keep silent.

Silence would have been more than welcome from the BBC pundits. Instead, some of them could scarcely conceal their glee that Gatting's crusaders had struck a blow for so-called freedom in sport.

Jack Bannister and Tony Lewis, men who are known to enjoy both the climate and the cricket of Southern Africa, watched every word with exaggerated caution, but Ray – 'a cricketer's got to look after himself' – Illingworth grew so enthusiastic that he finished a sentence for almost the first time this summer.

Yet if television's performance was depressing, then radio's Test Match Special was positively abject. The BBC's cricket correspondent, Christopher Martin-Jenkins, announced the news with the air of a head prefect proclaiming a half-holiday.

Brian Johnston, his headmaster, smugly observed that: 'They are in no way "rebels". They are merely following their profession.' 'Absolutely!' gushed CMJ.

A programme which once was a jewel in radio's crown has descended to self-parody, lurching between chocolate-cake chortles and the bovine pomposities of the golf club bar.

How we yearned for the articulate moral authority of a John Arlott, the one man who would have addressed greed and treachery by their real names.

Mercenaries will go and, in the short term, they will prosper. Consciences will be soothed by hard cash and opponents will be dismissed as malcontents and hypocrites.

A few of those opponents, slogans scrawled on makeshift banners, were awaiting Gatting as his Rover pulled away from Lord's the other evening. They did not concern him. 'People are entitled to their own views,' he said. 'It's a free country.'

Indeed it is; a country in which we can live where we like, eat and drink where we please and vote for whom we choose. There is one country, however, where such freedoms are reserved only for men and women of acceptable colour.

And in this shameful week, Mike Gatting – who doesn't know much about apartheid – has unwittingly proved himself a true and valued friend of that squalid tyranny.

1990

Shuffling through Bucharest in history's footsteps. Hurrying across Rome to watch the Americans at the World Cup. Stepping out on the long and winding road from Hull to Grimsby on an ill-advised attempt to keep up with Mr Botham. There were times, I can tell you, when your correspondent felt quite overwhelmed by the pace of events.

But never remotely as overwhelmed as Buster Douglas, who had secured his place in folklore as the unlikely conqueror of Mike Tyson and was now making almost $20m for lying on his back and dreaming of room service. For all his slothful ineptitude, Buster had beaten the system. He was leaving boxing with his brains unscrambled, having earned almost as much money as his promoter. I voted him Sportsman of the Year for 1990. He lost that contest as well.

Jugglers on History's Stage

Mail on Sunday, 6 May 1990

UNIVERSITY SQUARE IN Bucharest is never silent; there is too much to discuss.

By day it hums with passionate argument; by night it throbs to the thunderous roar of mass rallies.

In the shadow of the National Theatre stands a tented village, where fiery young men from Timisoara plot the preservation of the revolution they helped to create.

Across the way, beneath the Faculty of Architecture, large pictures of the deposed tyrant Ceausescu stare down upon the crowd, the letters 'S' in his name replaced by swastikas.

In the centre of the square is a tall, wooden cross, its base surrounded by burning candles and its stem supporting long-hidden lithographs of the Blessed Virgin and flimsy pictures of the martyrs who died in the days before Christmas: Petre Maryan, Constantin Vania, Oancea Cristian; the names and faces plucked at random from a toll of thousands.

Two weeks from today, Romania will embrace her first free and democratic election, and all her doubts, fears and conflicting aspirations are concentrated upon this single square in Bucharest.

Every day this week, a group of British tennis players has crossed this square; first to prepare, then to play in a Davis Cup tie. Their backs are thumped and their hands are pumped, but they do not relish their celebrity. Like a troupe of jugglers shuffling innocently across history's stage, they are deeply embarrassed.

'Absolutely ludicrous,' says Andrew Castle. 'These people are debating issues of life and death, and we're talking about serve and volley. You have to come to a place like this to find out what's really important. God, I feel so pathetic.'

His emotional response was entirely admirable, and you found yourself wishing that other British sportsmen could be so sensitive. Yet there are those who insist that he is wrong.

'It is important for them to come here,' says Petre Roman. 'I welcome them as ambassadors and I admire them as tennis players. Truly, you don't know how much I admire them.'

Despite his vibrant youth and cruiserweight shoulders, Mr Roman is not an accomplished tennis player. But, as Prime Minister of Romania, he doesn't get too much time to practise.

Unsurprisingly, his Cabinet allies endorse his sentiments. Mircea Angelescu, the Minister for Sport, emphasises the new freedoms; passports being properly provided, athletes being allowed to retain most of their earnings, footballers who choose to stay at home being justly rewarded.

In truth, the past is not so easily buried. In Victory Square, the secret police headquarters of the Securitate stand haggard and derelict against the clear May sky.

Ceausescu's Royal Palace, from which he made his final, unavailing address to the nation, bears its bullet wounds like a rash of eczema. The grounds are tended by a solitary soldier.

The babble continues in University Square, befitting an election which encompasses 70 parties and 5,800 parliamentary candidates. The infant democracy comes squawking into the world as the public worries, with some justification, about its parents' dubious ties with the Ceausescu regime.

But over at the Progressul, all the criticism is reserved for the tennis, as if it were genuinely important. From his courtside box, Ilie Nastase yawns through a laborious singles: 'Nobody is alive out there. I think I may go to sleep. These are matches between dead people.'

His audience giggles at the phrase, and Nastase preens. And as you watch the indifferent tennis on show you join the easy laughter.

But when the laughter is done, you return to University Square. The candles around the wooden crucifix have become a field of fire. Old ladies and young children genuflect discreetly and murmur prayers for the martyrs. The contending parties prepare for the evening's exertions.

And the young men who play tennis return to the shelter of the Inter-Continental Hotel.

'We don't understand, do we?' says Andrew Castle. 'We don't bloody understand. But we suspect we might be seeing something marvellous. Sure, what we're doing may be totally frivolous, but I'll tell you what: I'm glad we're here.'

The buzz of argument yields to the roar of a rally. The men from

Timisoara emerge from their tents to add their voices to the tumult.

And the British tennis players look down from their rooms on the 19th floor, staring from history's baseline as a new nation is assembled and a new world acquires its uncertain shape.

In a square, in Bucharest, in the opening year of a better and braver decade.

America Comes of Age

Mail on Sunday, 17 June 1990

A T SIX MINUTES PAST midnight, in a room at the rear of the Olympic Stadium, the United States of America took its place among the football nations of the world.

It happened when Mr Bob Gansler sunk his hands into his pockets, shook his head and informed us that: 'Football's a funny game.'

Now when the manager of the USA can reach instinctively for the oldest cliche the game has to offer, then you may be quite certain that things are starting to happen in that great democracy beyond the ocean.

An hour or two earlier, the land of Babe Ruth and Joe Montana had restricted the nation of Dino Zoff and Paulo Rossi to a single goal.

The fact that they defended in droves, kicked Italian limbs when no ball was available, and sought managerial approval before crossing the half-way line is of small consequence.

As one member of the American Embassy staff observed: 'That was the Little Big Horn out there tonight. And we came through.' General Custer, as I recall, was rather less fortunate.

Sadly, the folks back home will be largely unaware of the service their soccer players have done them, since in America the World Cup is receiving the kind of television ratings normally reserved for repeats of I Love Lucy. Naturally, this rampant apathy offends the manager, especially as it calls into further question the outrageous decision to award the 1994 finals to the United States.

But he brushes it aside, like a man who will have no truck with negative thoughts: 'I'm not thinking '94,' he said. 'I'm thinking '90. Because '90 is now.' And nobody could give him an argument.

In fairness, and despite that remark about football being a funny game, Gansler does not fit the managerial stereotype. With his impeccable grooming, his slender figure and his cornflower blue eyes, he looks like a junior Senator for Idaho; Dan Quayle with the power of speech.

165

He also has a disconcerting tendency to burst into fluent German at the click of a heel, a facility which Dan does not enjoy.

When the Czechs poured five goals past America in their opening match, Gansler's team suffered a small crisis of confidence. The manager was equal to the challenge. 'We sat around. We talked hard facts. We did a lot of one on ones,' he said. 'And I got the answers.

'They knew what they were facing. I told them: "Hey, you're playing in the lion's den here. And you're up against the favoured lions."' It was the sort of team talk which English footballers hear before a match at Millwall. And, up to a point, it worked.

It worked because it was shameless. When a team has no desire to win; when the height of its ambition is the avoidance of heavy defeat, then it can make things infernally difficult for the best of sides.

And 'Iddaly', as the members of Team America are wont to call the host nation, remain one of the best.

Although they departed the stadium to the jeers of 73,000 frustrated followers, the Italian manager, Azeglio Vicini, knows that his team's American experience has changed nothing. The points were delivered, even if the goals did not flow, and players as gifted as Giannini, Vialli and Donadoni will surely grow with the tournament.

'We should not under-estimate the Americans,' said Vicini. 'Some of them can play football well. Remember.' And he said it with the air of one who will not spare them another thought for the rest of the summer.

But Gansler will never forget the evening; the small bank of stars and stripes, fluttering among the vast swathes of red, white and green, that rare moment of second-half aggression when only the Italian goalkeeper's hip prevented an equaliser, and the embarrassment of the scribes who had forecast ten Italian goals.

One such scribe was already munching his words: 'We've just gotten better,' he said. 'Better on the floor, better in the air, we're even better at fouling guys. And getting away with it.' Such is progress.

But Gansler didn't hear. Suddenly he was a football manager with an audience which demanded a ringing phrase. And he did not fail.

'Some match, huh?' he said. 'You know what, my team came back from the ashes. That was a Phoenix you saw out there tonight.'

A ballpoint scribbled at a notebook. That phrase would sit splendidly in the columns of the *Dallas Morning News*.

After more than half-a-century and a thousand false dawns, America had joined the football club. Bob Gansler smiled. It really was a funny game.

Jacko and the Ring of Steel

Punch, 15 June 1990

THE PRESS CENTRE IN Buenos Aires was large, slightly larger than the Royal Albert Hall. Five days before the opening of the 1978 World Cup finals, around 3000 journalists were sitting at typewriters and staring at empty sheets of paper. As I sat and stared with the rest, Jacko tapped me on the shoulder. 'Slow day?' he said. 'Nothing happening? Oh dear! You could always try "Gun-Toting Cops Throw A Ring Of Steel Around This Frightened City". But I think I've done that one already.'

Now Jacko was a tabloid reporter of the old school; a chunky, dapper fellow who knew his market and serviced it brilliantly. He had endured a thousand slow days of his own, but somehow he always found the words to fill them. And, as ever, he wanted to help. So he gave me a story about Scottish fans hitch-hiking down from New York to support their side. 'Very hard trip,' said Jacko. 'Sleeping rough, nowhere to wash and change. They're in a right state. People in Buenos Aires are complaining about the smell. Great story: "BO in BA". Geddit?'

But whimsy, however contrived, is not really his forte. 'You heard this rumour about the Red Brigades' threat to kidnap the Italian squad?' he asked, conversationally. 'I'm checking it out. My office wouldn't thank me if someone nicked a World Cup team and I hadn't told them.' Jacko went off to take on the forces of international terrorism and I returned to the empty sheet of paper.

As any long-serving hack will tell you, World Cups are like that: brief spasms of activity when the football is stunning and the clichés hurl themselves at the typewriter. And long days of gripes, grumbles and groin strains.

By comparison, the players have it easy. They sit around luxury hotels, placing calls to their agents, totting up the profits from their chart-topping theme tune and swapping lies about the size of their salaries. Occasionally they toddle off to the stadium for a football match, safe in the knowledge that if things go wrong, everybody will blame the manager. They neither know nor care about the problems of journalists, in fact they rather despise the breed. As one England footballer remarked after the last World Cup: '"Press" is a four-letter word.'

There was a time when that kind of hostility would have disturbed the sensitive football writer. But no longer. The odd sycophant still remains, to slap a back or giggle at an ingratiating joke, but most hacks adopt the admirable example of their tennis cousins at Wimbledon: We'll tolerate our lot until they're knocked out, then we can get on with the tournament.

Of course, such tolerance is not extended to the manager. Over the past eight years, Bobby Robson has treated the Press with decent courtesy, and he still seems genuinely shocked when he is abused in the grossest terms by men with whom he has shared a late drink or a cordial meal. The excuse they offer carries Mafia overtones: 'It's not personal, Bob. It's business.' And, in a sense, they are right. The persecution of Robson has sold a lot of tabloid newspapers – which is its single justification. How they will miss him when he goes.

By and large, the Robson-baiters tend to keep their own company at the World Cup, dining in small groups and chuckling over the latest malevolent headline dreamed up in London. The loyalists dine at a distant table, with expressions pained and haughty.

The television crowd, haughtiest of all, seek out a superior restaurant, far from these rough fellows. They guzzle Perrier, exchange compliments and list the satellite companies which have solicited their services with six-figure seductions; all loftily rejected. In the hacks' eyes, they are a mite precious, and the tale is told with some relish of how one telly-person, deep in conversation, accepted a large card from a waiter and scribbled his autograph. The waiter was puzzled. 'That, sir, was the menu,' he said.

Telly-men, loyalists and amateur assassins, they all have one prejudice in common; they all regard the news hounds, the Ring of Steel tendency, with the deepest distrust.

Jacko is aware of their feelings, and he cares not a toss. I once saw him hammering a typewriter with demented energy, taking care to cover the paper so that not a word should be revealed. An anxious football hack watched him at work. 'God knows what he's up to now,' he said. 'These people are capable of anything. And we're the ones who have to pick up the pieces.'

Jacko sensed his unease from 30 paces. 'Got a nice little tale here,' he said. 'How many a's are there in Baader-Meinhof?'

Beefy in the Parlour

Mail on Sunday, 21 October 1990

THE MAYOR OF Grimsby surveyed her parlour, smiled through a steaming cloud of sweat and embrocation and remarked to nobody in particular: 'I don't know when we last had a crowd like this.'

You could easily see what she meant. There in a wheelchair, supping a pint of bitter, sat a man with no legs who once had scored goals for Doncaster Rovers. Over there a carnival queen, draped in a red cloak, chatted with a former member of the SAS. In a corner of the parlour stood a man who, for no obvious reason, was dressed as a penguin.

And in the centre of it all, sprawled in the mayoral chair, huge feet upon the mayoral stool, Scotch in hand and a silver foil blanket around his shoulders, sat the finest all-round cricketer England has ever produced.

'It's good, this, innit?' said Ian Botham. And indeed it was.

A few moments earlier, the town of Grimsby had turned out to greet Botham's band of walkers as they tramped through the final soggy mile from Hull.

The East Coast March, which began in Aberdeen on the first day of October, had benefited by several thousands of pounds. Botham himself had clocked up a total of 2,175 miles of charity walking. And his latest venture, which ends in Ipswich next weekend, was on course to raise more than half-a-million pounds for the Leukaemia Research Fund.

A mayoral attendant, circulating with sandwiches, paused to stare at the big man. 'He's got his critics, has Ian Botham,' he said. 'But after this, I shan't have a word said against him.'

And, for what it's worth, neither shall I.

There are those who suspect that Botham has used these walks to enhance his frequently dubious image. After attempting to match his stride on a single 25-mile, six-hour slog, I can give the lie to that cynicism.

A man who puts himself through the agonising equivalent of a marathon every day for 26 days has far higher motives than image-building in mind.

On Thursday morning, while England's Test cricketers were assembling for their tour to Australia, Botham gathered his footsore forces at the Humber Bridge.

Over the next four months, we shall hear many tales of the stress and discomfort of a cricket tour. Let them come to the Humber, where the mist sits on your shoulders and the drizzle drools down your neck and the man at the front insists that you match his pace of four-and-a-half miles per hour.

The marchers were studded with moving stories. There were the three young lads who had lost a father to leukaemia and had raised £100 by selling apples. There was the man who appeared in the village of Barton Upon Humber to hand over a cheque for £1,300: 'Take that, our Ian. Three of my family have died from that disease.'

There was Clarrie Jordan in his wheelchair, telling tales of the old days at Doncaster Rovers and being pushed along by Fred Powey, once a welterweight contender, now soaking, steaming and raising money like the rest.

There was a flock of young ladies from the Spa supermarket chain, halting cars, clambering on passing buses, rattling collecting tins.

And there was Botham, bringing out the crowds in each village, in Barrow and Ulceby, in Brocklesby and Thornton Curtis; responding to every greeting, thankfully accepting every donation, never once breaking that relentless stride.

'I think we've got it right this time,' he said. 'There's just family and close friends involved, so nobody's creaming it off.

'Every penny goes to the Fund. Sure it's a struggle. I mean, after about an hour every day, my hands start swelling incredibly and my feet feel like they don't belong to me. But I get a good rest every night, and I'm ready again next morning. It's got to be done, hasn't it?'

Kathy Botham appears at intervals along the course; checking details, negotiating with police.

She has spent 18 months working on this walk and her organisation is impeccable. She shares with her husband the sense of mission which was born several years ago on a chance visit to the children's ward of a Somerset hospital.

'It's been hard work for a lot of people,' she says. 'But we'll get into Ipswich in one piece. You'll see.'

On we march, out of Yorkshire and past the desolate fields of north Lincolnshire, where they sow potatoes and barley and wheat. Village schools suddenly empty as the children throng the pavements. They scream their recognition. Botham waves and smiles.

After 17 miles, your correspondent is flagging. An elegant lady appears with a pint of ale: 'Take this,' she says. 'Much better than those bloody health drinks.' I ask for my benefactor's name. 'People just call me . . . Garbo,' she says. And disappears.

At the head of the march the Daily Mirror sports writer Chris Lander, who has trudged every charity mile with Botham, calls head office on his mobile phone to order more signed pictures.

After 21 miles, your correspondent succumbs to blisters, exhaustion and a kind old lady's observation that: 'You ought to be going a bit quicker, love.' Pathetically, he boards the accompanying bus.

But Botham strides on into Grimsby; past the surgery whose patients come clambering down the front steps, past the hairdresser's ('A Cut Above') and on through the crowds to the Town Hall and the sanctuary of the mayor's parlour.

'Another day gone, another week to go,' he says, and dreams about the bath which awaits him in the hotel.

I point out that the Test team departs in half-an-hour, that he could still make the plane if he tried. 'Not for me, mate,' he says. 'I don't want it any more. I wouldn't swop this for anything.'

Time was when you would have taken that remark with a pinch of salt. But now you are seeing the man in a different light. Now you can really believe him.

Demise of a Dumper Truck

Mail on Sunday, 28 October 1990

WITH HIS SHOULDERS SAGGING, his cap tugged over his eyes and the sound of righteous indignation assaulting his ears, James Buster Douglas mumbled his excuses and waddled into oblivion.

'Fink! . . . Quitter! . . . Bum!' The insults came screeching past the protective shoulders of the green-jacketed minders as the fight patrons paused in their indignant march from ringside to casino.

Inside that Mirage casino, a large man from the Mid-West was mundanely feeding 500 dollar tokens into a slot machine: *Chink, chink, chink*. Without a trace of irony, he spoke for the assembled hustlers and hookers and sky-high rollers.

'The guy was a disgrace,' he declared. 'Lazy fat sonofabitch just wanted to make a quick pile of bucks and get the hell outta here. Truly a disgrace.' *Chink, chink, chink*.

Now the high moral ground usually induces vertigo in Las Vegas, but in the early hours of Friday morning, words like 'shame' and 'cowardice' were the currency of conversation.

This reaction was palpably unfair to Evander Holyfield, the worthy and talented new heavyweight champion of the world. And, in a more complicated fashion, it was also unfair to James Buster Douglas.

In nine weeks of allegedly intensive training, Buster had laid to rest the myth that the best fighters are hungry fighters.

His insatiable appetite for junk food had draped 15 flabby pounds of excess baggage across his immense frame. As he stood upon the scales at the weigh-in, watching the needle flicker up to 246lbs, he seemed embarrassed by his own body; sucking in a great deep breath, he clenched his stomach muscles, like a middle-aged father at a holiday swimming pool.

His handlers wore the look of men who had set out to design a Ferrari and had somehow come up with a dumper truck.

By contrast, Holyfield seemed to have been chiselled from marble. In the past six years, he has put on 30lbs of solid muscle and now he nudges 208lbs; a small heavyweight by modern standards, yet more than a stone-and-a-half heavier than Rocky Marciano in his prime.

But after the damning evidence of the weigh-in, he didn't need to be Marciano; he simply needed to be Evander Holyfield at his most efficient. Events would take their inevitable course.

And so they did. Holyfield moved with a sense of grim purpose, while Douglas wobbled warily; a terrible testimony to the perils of junk food and a grotesque caricature of a heavyweight champion.

You found yourself remembering the fat boy in Bugsy Malone, the lad who trembled with fearful apprehension while the other kids sang: *So You Wanna Be a Boxer?*

The truth, I suspect, is that Buster never did want to be a fighting man. All that pain and discipline could find no echo in an essentially gentle nature.

But he had stumbled into the trade because times were hard and the money was promising, and eight months earlier that promise had been delivered when the finest night he will ever know coincided with the worst performance Mike Tyson will ever offer.

A real fighting man would have driven himself into shape for the title defence; pride and self-respect would have provided motivation, if not the absurd sum of $19,450,000 that he was about to receive.

A real fighting man would not have been blowing hard after two rounds, would not have hurled that optimistic uppercut in the third and exposed himself to the short, murderous right-hand counter.

And when his head had stopped singing and his brain had unscrambled, a real fighting man would have forced himself to his feet.

But that is not Buster's way. He had fought his fight like a man passing time between meals. Now he lay there comfortably, possibly dreaming of the room-service banquet he could order within the hour.

Cowardice is a fatuous charge, since cowards do not keep company with the likes of Tyson and Holyfield.

Shame is equally irrelevant, since Buster's nature does not embrace that lofty concept. Instead, he was content to congratulate his conqueror and reflect that: 'I had a bad night. I got caught. Sometimes it happens that way.'

The Holyfield camp affected indignation that a beaten fighter should attract more interest than the new champion.

Holyfield himself was entirely unconcerned. He is courteous and dignified even if he has yet to acquire the charisma which the title usually confers.

Since Thursday evening, he has discovered that people laugh more loudly at his jokes and react more smartly when he requests a soft drink. He seems a touch embarrassed by his daft nickname of Real Deal.

And he positively winced when the presenter of a post-fight Press Conference turned his back on Douglas and babbled: 'You're in charge now, Real Deal. You're calling the shots.'

In the course of a few modest speeches on Thursday night and Friday morning, he thanked everybody from Jesus Christ to the ladies in his car salesroom.

In that small husky voice, he even found kind words for the beaten Buster. Referring to the Tyson encounter, he said: 'Buster made history. He did what nobody ever thought he could do. I respect the guy.'

Yet, as a genuine fighting man, Holyfield knows he could never have prepared so wretchedly nor succumbed so willingly. His own ambitions run along the lines of improving with every fight and retiring undefeated.

Indeed, the nearest he came to boastfulness was his declaration that: 'All my life people have told me what I couldn't do. But I can do anything. All I needed was the opportunity.'

His next gainful employment will be found against George Foreman next Spring, when America's appetite for fat and cumbersome heavyweights will be put to the test. 'At last!' yelled Lou Duva, Holyfield's septuagenarian corner-man. 'We're finally fighting a guy that's older than me.'

But the fat man of the moment wasn't around to hear the crack.

Buster had departed much earlier, leaving the Mirage to its conventional diversions: the slot machines and the craps tables, the caged white tigers and the erupting volcano. All those endearing attractions which render Las Vegas a lurid blot on a perfectly good desert.

As he shuffled away, a Mirage official shook his head. 'There goes one dumb fighter,' he said. 'If he'd stayed in shape, he couldda made squillions. Dumb!'

The dumb fighter left town with his reputation in shreds and $19,450,000 in his pocket.

A man could buy a whole mountain of junk food with that kind of money. James Buster Douglas seemed content with the bargain.

1991

The best of '91 is easily identified. It was that glorious week in high summer when they sent me to the Pyrenees with orders to 'taste' the Tour de France. I loved it to distraction; extraordinary athletes blessed with improbable reserves of nerve, stamina and concentration, streaming in great swathes across breathtaking terrain and routinely reducing mountains to molehills. In the entire world of sport, the Tour stands alone.

The worst moment is equally easily recalled; it was the September evening at White Hart Lane when young Michael Watson fought Chris Eubank for a world title and suffered brain injuries so severe that he was condemned to a coma for months and a wheelchair for the rest of his life. Police had to clear a way through fighting fans as his stretcher left the ring. In normal circumstances, 'obscene' is an adjective best resisted. But, on that terrible night, it was the only one which seemed to fit.

Allez the Toasted Whippets!

Mail on Sunday, 21 July 1991

MIGUEL INDURAIN SAT IN a tent on the top of a mountain and talked about cycling. An agreeable fellow, he chatted for two hours and answered a few hundred questions in French and Spanish. Then, remarking that he felt a touch jaded, he climbed on his bike and rode off to his hotel.

Earlier in the day, he had cycled from the Spanish town of Jaca to the French ski resort of Val Louron. His journey of 145 miles had taken him seven hours and eleven minutes, during which time he had pedalled up and down five mountains. To mark this improbable achievement, they gave him a yellow jersey.

Now I suspect that Señor Indurain may be a little insane, but if so, he is in excellent company. For nothing in the whole world of sport can match the magnificent insanity which seizes this nation each July. And nowhere is that insanity more gloriously revealed than in the peaks and valleys of the Pyrenees. The first eleven stages are a pleasant deceit, a freewheeling feast of unassuming hills. Then, after a day of rest and apprehension, the race turns its face to the mountains. And the truth dawns: the Tour de France is an event devised by sadists for the persecution of supermen.

On Thursday morning, as the sun burns off the lingering mist above the town of Pau, the riders report for work with an air of bogus tranquillity. They are a curious physical breed, slender yet imposing. The muscles of calf and thigh are dramatically defined. Faces and forearms are baked a deep brown, with stark white lines at brow and bicep where the sun has been repelled by cap and jersey. Imagine a bunch of toasted whippets, and you have the general picture.

The teeming crowds urge them through the foothills; old ladies peering from doorways to offer gracious waves; young lads in yellow jerseys, watching and dreaming; middle-aged men in cycling shorts, wondering what might have been. After two hours, the climb begins; 5,000 feet to the summit of the Col de Soudet. A brief plunge, then another, longer climb to the Spanish border and the peak of the Col du Somport at 5,330 feet. The shade temperature has reached 95°F, and you start to understand how a man's brain might boil under such stress, and how poor Tommy Simpson perished all those years ago.

The white-painted signs on the road shriek encouragement; Allez Mottet! Allez Fignon! on the French side, yielding to Aupa Delgado! Aupa Indurain! across the border. On such a stage, a rider burns up more than 8,000 calories. These he attempts to replace by eating bread, jam tarts, fruit and muesli bars and swallowing five pints of fluid to combat dehydration. It is a daunting equation, and yet it brings the leaders through to Jaca in some five and a quarter hours.

There are two major surprises: Greg Lemond, the American winner of three previous Tours, has lost almost seven minutes on the stage, while the leader's yellow jersey has been acquired by the French novice Luc Leblanc. The crowds have discovered a new hero, but the experts insist that he will not survive. Tomorrow, they say, will tell a different tale. They mention the name of Miguel Indurain.

The riders retire for massage and sleep. They are called for dinner, then they return to their rooms. They wake for an early breakfast, then eat again, just before departure. The heat has relented by ten degrees, but the mountains are undiminished. Five of the awesome brutes must be scaled before the sanctuary of Val Louron. Such a day could decide the destiny of the Tour.

The Caravane Publicitaire leaves Jaca an hour before the riders; a hooting, whooping circus hustling the wares of 28 sponsors. They shower the fans with leaflets, trinkets and all manner of imperishable junk as they trundle through the mountain passes. After negotiating the first two Cols by abusing the lower gears of a rented saloon, I become embroiled with the Caravane on the ascent of the Tourmalet, a 7,000-foot giant and the highest point of the entire Tour.

Passing a fleet of Coca-Cola trucks, I am suddenly trapped between a huge plastic éclair, mounted on a three-wheeled motor cycle, and a large red boot perched upon a supercharged go-kart. Incited by the crowds, this demented trade fair slowly attains the summit. Whereupon the drivers stare down on the sinuous bends and react with a communal stamp of the right foot. We blast down the Tourmalet at 50 mph. Terrified, I contemplate the indignity of entering eternity between a red boot and a chocolate éclair.

Young Leblanc is also experiencing a few problems. As the

experts predicted, the yellow jersey is proving an onerous emblem. Inexperience impels him to cover every break, and the desperate bursts are destroying him. Eventually, on the 4,800-foot climb to the Col d'Aspin, he is broken. He pushes urgently at the pedals, but his calves are exploding and his body is spent. Lemond, too, is losing contact; the favourite drifting from the betting. Poor Laurence Roche, brother of Stephen, was never in that betting. At Val Louron, only five of the 176 survivors are behind him. But on he goes, and you tremble at his courage.

Yet Indurain is as strong as ever, the man grasping his moment. He makes the final, unreasonable climb to Val Louron just one second behind the stage winner, and he is pulling on the new yellow jersey long before Leblanc is home. It is, he says: 'Mon rêve d'enfance', my childhood dream to wear the tunic, and he hopes to defend it all the way to Paris. If he succeeds, he will win a prize of £200,000, which he will promptly distribute among his team-mates while he studies the small print of a new and lucrative contract.

You wish him well. He may be a little insane, but it is the sublime madness of a man who believes he can reduce miles and mountains to the demands of his will. Aupa Indurain! indeed. Vive le Tour! Allez the toasted whippets! And long may dull sanity be kept at bay for these three blessed weeks of July.

'I am the Bishop of Lima . . .'

Punch, 18 September 1991

YOU WOULDN'T RECOGNISE the pavilion, swept and dusted for the first time since April. And the trestle tables, which these past few months have carried humble ham sandwiches and jugs of bitter, are now covered with plates of lamb chops, and glasses of Sainsbury's finest.

The ladies are responsible for the catering, of course, and they are rewarded with a toast: 'The Ladies – God bless 'em. What would we do without them, eh?' Whereupon there is much tittering and the second team wicket keeper, a ribald fellow, bellows his usual joke as the captain's wife hurries her charges to the kitchen before the speeches begin.

Ah, the speeches! Having laid down bat and ball, the cricketers are currently reaching for knife and fork, and the shires are echoing to the sound of the same old speakers seeking the same old laughs, from the same old stories.

At some stage in his oration, the speaker will tell the tale of the late Bill Edrich who, slightly the better for drink, appeared at an MCC tour function in Peru and allegedly requested the next dance from a lofty vision in purple. He was rejected on the following grounds: '(a) The band is playing the Peruvian national anthem, (b) you are drunk. And (c), I am the Bishop of Lima.'

Everybody told this tale for the better part of two decades until Edrich protested his innocence and called in m'learned friends. But it remains the quintessential cricket dinner story in that it is vaguely amusing, mildly scandalous and hints at an intimate knowledge of the social misdeeds of a famous cricketer.

Likewise, every speaker will have a story about Geoffrey Boycott; none, I make haste to add, involving alcoholic indiscretion, but most making great play of that part of his nature which may safely be called 'single-minded.' 'He's a great judge of a run,' Trevor Bailey once said. 'His own run.'

Of course, if the cricket club has real influence, it will attract one of the resident sages of *Test Match Special*, who will tell any number of such tales. Moreover, his presence guarantees that at some stage of the following summer, probably on a slow day at Trent Bridge, he will mention the club by name, and recall the evening at Old Tosspottians: 'when we were looked after rather well.'

Naturally, there are penalties involved in having a *TMS* man as guest speaker. For one thing, the audience must have a connoisseur's appetite for schoolboy smut. They will be reminded of Mr Brian Johnston's immortal lines: 'He's standing in the slips with his legs apart, waiting for the tickle,' and 'The batsman's Holding, the bowler's Willey.' They will also be told of Johnston's breathless, giggle-racked seizure this summer when Jonathan Agnew observed that Botham had dislodged a bail while: 'trying to get his leg over.'

Brian Johnston is 79 years old, yet despite being marooned in the third form for the past 66 years, he is a thoroughly engaging character. Some of his colleagues are less obviously appealing.

Imagine, if you will, the lugubrious tedium of listening to Don Mosey celebrate the wit and wisdom of Fred Trueman. Still worse, imagine attending a dinner at which Mr Trueman himself is asked to reply for the guests. I once heard the great man deliver an after-dinner speech which included a ten-minute ode to farting. He's a character, is our Fred. Almost everybody says so.

And then there is Mrs Rachel Heyhoe-Flint, compared with whom Trueman is a Michael Foot, a John Biffen, a veritable Demosthenes. Earlier in this century, she captained the English women's cricket team, which has provided her with a rich seam of source material for jokes about bouncers and fine legs and the buxom fast bowler who could swing them either way.

She was, you may recall, at the forefront of the campaign to persuade the MCC to admit women to membership, and there was much public disapproval when her attempt failed. In truth, I found it difficult to blame the members of the MCC. Forced to choose between male chauvinism and the wacky, zany, fun-packed twitterings of Mrs Heyhoe-Flint, I know how my vote would have been cast.

Still, the best of the cricket speakers perform with a fair degree of style, although none, in my experience, has achieved that note of whimsical candour which marked a speech by the ex-footballer and reformed drinker, Mr Jimmy Greaves.

Mr Greaves was once asked to speak at a function organised by the Bell's whisky company, and he was reluctant. 'Why should I put myself out for Bell's?' asked Jim. 'Because Bell's have done a lot for football,' he was told. 'Oh, yeah?' he said, 'well, they've done f*** all for me.'

Jimmy Greaves has never been asked to address the Old Tosspottians. And they don't know what they're missing.

The Last Fight of Michael Watson

Mail on Sunday, 22 September 1991

A T THE END OF A NIGHT of ugly, primitive drama at White Hart Lane, Chris Eubank was WBO super-middleweight champion and Michael Watson was carried unconscious to hospital through the remnants of a riot. Chairs, kicks and punches flew at the ringside as police fought to clear a way for the stretcher which bore the beaten fighter to safety. It was an obscene ending to one of the fiercest, most brutal fights the British ring has seen these many years.

The new champion, who had won his title after 29 seconds of the twelfth and last round, stood virtually ignored in the ring as the fans fought and the still body of Watson proceeded with pitiful slowness through the chaos. The final bout was cancelled by order of the police and all the personal antagonism which the pre-fight hype engendered took its dangerous form in the fury of the crowd.

Your concern for Watson's health overwhelmed your sympathy for his defeat in a fight he had dominated. When the end came, I made him three rounds ahead and he was leading on the cards of all three judges. But Eubank's improbable strength had proved ultimately decisive.

That strength, and the raw courage which attended it, had lifted Eubank from the very brink of overwhelming defeat. For much of the fight he had been outmanoeuvred and frequently outclassed by a man who revealed none of the inhibitions which had marred his performance in their first fight in June. He set a frantic pace, moving forward relentlessly, scoring with crisp, measured punches and inflicting stern damage with his punishing right hand. Eubank was never allowed to indulge in his customary posing and posturing as the punches flooded in with jolting precision.

Although Eubank stole the second round, the pattern of the fight was being shaped by the pitiless accuracy of Watson's right hand. In the fourth, a small gash appeared above Eubank's left eye, the injury

182

lifting Watson's buoyant confidence to still greater heights. But the pace of the whole affair was almost manic and the intensity of their mutual dislike filled every punch that was thrown.

Watson was boxing like a man who felt he had the measure of his dangerous opponent. His work was fluent and chastising and his points advantage was widening with each passing round. The arrogance had long departed Eubank; what remained was the fighter's primitive instinct. And after surviving a protracted crisis, that instinct seemed about to save him in a tenth round fought with savage intensity. Yet again Watson came through, insisting upon his supremacy, turning aside the onslaught and responding with lacerating punches of his own.

The intensity of the tenth provided only a prelude to the mayhem of round eleven. Watson, raising the pace to a terrifying level, eventually punched his man to the floor halfway through the round. At that moment, the title was within his grasp. But Eubank amazed the White Hart Lane crowd, and probably himself, with the ferocity of his reply. In the last moments of the round he found a right hand to floor Watson. The Islington fighter struggled to his feet and the bell saved him from immediate punishment. But he was no more than semi-conscious as he returned to his corner, to slump and stare as his seconds worked with blind desperation.

Full consciousness had not returned as he lurched out for the last round and Eubank was on him instantly, throwing punches without retaliation as he pinned his man in a neutral corner. Referee Roy Francis watched for a few moments, then forced his way between the fighters. It was all over. Eubank was the new champion. And poor Michael Watson was a beaten, broken man.

Twickenham Man

Mail on Sunday, 6 October 1991

S THE 12.53 ROLLED OUT of Waterloo Station, he burst
through the door and flopped into a corner seat. His uniform revealed his destination: waxed jacket by Burberrys,
tweed hat by Dunn's and complexion by John Courage.
The ensemble screamed: 'Twickenham!'

And he was agitated. Small rivers of sweat ran from his temples,
trickled down his jowls and gently soaked the soft collar of his
Viyella shirt. 'Knackered!' he announced to the carriage at large.
'I'm bloody knackered!' From Waterloo to Clapham Junction, he sat
and gasped, as his chum fanned him with a copy of the *Daily
Telegraph*. Briefly, he attempted to launch a song: 'Swing looow,
Sweet Cha-ri-o-ot . . .' His chum took up the chant, but the rest of
the carriage remained stubbornly silent. 'Sod you lot, then,' he said,
with a touch of petulance, and lost himself in the sports pages.

Just before Richmond, he looked up from the paper. 'They're
going to have a pre-match song,' he said. 'Spose it'll be that big bird.
New Zealander. Dame Kitty Whassername?' His chum nodded
wisely. 'Spose so,' he said.

'Twickenham! This is Twickenham!' boomed the Caribbean
tones of the station announcer. Twickenham Man accepted the cue.
'Tweeckenham! Dis am Tweeckenham, man!' he yelled. 'Oh my
Gawd, where do they find 'em?'

His chum chuckled as they bustled past the old gentleman collecting for lifeboats. Like a subaltern rejoining his regiment,
Twickenham Man mingled with the waxed jackets and tweed hats
marching along Rugby Road. A young man offered him souvenir
song sheets; 'Sweet Chariot', of course, and Blake's 'Jerusalem'. He
seized a copy and marched on, with the stern glare of one who
would not cease from mental fight. At least, not until the All Blacks
had been put in their place.

Before he reached his seat, high in the South Stand, Twickenham

Man had encountered a dozen friends. They punched him warmly on the bicep. 'You old bastard!' they said. 'Good to see you sober.' He knew none of their names and all of their clubs: Esher Thirds, Askeans Seconds, Rosslyn Park Extra C. He returned their punches, accepted their hip flasks and exchanged reminiscences of Easter tours long ago, when a man could drink all night for thirty bob and still find the strength to chase the chambermaid.

Looking back, he knew he could have been a real player. Trouble was, he was 30 years ahead of his time. With all his speed, strength and tactical flair, he'd have strolled into this English side, no question. Then it would have been magazine covers, game shows, perhaps even *Blue Peter*. Yeah, he'd have coped with all that. You see, the talent was there.

He recalled the try he scored against Old Gravesendians in November '61; change of pace, outside break and in under the posts without a hand laid on him. 'Class,' their skipper had said in the bar that night. 'Sheer class. You'll go a long way.' But times were different then. He had his career in the bank to think of, and anyway, he'd spoken his mind too often. The Committee didn't like that. They saw to it that he never got beyond the Seconds. Conspiracy, really.

His wife had been a brick. 'Rugby's loss is Barclays' gain,' she'd said, when he hung up his boots at the age of 36. 'And anyway, a chief cashier's place is on the golf course.' But it wasn't the same; never could be. Down on the pitch, the competing nations paraded. Argentina: 'Boo!' Japan: 'Boo!' Wales: 'Boo! Jeer! Whistle!' 'But we've never had a war with Wales,' protested his neighbour. 'Not yet,' said Twickenham Man.

A young man mounted the rostrum and the pre-match song blared from the tannoy: 'We can always do better, we can always do more. We can always go further than we've been before.' Uplifting stuff, and Michael Ball acknowledged the applause. 'That's not Dame Kitty Whassername,' observed Twickenham Man, perceptively.

Prince Edward climbed the same rostrum to deliver a message from the headmaster of Rugby School. More uplifting stuff, which concluded with the hope that the eventual winner of the rugby World Cup would be 'the game itself'. A young Australian lost patience: 'Yawn, yawn. Clee-shay!' he bellowed. 'Bloody cleey-shay!' Twickenham Man was scandalised. 'Belt up, you convict!' he screamed. 'He's a sodding Prince!'

The anthem sounded and the crowd leaped to attention.

Twickenham Man removed his hat, threw back his shoulders and aligned his thumbs with the cavalry-twill seams of his trousers. 'Send her victor-i-ous, happy and glor-i-ous!' The young Australian bore a grudge: 'Sing up, mate,' he called. 'Much bloody good it'll do yer.'

And he was right. For 80 minutes, Twickenham Man shouted and cursed in England's cause. He did not remotely understand what was happening on the pitch, since the laws of the game have been changed a time or two these past 30 years. But he wielded his ignorance like a cutlass. It did no good. England were beaten, the black-shirted colonials were triumphant and the Word Cup was a receding fantasy.

The man from Esher blamed the referee. The man from Askeans blamed the insatiable greed of modern players, for whom the white shirt of England was no more than a flag of commercial convenience. The man from Rosslyn Park laid no blame, but said he knew a pub near Waterloo where matters might be discussed in depth.

And there they stayed, exchanging tall stories and strong drink, until the gloom had dissolved and their eyes were lifted to a hopeful horizon. Twickenham Man consulted his programme. 'D'you know who we've got next?' he demanded. 'Italy! Didn't know they had a rugby team! Bet they play on the retreat, eh? Bloody Italy! We'll see them off all right, won't we?'

And with confidence restored and prejudices reinforced, he staggered off into the Waterloo Road. In search of a passing chariot.

'Funny Game, Innit?'

Mail on Sunday, 8 December 1991

P AUL IS DEPRESSED; you can hear it down the telephone line. A Southampton fan, he had followed his ailing team to Coventry and had walked out in disgust at half-time.

As football fans do, he finds brief comfort in nostalgia: 'Channon, Keegan, Ball, Charlie George; we had half the England team. All gone. This is the year when there's no side worse than us. Well, p'raps Luton.' Then, from his black depression, he produces his 'master plan'. 'The best thing they could do,' he says, 'is sell Le Tissier and Shearer, get as much money as they can, hand it out to the fans and say: "We're very sorry for the last three years".'

Danny is swift to agree. 'Perfect sense,' he says. 'Instead of buying journeymen players, clubs should give everyone a fiver as they come through the gate. Never mind your crèches, your old folks' centres, your family enclosures. Give us all a fiver and our hats will be in the air.'

In fairness, Danny Baker is also depressed. He has spent his Saturday afternoon on Millwall's terraces, watching his team lose to Bristol Rovers. You could sense his mood when he entered the studio at Broadcasting House. 'We're worse than bad,' he said. 'We're boring. That's the real killer.' He pulled off his coat, clamped on his headphones and addressed the nation thus: 'Sport, my friends, is the rich marrow within this radio bone. If you've just left the ground swearing, as I may have done, that you're never gonna go and see that rubbish again, tell us.' And, for the next hour and a half, the nation responded.

Baker's *Six-O-Six* show on Radio Five is as old as the current football season, yet already it has acquired a cult status. From League pros in luxury coaches to faithful fans in ageing Fords, the audience is growing by the week. And rightly so, for it is perhaps the only programme on radio or television which addresses the whims, fancies and genuine concerns of that despised breed, the football supporter.

In Baker, the tubby, breezy, thirty-something South Londoner, the fans recognise a kindred spirit. He is saying all the things they would wish to say, if only they possessed the wit and imagination. So he sits in the tiny studio and awaits the calls, his only props a pile of middle-of-the-road CDs and a list of the day's results.

Stewart, a Luton fan, calls in on the way home from Sheffield to complain about the inconvenient location of Bramall Lane. They fall to discussing the problems of finding football grounds. 'You go along,' says Baker, 'and one of your mates says: "Oh, look, there's the floodlights over there." So you make for them, and they always turn out to be the British Rail sidings.' Hundreds of thousands of people nod in recognition.

Stewart is asked to name the most inaccessible League ground and, to popular acclaim, he names Crystal Palace. Baker nods furiously: 'I'll buy that,' he says. 'In 1936 the wrong Crystal Palace burnt down in my book.' Pete, from Walsall, receives a yellow card for saying: 'At the end of the day'. It is the kind of phrase which slack-jawed managers tend to employ when speaking to Mr Elton Welsby.

John, calling from the M1, is driving home from Chelsea and is 'fed up with seeing Forest lose away'. Under Baker's mischievous coaxing, he thinks the unthinkable: 'Well, an awful lot of Forest fans are saying: "Is it time we changed the manager?"' You could almost hear the 'click!' as the radio was extinguished on the Forest team coach.

Baker asks about Teddy Sheringham, the striker sold by Millwall to Forest at great cost. He beams at the enthusiastic response. 'D'you know,' he says, 'we used to sing his name so often, that we thought when he got married the vicar would say: "Do you, Oh Teddy Teddy, Teddy Teddy Teddy Teddy Sheringham, take thee . . ." Top man, Ted. Funny, though. When it comes to exporting players, Millwall's got a reputation like East Germany has for making cars.' He becomes genuinely passionate about a couple of calls which attack the debenture schemes devised by clubs like West Ham and Arsenal; schemes which seem likely to set the price of football-watching far beyond the ordinary fan. 'It's the most evil thing that's happened since the League was formed,' he says. 'If football supporters had any guts at all, there'd be some kind of a walk-out.'

Bernard from Marlow sympathises. 'We should stay away, but it's our team, innit?' 'Yeah,' says Baker. 'I'm afraid that's how we are; suckers and lifetime victims.' A loon calls from Scotland, asserting that women should only be admitted to football matches if there are tickets left over. Baker winces and slaps on another CD. 'They're out there, walking around. That's the terrifying thing,' he says.

Melissa rings from Luton to re-affirm the right of women to watch football. Then she sabotages the feminist case by nominating Sheffield Wednesday as the best-looking team in the country. 'That gunshot we just heard was Mrs Pankhurst's great, great granddaughter, walking out into the woods,' declares Baker.

But the prize call, the pitiful *cri de coeur* of the genuine fan, comes from Mike in Reading. 'Why is it,' he asks, 'that when you go to matches, you can only ever buy Wagon Wheels? You can't buy them anywhere else. You go into Tesco's and ask for Wagon Wheels and they'll laugh at you.'

It is a googly which would bewilder Gooch, but Baker plays it off the middle of the bat. 'Because, Mike, they are the original stock. They take them into the chairman and say: "Mr Chairman, this is the sixteenth year we haven't sold these Wagon Wheels." And the chairman says: "Nonsense! Send them back out there till they're sold!" Can you imagine football clubs chucking anything away?'

They play the closing theme. The switchboard closes down with a gasp of relief. Baker tugs off his headphones, pulls on his coat and shuffles out of the studio, shaking his head. 'Wagon Wheels!' he says. 'Bloody Wagon Wheels! Funny game, innit?' He awards himself a private yellow card for the cliché. It is his first lapse in 90 minutes. Which is more than his beloved Millwall can claim. At the end of the day.

1992

As Olympic revelations go, Jason Livingston's tale will not take its place alongside that of Ben Johnson. But it provoked a degree of sadness and shame, and it threw a shadow across Britain's efforts in Barcelona. Then along came Linford, and out came the sun.

Christie had achieved something astonishing, and he was justly feted for his efforts. But, just a month or two later, my attention was drawn to the deeds of a gentleman named Max Woosnam. And, quite suddenly, 'astonishing' seemed a wholly inadequate term.

From Hull to Eternity . . .

Punch, 12 February 1992

B Y HIS OWN ADMISSION, Mr Ian Martin has know a deal of melancholy in the course of his 15 summers. In fact, he sometimes feels 'as tho' part of me has died'.

In April 1990, he launched a football fanzine for the discriminating sportsmen of the East Midlands. It was called *Alternative Mansfield Matters*, and it covered the activities of his local football team.

Although his efforts were well received, the young editor became a victim of his own success. He ran off 200 photocopies of what proved to be the final issue and offered them for sale at a cup tie with Sheffield Wednesday. They went, he recalls: 'like hot cakes', but his attempts to produce a further 100 copies were frustrated by a faulty copier.

The pressure of production defeated him. 'I was trying to juggle GCSE course work with running a fanzine and it just wasn't on,' he concedes. So *AMM* was laid to rest, with Mr Martin's message to his public: 'You, the reader, have got to get involved. The amount of work done by the editor is immense and it is for your benefit . . . Don't let the fanzine scene die because of your laziness!'

It is a story to touch the flinty old heart of Mr Punch himself and it can be found in a new collection of fanzine writing, *It's Twelve Inches High . . . And It's Made Of Solid Gold*, published as part of the Football Against MS campaign.

It was that bit about not letting the fanzine scene die which caught my eye. As one of those hacks who is incapable of spotting a trend until it has become a tradition, I had imagined that the scene was still in its infancy.

Those of us who had been reared on official club programmes – 'Today we welcome the directors, players and fans of Slagthorpe United' – were mightily relieved by the emergence of publications which were written by football fans and took their tone from their titles.

Rotherham, for example, offered *Me Whippet's Dead*, while Brighton, trying a touch too hard, came up with *Seasons Of Missed Opportunities And Mellow Unfruitfulness*. The Scottish fanzines were distinguished by their doleful candour: *It's Half Past Four And We're Two-Nil Down* (Dundee), *Still, Mustn't Grumble* (Hearts), *Waiting For The Great Leap Forward* (Motherwell) and, starkly, *Worse Than East Fife* (Partick Thistle). In addition to *From Hull To Eternity* and *Dial M For Merthyr*, I must confess something of a soft spot for QPR's effort called *Ooh, I Think It's My Groin!*

Now some critics believe that fanzines have become exercises in self-indulgence under the camouflage of cute titles, and certainly there is much in the latest collection to support this view. Witness the rantings of a Crystal Palace fan, describing the 'truly orgasmic experience' of beating Liverpool in the FA Cup semi-final: 'Everywhere people were blowing up balloons. Many had two in each hand . . . Occasionally one would burst and those in the vicinity would be covered in spittle.' And so on. For 74 paragraphs.

Yet there are jewels to be found amid the dross. I loved the Everton fan's recollection of a rare trip to Rotherham: 'Since we were hungry, I was encouraged to partake of the club snack bar. "Have a sausage roll," said Peter, "they are in the club colours." "I hope it's not the away colours of yellow and blue," I thought to myself.'

And in Gillingham's excellent fanzine, entitled *Brian Moore's Head (Looks Uncannily Like London Planetarium)*, it is revealed that 'Gillingham have only ever won promotion in a year in which Labour has won a General Election, and have been relegated under every Conservative administration since Baldwin (bar one).'

Now that kind of socio-political reflection is what I look for in a fanzine; that and a readiness to savage club directors, name the guilty players and mock Elton Welsby. And if they can regurgitate some well-loved stories, then so much the better. The national fanzine *When Saturday Comes* recently had a cutting from the Sheffield Green 'Un: 'There were two new dads, one a Wednesdayite, the other a Unitedite. Each agreed that if his team lost the Sheffield derby, he would name his son after the winning side. So down went the Wednesday fan to the register office, and when asked for his lad's name he replied sadly: "Rubbish, rubbish, rubbish, rubbish, rubbish, rubbish, rubbish, rubbish, rubbish, Brian Deane, rubbish".'

If poor, young Ian Martin had turned out that kind of material, then you feel that *Alternative Mansfield Matters* might still be in business.

Christie: The Dream is Delivered

Mail on Sunday, 2 August 1992

O N A GOLDEN EVENING OF surging pace and soaring emotion, Linford Christie delivered his dream. Glorious reality came crowding in as he accepted the highest place on the Olympic rostrum. The anthem was played, the flag was raised, and the athlete was left to fight back his proud tears. Champion of the Olympic 100 metres, the fastest man on Earth, winner of the 'blue riband' event of these Barcelona Games. Christie claimed all these coveted prizes last night. Yet the glittering facts of victory were overshadowed by the majestic manner of his triumph.

He was confronted by the most talented array of sprinters, with the notable exception of Carl Lewis, which this planet can assemble. And he simply slaughtered them. His margin of victory was six one-hundredths of a second; the merest blinking of an eye yet an eternity in sprinting terms. And the Catalan crowd yelled in awe-struck disbelief at the full stride of space which separated Christie's 9.96 seconds from his nearest pursuer, Frankie Fredericks of Namibia.

At 32, he is the oldest man to win the Olympic sprint. He is also the third Briton to seize the prize, following in the footsteps of Harold Abrahams, who rode his fiery chariot to victory in 1924, and Allan Wells, who took his title a dozen years ago in Moscow. Christie has well-earned the right to keep such towering company.

Before the race, he had been told by his room-mate Colin Jackson: 'This is the gold medal room. Don't you dare come back with anything less.' There was never a chance that Jackson would be disobeyed. Christie was palpably the most relaxed man in the field; ignoring the two false starts which unsettled less experienced competitors, staring down the length of lane five, concentrating intensely upon the task before him.

His start was all he could have wished, his acceleration at 40 metres was more fierce than he could have dreamed. By 60 metres, the race was effectively over. The man had flung down his cards and none could match his hand. Fredericks gave token pursuit for the silver in 10.02 seconds. American Dennis Mitchell took the bronze in 10.04. But at 9.96 seconds, Linford Christie was untouched and untouchable. Nothing could stand between the man and his golden destiny.

And when the race was run, he jogged off around the curve of the track, beaming through the waves of applause which rolled down the slopes of Montjuic. It was a strangely moving moment; the young black from the meaner streets of West London, wrapped in his country's flag, accepting the acclaim of those full-throated pockets of Britons who had travelled to Barcelona in the hope of witnessing such a moment. Among them was his coach, Ron Roddan, who had conducted Christie's final preparations in Monte Carlo, was to have returned home at the start of the week but, on impulse, changed his mind to guide his charge through the final, crucial steps.

On Thursday, Roddan was stricken by the news that his other sprinter, Jason Livingston, had failed a drug test. Last night, Roddan shed tears of pure and justified pride. But then, on such a night Barcelona was awash with British tears. And Linford was leading the parade.

'I'm going to have a right good cry now,' he announced. 'It's always been my ambition to be number one in the world. I've done it, and what's more I'm clean. Ever since I started in athletics, people have been telling me I'm too old. But age is just a state of mind. The legs go on and the mind gets wiser. Sure, we've had some troubles in the British camp this week, but we put them all behind us. Life goes on, and I was the most relaxed I've ever been for a major championship. Just walking around, smiling. Wicked, wicked!'

Wicked it was; wicked and wonderful. The performance of a man who suddenly finds himself sprinkled with stardust. The disappointments of the past were forgotten. The bronze medal in Seoul, later upgraded to silver when the evidence of Ben Johnson's treachery was revealed. The fourth place in Tokyo's World championships, when even a European record of 9.92 seconds was swept aside by the world record pace of Lewis. Carl Lewis was absent last night, a victim of the American trials. And Johnson, required to perform without chemical assistance, was mercifully eliminated in the semi-final. Glory was offering its final chance, and Christie seized it in stunning fashion.

Later, as his rigorous discipline yielded to bewildered joy, he remembered his oldest allies. He thanked his family, he thanked Ron

Roddan, most touchingly he remembered Ron Pickering, that great man of athletics who died last year: 'Ah, Ron,' said Christie. 'He'll be leading the cheering tonight.' And our tears fell still faster. For this was the culmination of one of the most remarkable careers British sport has known. Trophies and records, he has seized them all in dazzling profusion. But this was the one which mattered above all. And for the next four years it will rest in the hands of the man who has sought it most hungrily, most persistently.

Linford Christie is the Olympic 100 metres champion. The impossible dream has been gloriously delivered.

'How's He Going to Cope?'

Mail on Sunday, 2 August 1992

JIM FAICHNIE TOOK THE call at his London office in the middle of the morning. It was his wife, Joyce, repeating the newsflash she had heard on the radio. She was agitated and distressed, and he asked her to repeat the message. He registered the words: 'Jason . . . drugs . . . sent home', and he put down the telephone. He spent the rest of the day in a daze.

At the close of a week dominated by sleazy tales of tablet and needle, a week in which names like Methandianone and Clenbuterol have tripped from the tongue with depressing facility, the private anguish of Jim Faichnie may seem of small consequence. But when we assess the damage done to British sport by the shaming events of Barcelona, we may conclude that it is men like Faichnie who have suffered the greatest betrayal.

Faichnie was a coach, one of that unregarded army of enthusiasts who accommodate the dreams of the best and the brightest of our young athletes. This morning, in every park, track and recreation ground across this land, they will be out with their charges; coaxing, cajoling, seeking out the single nugget which will make their work worthwhile.

Jim Faichnie found his nugget seven years ago, and his name was Jason Livingston. He was fourteen years old, he wanted to be a sprinter and he joined Faichnie's group of 30 athletes. 'Lot of ability,' recalls the coach. 'He was probably the star among my crowd. And he wanted to learn. He took it seriously. School didn't interest him. He was always playing truant, always going off to the pool hall when he should have been in class. I suppose he could have gone off the rails, but athletics was his salvation.'

Livingston started to acquire a reputation with success at the English Schools championships. The foreign trips began to arrive. Faichnie has fond memories. 'He always behaved himself,' he says. 'Never took liberties. You get kids who check into a hotel, drink the mini-bar dry then expect you to foot the bill. Not Jason. He'd have a lemonade and he always made sure he paid for it.'

Faichnie guided him to a silver medal at the World Junior championships in 1990, devoting countless hours of unpaid time to the gifted young sprinter. But the pressures of his task were becoming too great. 'Coaching was taking over my life,' he says. 'I didn't have an hour to call my own. I wanted to do the things other people do; play a bit of golf, have a pub lunch on a Sunday. I just stopped enjoying it.'

In February of last year, he decided to quit. He first informed Livingston, then the entire squad. 'Most of them took it well,' he says. 'They thanked me for what I had done for them and wished me well. Jason didn't thank me. Didn't even say goodbye. I thought he'd call and say sorry after a couple of days. But he never did. It was a bit hurtful, really.

'I followed his career, of course. Mostly on television. I've sent him a couple of cards when he's done particularly well, but he hasn't responded. Ah well, that's his choice. Mustn't dwell on it.'

Livingston joined forces with Rod Roddan, the mentor of Linford Christie and a fine coach of impeccable reputation. But soon he was confronted by other, more worrying choices. Christie's pace on the training track was a constant reminder of the standards which had to be achieved. Yet to achieve those standards, it was necessary to become a full-time athlete. Without money and without an indulgent employer to allow him endless time off for training, Livingston could not contemplate such independence. He would have to settle for being just another talented athlete who fell short of the highest level.

The temptations were crowding in. He began to drift away from Roddan, who remained his coach in name. And, in hindsight, worrying tendencies started to emerge. In Birmingham, at the last major indoor meeting of the winter, he was narrowly beaten by Christie over 60 metres and he reacted with the smouldering aggression of a street fighter. 'I know I can do it this year,' he said. 'Nobody's going to be running past me like they used to. Not this year.' At the Olympic trials, after surviving a controversial false start, he won his semi- final and reacted with an extravagant piece of posturing; pouting, hands on hips, as if he had just won an Olympic title in Barcelona instead of defeating an undistinguished field in a sluggish time in Birmingham.

The prospect of actually winning the Olympic 100 metres could never have entered his wildest dream, but even a place in the final would transform his life. 'Olympic finalist, Jason Livingston'; the introduction would secure lucrative contracts and fat and regular fees at Grand Prix meetings. That money would deliver his independence.

The temptation became irresistible, but the illusion dissolved with a late-night knock on the door of his room at the Olympic village. His modest fame had been transformed into massive notoriety. The random drug test had told its damning tale. Brendan Foster spoke for the overwhelmingly decent majority. 'When I was a kid,' he said, 'my idol was Emil Zatopek. I dreamed about being like him. But where do the kids find their idols now? When athletes climb on a rostrum, we have to wonder what they've been taking.'

Jim Faichnie would agree, but he is moved by a lingering compassion for the kid who approached him all those years ago and told him he wanted to be a sprinter. 'I really thought he'd have more sense,' he says. 'He must have known he'd be found out. Now what's he going to do with his life? He's got no qualifications, so who's going to give him a job? How's he going to cope with people pointing fingers?

'The comparison with Ben Johnson is ridiculous. Johnson was a wealthy man and he went on to make a lot more money from being notorious. Jason would find it hard to get £100 together.

'I feel so sorry for his family. Nice people, and they gave him such tremendous support. I feel for Ron Roddan, who'd be insulted at the mention of drugs. But most of all, I'm worried about Jason. He hasn't been able to do this on his own. He wouldn't know enough about steroids to supply himself. No, some wicked bastard's corrupted him. And it's bloody shameful.'

Shameful indeed; shameful and sickening. For if children may not dare to dream, then the noblest of sports has surrendered its future. And the bastards have corrupted us all.

Works Outing of the Gods

Mail on Sunday, 6 September 1992

G EORGE BEST IS SITTING in the foyer of the Wembley Hilton, wearing the fraught expression of a man who has been waiting for two hours. Then the swing doors jerk, and the frown becomes a broad beam.

For in they come, roaring greetings and pumping hands; Law and Charlton; Crerand, Stepney and Foulkes; Stiles and Sadler; the Irishmen Brennan and Dunne and the youngsters Aston and Kidd. A works outing of the gods. Among them is an elderly gentleman, slim and stately, with the bearing of a cardinal. 'Hello, boss,' says George. 'How are you, son?' says Sir Matt Busby, and he gathers him into his arms.

They have come to Wembley to visit their past, to linger on the ground where, almost a quarter of a century ago, Manchester United became the first English side to win the European Cup. They had been young men then, brimful of running. Matt's boys; sublimely talented and blissfully entertaining. Now, in their middle years, the swagger still clings to their step and the sense of style has not deserted them. Greyer, stouter and slower, they remain Matt's boys.

They assembled on Friday lunchtime at Old Trafford, a gift beyond price to the autograph seekers. A small lad climbs respectfully aboard the team bus, clutching his book. Denis Law signs with a flourish: 'Give that to your grandfather, son,' he says. 'Hey, that's Pat Crerand. Your great-grandfather remembers him.'

Sir Matt sits in the front seat, alone with his thoughts. Occasionally, a player breaks off from the card school for a quiet word and Busby awards him a brief and cordial audience. At 83, he retains the knack of making each man feel like an honoured guest.

They are all aware of the debt they owe him; Bobby Charlton more than most. 'That was so important to him, winning that trophy,' says Charlton. 'He knew that history won't consider you a great side unless you win it and he knew that the club deserved to be in that kind of company. Maybe we weren't the players who should have won the first one. Maybe that should have been reserved for the lads who died at Munich. But Sir Matt was the happiest man on earth the night we beat Benfica. He sang "What A Wonderful World" at the reception afterwards. And he meant every world of it.'

Munich: the name is inescapable in any United conversation. Bill Foulkes, Charlton's fellow survivor, has lived with his loss these many years. 'I was aware of the responsibility we had to that team of '58,' he recalls. 'I just knew we were going to win the Cup for them. There's not a day goes by when I don't think of those lads. But it's not in a sad way, not any more. I played 700 games for United, won four championships. But that was the match for them. For my friends.'

The bus thunders on down the M6. Law is in the kitchen, making coffee. 'I know my place,' he says. 'Always have.' His place on that historic night was in a hospital bed in Manchester, recovering from a knee operation. 'I remember I had a few friends in before the match. About two hours before. We has a few shandies and sang a few songs and I don't remember much about extra time. I know we won, because they rang me up later. All pissed, the lot of them. And me on my bed of pain!'

'Course we missed him,' says Crerand. 'Who wouldn't miss a player like that? But we'd have just won it a bit easier if he'd been there. Honest, it was never a race, that game.'

They arrive at the hotel, hugely amused at having kept Best waiting. There are drinks, a dinner in a private suite. 'It's beautiful that everyone's here,' announces Law. 'But who are we going to talk about?' There is no shortage of good talk.

Crerand escorts Sir Matt down from his room. 'We can't go out tonight,' he says. 'The boss is staying on the same bloody floor.' Busby smiles: 'Ah, Paddy,' he says. 'That was all in the old days.'

Chrysalis Television, preparing a commemorative video of the triumph of '68, film their reactions as they adjourn to watch a film of the match. Charlton flings an arm around Best. 'I can't remember a thing about this game,' he says. 'Me neither,' says Best, 'but it's a got a happy ending. I do like happy endings.'

They become engrossed in the match; shouting, cheering, cursing. A large Benfica defender upends young Kidd: 'Chin him, Brian!' exhorts Crerand. Three United passes go astray, and Law grunts his disapproval: 'Besty,' he calls, 'how did we win this game?'

Charlton goes off on a mazy run and the middle-aged man purrs at his golden youth. 'My God,' says Bobby, 'I really was a genius, wasn't I?' Best seeks assurance from Busby: 'What do you think, boss?' Sir Matt sucks at his pipe and smiles: 'We're playing quite well now,' he says. 'I'm quietly confident.'

Charlton heads the opening goal, and the room leaps to its feet. 'The boys are back in town!' yells Best, as the ball loops into the net. 'Vicious header, Bobby,' snipes Law. Charlton offers him a smug grin.

Shay Brennan explains why he is so rarely in the picture. 'You never see defenders,' he declares. 'Not good ones, anyway.' Benfica equalise, then in the dying moments of normal time, Eusebio strikes a thunderous drive and Alex Stepney makes his astonishing reflex save. Wild applause. Stepney is bashful. 'He couldn't score an ordinary goal, that feller. Always wanted to break the net. Now Jimmy Greaves would have taken it round me and destroyed me. He did that once at Old Trafford. Danced round and shoved it in. Dead silence at the Stretford End. As he was running back, Greavesie said: "If you don't believe I've scored, Al, look behind you."'

Kidd just sits and stares as victory takes its course. Still the youngster. 'I went into that game as an apprentice and came out a tradesman,' he says. 'It was having all those good pros round me. They brought me through.'

Best celebrates his extravagant goal in extra time, the kind of goal scored by the most gifted kid in the playground. 'I had this idea,' he recalls. 'I was going to go round the keeper, get to the goal-line, flick the ball up and head it in. But the keeper kept at me, so I thought: "Sod it." And I just gave it a poke.'

The night drifts on in celebration. The boss is enjoying himself enormously. The players watch over him as if he were an aged, well-loved father. 'Silly, I know,' admits Brennan. 'But after all these years, I'm still in awe of that man. Always will be.'

Next morning, they stroll out on a Wembley awash with sunlight and memories. Nobby Stiles thinks about Eusebio. 'Some player,' he says. 'But he never liked playing against me. He told me so, years later. Didn't say why, though. S'pose it was because I was a narky little sod. Or so they tell me.'

Best has his own, bitter-sweet reflections. 'The European Cup final was the night of my life. The absolute peak,' he says. 'They talk about "fallen-idol", "ex-superstar", stuff like that. But I had that night, and nobody can take it away from me.'

Sir Matt stands by a goalmouth, staring across the empty stadium. 'We've been here a time or two, eh?' he says. 'Ah yes, we've had some fun at this old place.' But soon he has had his fill, and he retreats towards the players' tunnel. Best follows him, guiding him across the turf with a light touch at his elbow. Together, they walk away from Wembley; a man in middle age, his black brush of beard tinged with grey. And an elderly gentleman, slim and stately, with the bearing of a cardinal.

Jackpot for a Regular Guy

Mail on Sunday, 27 September 1992

JIMMY CONNORS STOOD IN the centre of the tennis court at Caesar's Palace and addressed the sporting citizens of Las Vegas. Truly, he declared, it had been a wonderful evening, a glittering occasion, a landmark in the history of his own beloved sport. As he spoke, he toyed with a scrap of paper, folding it carelessly, flicking it with his fingernails, occasionally waving it to emphasise a platitude. The paper was a cheque for half a million dollars.

He had acquired that enviable prize by defeating Martina Navratilova in straight sets, 7–5, 6–2, within the space of 88 minutes. And, since he had already received a similar amount for agreeing to take part in this extraordinary venture, you could easily understand his satisfaction.

Las Vegas loves Jimmy Connors. He is loud, brash, shallow and self-regarding; in short, he possesses all the character traits which this city cherishes most dearly. Moveover, he refuses to grow up. He is 40 years old, and still he answers to the nickname of Jimbo. This is one regular guy.

Whereas Martina, well, she's different. For one thing, she's a woman, and Las Vegas is reluctant to recognise women who are neither broads nor barmaids. For another, she describes herself as a 'liberal feminist', canyabelieve it? The dame needed her butt kicking, and regular Jimbo was just the man to kick it.

So a sell-out attendance of 13,832 – 'the largest crowd ever to witness tennis in the history of Nevada. Wow!' – temporarily deserted slots, craps and poker tables to watch Connors go to work. This being Caesar's, where nothing is knowingly undersold, the chance was seized to advertise this weekend's super-welterweight world title fight. So they staged the weigh-in right there, on the baseline. And a fanciful man might have caught an: 'Oooh, I say!' from some ethereal Maskell, suffering an attack of the vapours, when, with a booming 'Let's Get Ready To RUMBLE!!!' from the stadium announcer, the battle began.

In truth, 'battle' is an excessive term for the events of the ensuing 88 minutes, for the tone of the match rarely rose above an animated squabble. Connors was handicapped by rules which decreed that he be allowed only one service. Moreover, while he was required to deliver the ball within the singles lines, Martina played lines placed halfway between the singles and doubles courts, giving her an extra target area of 2ft 3in.

This formula was arrived at in the happy-go-lucky fashion so typical of Navratilova's attitude towards tennis. Her lawyers re-drafted the match contracts only seventeen times before obtaining the rules they required.

For a while, it seemed that this meticulous preparation might yield dividends. Connors, the 1–5 betting favourite, lost his opening service game, patting them across in his efforts to keep them legal. The crowd was remarkably restrained. There was the odd, throaty bellow for 'Jimbo', the occasional squeak for 'Mar-ti-na!', carrying echoes of wet Wednesdays at Wimbledon. But mainly, their mood reflected the grimly serious intent of the participants.

As the desert sky grew dark and the unlovely bulk of Caesar's Palace threw a bilious green glow across the proceedings, Connors started to solve his problems. He forced Martina to the brink, and a blundering double fault cost her the first set in 52 minutes. The finest woman player of all time, Wimbledon champion on nine occasions, she seemed reluctant to exploit her wide-court advantage. After spending 30 years training herself to hit the ball inside the line, it seemed an offence against nature deliberately to play outside.

Connors grew still more confident, even at a damaging pace. 'Get him, Martina! He's tiring!' screamed a woman. 'Very observant, ma'am,' responded Connors. But he ploughed on until his deep fore-hand approach shot was met by a tired and errant return. Game, set and Jimbo.

Later, he cursed the rules which had caused him such discomfort: 'That was too damn much court for me to cover', and boasted, at some length, of how he had taken tennis away from 'the country club set' and given it to the 'yelling, screaming fans'. Martina was more reflective. She thought there were women players who hit the ball harder than Connors – Steffi Graf, Monica Seles – but there was none who placed it so well. She even mentioned finance, with the authority of one who has made more than $18 million (£10.5 million) in prize money alone. And she dismissed the frivolous notion the event had been the 'Battle of the Sexes'. 'It was,' she said, like a liberal feminist, 'the Battle of Genders.'

But the organisers were not ready to concede their selling-point so readily. 'So the guy won, huh?' said a Caesar's executive. 'We all walk a little taller tonight, eh fellers?' And he was only half-joking.

Along the Strip, the neon signs were hailing the current attractions: Sinatra at the Desert Inn, Johnny Mathis at Caesar's, the Righteous Brothers, God help us, at Ballys. Ageing entertainers, long past their prime, yet still capable of skipping merrily to the bank. It is an exclusive club, and it has just elected a new member.

Max Woosnam – The Unknown Hero

Mail on Sunday, 11 October 1992

MAXWELL WOOSNAM WAS born in Liverpool, 100 years ago this autumn. The centenary of his birth has passed without notice, since his name and his deeds have been buried with his bones. And that is a pity. For Max Woosnam was, quite simply, the most extraordinary sportsman that this nation has ever known.

It is a considerable claim, yet the evidence is overwhelming. In the course of his sporting career, Woosnam won Olympic gold and silver medals. He won a Wimbledon title. He captained the England football team, at amateur and professional level. He captained the British Davis Cup tennis team and a Manchester City side which finished runners-up in the First Division. He also, in passing, captained the Cambridge University cricket and football teams, won Blues for golf (which he played to scratch), football, lawn tennis and real tennis. And he once scored a century against MCC at Lord's.

Now British sport is not so rich in heroes that it can afford to neglect such a man or such an astonishing record, yet Woosnam's achievements remain perversely uncelebrated.

His son, also Max, has learned to live with the oversight. 'Occasionally, the name will be mentioned and some old chap will prick up his ears,' he says. 'But, mostly, when people hear "Woosnam" they think it's that young golfer. Sad, really.'

Woosnam Jnr is now 70 years old, a retired chemical engineer who lives in a disused nineteenth-century Methodist chapel in Malmesbury, Wilts. He trawls through a clutter of sporting mementoes, sepia photographs and yellowing newspaper cuttings. And he assembles a remarkable story.

Educated at Winchester, where he was captain of cricket and golf, Max Woosnam first made his mark when he scored 144 for the Public Schools against MCC at Lord's. His university career was predictably dazzling, with blue following upon blue. Football was his chief love, and in the Christmas vacation he would turn out for Chelsea in the Football League. Although a life-long amateur, he was a sturdy champion of the professional sportsman and fiercely resented the class divisions which separated the paid from the loftily unpaid.

In 1914, he accompanied the Corinthians on a football tour to Brazil. On arrival in Rio, the team was told of the outbreak of the Great War. They took the first boat home and, to a man, enlisted in the colours. After serving in France, Woosnam returned to Cambridge.

'His life was one long party,' says Max Jnr. 'The College Fellows at Trinity fell over themselves to accommodate sportsmen. But he did get some sort of degree in between all that sport.'

Obliged to earn his living, he moved to Manchester in 1919 to work for a forerunner of the ICI company. United offered him a first-team place, but they played their mid-week matches on Wednesday and he found it inconvenient to take time off from work. So he took the advice of the legendary Billy Meredith and signed for City. At 5ft 10in and 12st, he was a centre half of the old school. He wore a handkerchief stuffed into his left sleeve with which he wiped his face and his technical speciality was the vigorous shoulder charge for which he was frequently reprimanded.

The professionals at City elected him captain, and he led them to second place in the League in 1920–21. In the following season he played against Wales and Ireland for the English amateur side and in that same year captained the full England side against Wales. They loved their commanding, flaxen-haired defender at City; indeed, they not only named a street after him but published an ode to the first goal he scored for the club, on 19 November 1921:

What a scene of jubilation and a round of great applause
The spectators are delighted, and you need not ask the cause
For Max Woosnam of the City, who at Cambridge won his blue
Has at last performed the function with the goal he had in view.

So fond were they of their goal-scoring centre half that they insisted he should lead out the team for the inaugural match at Maine Road, when a crowd of 56,993 turned up to see City play Sheffield United in August, 1923. And yet, as his son concedes, Woosnam forfeited some of the affection three years later.

'Father drove a bus during the General Strike of 1926. He wasn't a political man, he just thought it ought to be done. After that, we had to have a policeman patrol the grounds of our home in Cheshire. Some of the City fans saw him as something of a strike-breaker.' But by then, he had established his legend in a quite different sport.

In 1920, while still at Cambridge, he decided to devote his entire summer to tennis. He was rewarded with selection for the Olympics of Antwerp, where he won the men's doubles gold medal with Noel Turnbull and the silver medal in the mixed doubles with Kitty McKane, later Kitty Godfree. In that same year, he made his Davis Cup debut in the men's doubles with Randolph Lycett, and a year later the pair won the Wimbledon title.

Most men would have been satisfied with such a sporting record, but Max Woosnam was curiously unfulfilled. 'It was the cricket thing, you see,' says his son. 'My maternal grandfather, "Punch" Philipson, had played cricket for England. So, in order to impress the family, my father had to be jolly good at sport. But that side of the family had heaps of money, whereas my paternal grandfather was a clergyman, something of a poor relation. And mother's family never really coughed up.

'My father was condemned to be a Gentleman amateur rather than a Player, and he really couldn't afford the life-style. He had a family to support. It was such a pity. Had he concentrated on cricket, I really believe he would be spoken of as a Grace or a Hobbs by now. Not that he ever dreamed of earning money from sport. In all those years, he didn't earn a penny.'

The father went on to a successful executive career with ICI. The son made earnest, foredoomed attempts to follow in his sporting footsteps. 'He encouraged me to take up tennis but he never found time to coach me,' he says. 'I made Junior Wimbledon standard. I got into all the XIs at Winchester and I reached county standard at squash. But I just never had his talent.

'The sad truth is that I never really knew him. In those days you were sent off to boarding school because they didn't trust mothers to look after you. Then it was Winchester, then Cambridge; I never really saw him.

'I scarcely ever had a conversation with him. I do remember playing tennis with him in 1949, when he was 57. He beat me. In later years, when he moved down to London (where he died in 1965), I should have said: "Come on, let's have lunch once a week." But I never did. Strange, it was he who prompted me to father a child. I thought: "If there really is anything in this genes business, I should hate to think I hadn't tried to pass it on."

'I had a fine son, a splendid chap. But he was never the sportsman that his grandfather was. How could he be? How could anyone be that brilliant?'

When old men cast their eyes across the modern world of sport, they tend to insist that things are not what they used to be. Usually, they are quite wrong. But when they invoke the name of Maxwell Woosnam, born 100 years ago this autumn, the old men make a mighty case.

1993

They tell you that cricket is the game that God invented, and they do not lie. I always come to it in a spirit of wide-eyed incomprehension ready to be overwhelmed by its subtleties. It never lets me down.

This was a particularly splendid year. Any Antigua Test match is a memorable event, and a Test in the civilised company of Richie Richardson is doubly rewarding. Hythe was a singularly beautiful venue for an exploration of the grass roots and, towering above all, was the match in the real South Africa; a genuinely misty-eyed memory for all who were privileged to be present.

Richie and the Antiguan Way

Mail on Sunday, 9 May 1993

D ICKIE BIRD WAS ON his way to lunch. His shoulders were stooped, his step was heavy and he wore that air of agitated contemplation which is the stock in trade of the English umpire. He was a dozen strides from the pavilion when an intruder crossed his path. The intruder's name was Mayfield, and he wore a blue frock coat, a yellow sombrero and green frogmen's flippers.

He was being pursued by a figure in a crimson silk cocktail dress, clumpy platform shoes and a long black beard. His name was Gravy. Mayfield threw the umpire a wave. Gravy blew him a kiss, and the pair resumed their scamper across the outfield. Dickie's mouth dropped open, he paused for a second, then he hurried into the pavilion, shaking his head. You could almost hear him muttering that incantation of another famous Yorkshire cricketing person: 'Ah joost don't know what's going off out there.'

Richie Richardson knows, all right. Born and reared in this demiparadise, he understands that the fiercest commitment may be tempered by capering carnival. It is the Antiguan way.

Today, the West Indies captain will leave his island home. He will leave behind his family, his home by the bright sands and blue waters, his two shops and the stall at the rear of the Recreation Ground which sells vast numbers of his wide-brimmed red hats for £10 a time. And he will join Yorkshire County Cricket Club, most of whose members would not be seen six feet under in a wide-brimmed red hat.

Richardson will be only the second 'import' to represent Yorkshire, after last season's trail-blazing effort by Sachin Tendulkar. And there are those who suggest that he will find the burden a touch daunting. The skipper greets that suggestion with a small smile. A man who has spent his week leading his nation in his own island for the first time is not likely to be overwhelmed by anything which the broad acres may have to offer. 'I don't believe in getting excited about things,' he says. 'You've got a job to do; you do it. A cricketer gets excited, he can't do the job. Very simple.'

As he spoke, perched on a table in the dressing room corridor, the loudspeakers in the double-decker stand were pounding out the song which has become Antigua's unofficial anthem:

Who's de man wid de blade in his hand?
Richie Rich, Richie Rich, Richie Rich - ard - son.

Another small smile, a trace of embarrassment. 'It's nice to hear people singing about cricket again,' he says. 'For a while there, all the kids were watching baseball and basketball on the television. New sports, new heroes. I think maybe we've corrected that now.'

Indeed they have. Although the West Indies have not lost a Test series since 1980 in New Zealand, pretenders to the crown in the forms of Australia, Pakistan and the newly restored South Africa were starting to state their case. They have all been chastised, one by one, as Richardson has steered his ship into more familiar waters. His style has been markedly different from that of his predecessor and fellow-islander Vivian Richards. 'Viv was an autocrat, Richie's a democrat,' says Andy Roberts, the third member of the island trinity. 'Different men, different styles, that's all.'

In fact, there are many who tell you that Richards operated something akin to rule by fear, forbidding dissent and flaying those who fell short of his expectations. On many occasions, it is said, young Richardson was the target for his fiercest abuse.

Richardson shrugs: 'Viv did things his way, I learned a bit from him. Certainly he never put me under any pressure when it was my turn to take over. I just try and listen to everybody. They all have a contribution to make and I want to hear it. Sure, I take the decisions. But if people start talking together, pretty soon they'll be working together.'

He is, in truth, a deeply impressive character, with that calm air of authority which has already earned comparisons with Sir Frank Worrell, who remains the yardstick by which West Indies captains are measured.

Certainly Richardson has maintained a healthy perspective. In the Test at Brisbane, West Indies needed 200 to win with all wickets standing. Suddenly, they found themselves at 40 for 4, and needing to bat out the day to save the match. The captain watched the wickets tumble and walked across to the umpire. 'When you think about it, what a marvellous game this cricket is,' he said. 'What a really marvellous game.'

It is difficult to imagine his predecessor permitting himself a similar reflection. And yet, after just nine Tests as skipper, he admits to an awareness of the pressure. 'Sometimes, I feel like I belong to the public, body and soul,' he says. 'People make demands all the time. I try to please them, really I do. Without the public, I'd be a very insignificant man. But I can't please everybody, and people don't always understand that. And it upsets me when they're hurt.

'Cricket's a tough life these days. I'm not complaining; nobody makes me play the game, but it can be terrible tough. Physically, if you work hard enough, you can last a long time. But mentally, it's a different story. Thinking, thinking all the time. Worrying about everybody, everything. Your mind gets tired, you know? And travelling, always travelling. Sometimes I wake up and I look at the ceiling and say: "What hotel am I in? What town? What country?" Very strange questions, but lately I've been asking them more and more.'

In the summer ahead, he will continue to ask those questions, and an endless list of provincial towns will offer themselves as answers. Yet even as he anticipates the challenge of the English county game and breaking down the last few barriers which separate Yorkshire cricket from the twentieth century, he will look back with a touch of sadness to his last innings in Antigua. He walked in at the height of Waqar Younis's fastest spell of the series. The first ball whipped through his guard and scuffed his pad. A huge shout, a full second of consideration, and Dickie Bird's finger was jabbing the sky.

The steel band blared a consoling chorus as he trudged away, dragging his bat. He was halfway to the dressing room when Gravy of the crimson dress, who was performing an act of indescribable indecency upon a girder, crashed spectacularly to the ground, landing amid a tangle of arms, legs and platform soles. Richie Richardson didn't spare him a glance. Carnival is fine, but it doesn't soothe the agony of a first-ball failure.

And as he fumed his way into the pavilion, you suddenly realised that this gentle character has all the makings of a true Yorkshireman.

Bobby Speaks for Manchester

Mail on Sunday, 30 May 1993

BOBBY CHARLTON WAS LATE for dinner. He arrived between the avocado and the duck, mopping his brow and muttering about the traffic on the M40. A courteous man, he apologised profusely; but there was really no need. After all, the Oxford Union had billed him as 'The Legendary Manchester United and England Football Hero'. And being a legend means never having to say you're sorry.

On the stroll from dining room to debating chamber, he signed half a dozen autographs; mostly for young men unborn in 1966, one for a dewy-eyed don who recalled seeing him score 'a corker' at Burnley in the early sixties. Bobby thanked them all, then offered a shy little nod to the applause which greeted his entry. He took his seat on the front bench and the terms of the motion were announced: 'This House believes that the International Olympic Committee will not choose Manchester for the 2000 Olympic Games.'

He shook his head in mute disapproval and his face said: '*Not* choose Manchester? Come on! We know better than that, don't we?' And we, on the other side of the gangway, glanced around the chamber and knew that our cause was lost.

If Manchester are to avoid humiliation when the IOC casts its votes in late September, then they must lean heavily upon the celebrity, the charisma and the plain, homespun decency of Bobby Charlton. This week, in Oxford, he did not fail them.

In truth, he was ably supported by Adrian Moorhouse, a breast-stroke gold medallist in Seoul and a man whose extrovert enthusiasm would infect far less sympathetic audiences than the one he encountered this week. Disdaining elaborate preparation, Moorhouse had scribbled his speech on his menu card over dinner. The topic headings were jotted down and vigorously attacked.

The Weather: 'I'm a northerner, and it's lovely up there in August . . . Sydney will be in the middle of winter. No good to anyone . . .

215

Beijing's hot and sticky. And, let me tell you, there's jungle in Beijing. Ugh!'

The Benefits: 'Granada's studio tours would be packed. They'd make enough to run *Coronation Street* on a separate channel all year round. Great!'

The Omens: 'Manchester sort of *sounds* different. And it's been nearly twenty years since a city beginning with the letter M won the Games. So there.' It was good, breezy, knockabout stuff. And the Union audience lapped it up.

David Pickup of the Sports Council made a sober, measured case for Manchester and the advantages which would accrue from a successful Olympic bid. While Bob Scott, chairman of Manchester 2000, faithfully regurgitated the arguments he has been proclaiming these past eight years. In the face of this Mancunian onslaught, the movers of the motion were forced on to the back foot.

Vyv Simson, the investigative journalist, and Dr Alan Tomlinson, the sports sociologist, emphasised their affection for that endearing city. They praised the undeniable virtues of its bid. But they sturdily asserted that the motion expressed a truth which is self-evident: Manchester will *not* be chosen for the 2000 Olympics.

Your own correspondent conceded all the virtues, but maintained that the city will fail because Britain's miserable record of investment in sport does not deserve success. The deficiencies were listed: we are a nation without a National Stadium; we have no athletics stadium capable even of staging a European championships; school playing fields are *still* being sold; local authority spending on sport has declined by 25 per cent over the past five years.

Most contemptible of all, the 'appeal fund' which the British Olympic Association organises to support our team at the Games continues to be the subject of tax – twenty per cent of almost £7 million for the Barcelona Olympics. According to the Sports Council, we are the only nation on earth which actually taxes its own Olympic athletes. A country which sets so little store by sport, it was said, has no business even bidding for the ultimate prize.

Honesty compels the admission that mine was probably the least effective address of the evening. Certainly the audience found the arguments deeply unpersuasive. But then, they were waiting for Bobby Charlton.

He walked to the despatch box, slipped on his thin-rimmed spectacles, thrust his hands into his pockets and spoke, virtually without benefit of note, for some twenty minutes. There were no oratorical tricks, no catchpenny gimmicks; just the gentle vowels of Ashington, tinged with the tones of his adopted city, drifting around the ancient hall.

'Why not?' was his theme. 'Why shouldn't we have just as good a claim to the Games as anyone else?' Sure, he played the patriotic card; but with a nudge rather than a flourish. 'I'm proud of being British, but not too proud that I let it affect my thinking. What's to stop us putting on a marvellous Olympics?'

He spoke of Manchester's image: 'Black buildings, the Industrial Revolution, *Coronation Street*'. And he shook his head. 'I know what people are thinking,' he said. 'I go to Australia and they say: Why Manchester?' And I say: 'Why Sydney, for goodness sakes. Look, within forty-five minutes' drive of Manchester there are more people than you've got in your whole country!'

His listeners chuckled on cue. They were, most of them, too young to remember the time when the words 'Bobby Charlton' were the most celebrated in the English language; when even the Germans would surrender their sun-loungers at the mere invocation of the name.

But their fathers had told them that this was a great man, and now they sensed that their fathers had not lied. So they cheered when he made his pitch: 'Let's have some good news for a change. A Manchester Olympics could be the greatest thing that's ever happened to this country. We could do a fantastic job. Let's go for it. Why not?' And they trooped through the lobbies to return their inevitable verdict. The motion was defeated by 92 votes to 73.

You speculated, silently, that this might prove the only Olympic election that Manchester is destined to win this year. You hoped, fervently, that this result would not encourage Oxford's students to gamble next term's grant on Manchester's chances. For Mr William Hill is currently offering 7–1 against them, and he is not a generous man. Yet even those of us who had proposed the evening's motion could not grudge The Legendary Manchester United and England Football Hero his debating triumph.

The legend was smiling as he stood by the front bench and signed order papers for a queue which stretched to the doors of the chamber. One undergraduate, joining the queue, asked to borrow my pen. 'That Bobby Charlton's some performer, isn't he?' he said. Indeed he is. But then, he always was.

The Men of Middle England

Mail on Sunday, 27 June 1993

THE YOUNG MAN WINCED at the clatter of timber. He didn't look back, he just swallowed a curse, tucked his bat under his arm and marched philosophically to the pavilion.

Sympathy awaited him on the steps. 'Bad luck,' said the skipper. 'Looked like it kept a bit low.' The young man never even broke stride. 'Rubbish,' he said, 'I played down the wrong bloody line. That's all.' And that was when you felt like cheering. Because, for the first time this summer, an English batsman was being completely honest about his shortcomings.

Now older, shrewder, Test-playing cricketers will shudder at his candour. Peering through sponsored sunglasses, they see a game in which excuses are seized, responsibility is declined and words like 'unplayable' leap readily to the lips. And when all else fails, Mr Ted Dexter can be wheeled out to blame the media, the weather and the untimely conjunction of Jupiter with Uranus.

There was a time, not so very distant, when club cricketers would revere international players as role models, masters of their trade. But down among the grassroots, reverence has been replaced with something close to contempt.

Press them hard and they will discuss our current ineptitude with much shrugging of shoulders and shaking of heads. But they find the subject distasteful. Instead, these men of 'Middle England' reserve their passion for a game they can recognise and respect; a game conducted upon an ancient, green and perfect oval, nestling between the Royal Military Canal and the English Channel. Hythe CC v Whitstable CC, in the qualifying round of the East Kent League Cup. Forty-five overs a side, and everything to play for.

Hythe had batted through the drowsy afternoon to compile a total of 183. 'Respectable,' was the pavilion consensus, 'but eminently attainable.' The early batting endorsed that prediction, but as sweaters were taken against the evening chill, the visitors' wickets began to slip away.

Bruce Campbell, once a detective and now, more stressfully, captain of Whitstable, grew anxious. 'If we lose this,' he threatened, 'heads will roll.' 'Too right, Goochy,' said a loyal lieutenant. Everybody giggled.

With seven overs left, they were eight wickets down and forty runs adrift. The last man was padding up and, curiously, the sight inspired little confidence. 'It's Eddie,' groaned a camp follower. 'Cometh the hour and what do we get? Bloody Eddie.'

Eddie ignored the jibe and strode out at the fall of the ninth wicket. An artless lunge, a top edge, a looping dolly into the hands of point. The two girls on scoring duty scribbled the last rites. Victory to Hythe, with something to spare.

The umpire, pausing to return a few lingering sweaters, was last to reach the bar. He adores his cricket, does Neil Jones, and yet he is seriously concerned for his sport. He worries about the slow death of cricket in schools. He worries about the narrow, financial expectations of too many talented youngsters. And, naturally, he worries about the English game.

'The administration's a disaster,' he said. 'They can't identify problems, so they've no chance of solving them. Then there's the skipper, poor old Gooch. A solid man, I'd say, but that dreadful business over Gower showed that he distrusts individualism.

'D'you know, individual talent is the really superb thing about cricket. It's what makes it worthwhile. Invention, resource, elegance; they're the qualities which should win the day. But what we're getting is sheer, tub-thumping grind. And look at the results.'

Across the room, Bruce Campbell stared glumly into his glass. 'I know it's not easy,' he said. 'But they make you wonder, don't they? I mean, look at the way they treated young Lathwell, for example. Picked him in the squad for the three one-dayers, lost the first two and still didn't give him a game! Madness, that was. And now it's too late for sweeping changes. We just seem to blunder from match to match.'

Gerry Willsher, the Hythe chairman, was equally gloomy. 'If you could be sure that people were coming through you could put up with a miserable standard at Test and county level,' he says. 'But the people in charge don't seem to realise just what we lost when school cricket virtually disappeared. I couldn't say I'm optimistic about the future of cricket. I wish I could.'

Dick Apps, the venerable stalwart of Hythe cricket, had a radical solution. 'We should sort out every player who might do a job and stick them in against the likes of the West Indies, New Zealand and Pakistan. Try everyone, and use those countries as practice for Australia. Because English cricket's about beating Australia. Nothing personal, but we've got to do everything we can to beat those bastards.' There was much nodding, murmurs of approval. Then somebody said: 'That'd stuff Sully, wouldn't it?'

'Sully' is one James Sullivan, a 28-year-old Antipodean who hails from a hamlet 'an hour outside Wagga'. A hugely engaging character, he lives in a caravan parked next to the Hythe pavilion. He plays for the Hythe club and on Sunday mornings he coaches 45 local youngsters.

He has achieved a degree of notoriety this summer by interrupting home games to announce the fall of England's latest wicket. 'Another one's gone! Useless bastards!' is his favoured cry. Tonight, he presides over a barbeque – 'I cook 'em a barbie one a week. Brilliant, mate. They bloody love it' – and pauses to speak a deal of sense.

'People keep asking me what's our secret,' he says. 'Well, we get 'em young for a start. Kid gets to be, like, four or five in Australia and he gets a cricket bat for Christmas. By the time he's nine, he's being coached in school. Then he's playing serious cricket; no bloody friendlies, play to win. We bat for three hours this Saturday, they bat their three hours next week. Proper structure.

'And the best keep coming through. You bat at six or seven in a State side, and you could play for Australia tomorrow. Couldn't say that of the English counties, eh? We take it seriously, and I'm not sure you do. Mind, some of your blokes amaze me. That Hick; what a good player! But why doesn't he prove it? Then there's Dexter, blaming the stars! I couldn't believe that! Can you imagine Miller or Lillee or any of that mob blaming the stars? Jeez!'

The thought intrigues him and he cackles again. The men of Kent, queuing for burgers and burnt sausages, join in his derisive laughter and the sound races across the silent field. A message from Middle England, expressed in the accent of Wagga. You hoped that out there, in some distant galaxy, Lord Ted was listening. And taking serious note.

'Swales Out! Swales Out!'

Mail on Sunday, 9 September 1993

Manchester City 3 Queens Park Rangers 0

PETER SWALES SAT in the directors' box and chatted affably to his neighbour as Manchester City's oldest and fondest battle cry boomed across Maine Road.

'Swales Out! Swales Out!' the yell came from 20,000 throats. But the old chap ignored it, just as he has done these many years past. For City will lose their chairman and football will lose its most remarkable haircut only when the price is right. And that price may reach some £7 million.

Four rows in front of Swales sat the man most likely to pay the price, the man whose face stared out from a forest of placards around the old ground. Francis Lee timed his entrances and exits adroitly, securing standing ovations before the start of each half and another when he left thirteen minutes from the end.

Swales ignored him. After a couple of decades in the City board room, the only thing capable of shaking him would be a kind word. The only one which came his way yesterday cropped up in the 38th minute of a match which saw City's players ignore the prevailing uncertainties and get on with the task of defeating Rangers.

Niall Quinn had taken the first after 18 minutes, after Mike Sheron struck a post. Then, in 38 minutes, Sheron himself accepted a simple chance after the Rangers' keeper Tony Roberts had been deceived by a corner.

'Swales In,' boomed a grandstand voice, which received the ovation it deserved. But even as City ensured a simple success with Garry Flitcroft's long, swerving drive in the 71st minute, the demands for the chairman's head were growing ever more shrill, the demonstrations rumbling long after the match.

In truth, the kindest term one could apply to Peter Swales' stewardship would be 'undistinguished'. After all those years and all those managers, City remain the butt of every bad joke in town. You are told of the video they produced last season: 101 Best Throw-ins.

You are warned about crowd congestion when arriving at Maine Road: 'There'll be two queues. Don't join the long one – that's for the chip shop.'

This is what they have come to, and Swales has played a major part in that sad process. But this season, and quite unexpectedly, the pressure has grown too great to resist. Again, Swales brought it on himself. Tiring of his reputation as a peerless sacker of managers, and seeking an obliging patsy to take the flak, he appointed as general manager one John Maddock. It was as if Blackadder had handed control to Baldrick.

Poor Maddock's idea of a 'cunning plan' was to sack Peter Reid, with the season just four matches old. Everybody knew that Swales was pulling the strings, and Swales himself realised that the game was up.

As in every earth-shaking crisis of this kind, high emotion fought a gallant draw with low farce yesterday. The Daily Mirror, sure-footed as ever, sent in a team of comely ladies to distribute badges bearing the motto: 'We Want Franny'. Sadly, there was a design fault, as one affronted gentlemen pointed out.

'This badge is *red*,' he said. 'I can't wear a *red* badge. Bloody United's red.' The lady, blonde and vacant in the manner of *Coronation Street's* divine Racquel, shrugged prettily. 'Don't tell me,' she said. 'Myself personally, I don't know nothing about foot-ball, I'm sure.'

In the forecourt, before the club offices, television cameras panned across the fans. One wild-eyed vicar knew just what they wanted. 'Right,' he instructed his raucous flock, 'when they point the camera this way, we'll give 'em "Swales Out! Swales Out!" then straight into "All We Are Saying Is Give Lee A Chance". Right?'

They performed on cue, and the cleric was mightily pleased. 'What's his name?' I asked a blue-shirted bystander. 'Dunno,' he said. 'I've always called him Prat.'

Inside the ground, City had laid on a marching band, a character obscurely known as Mr Blobby, and a curiously comfortable and convincing victory. But it will not serve to save the chairman.

'Swales Out! Swales Out!' the old tune was being bellowed more loudly than ever last night. And there were those who swore they had seen the chairman shed a regretful tear. He was, it is rumoured, on his way to the bank at the time.

Listening to the Trains

Mail on Sunday, 14 November 1993

THE DRINKERS SAT BY the bar window and stared out at the Lisburn Road. It was a drowsy afternoon, so still that you could hear the clatter of the Army helicopter suspended over distant Ballymurphy. Across the way, a policeman in a flak jacket checked the papers of a lad in a red Fiesta. 'Nice motor, that,' said a man in the bar. 'My brother had one of them stole off him once.'

An armoured car rounded a corner; two young faces peeping from its turret, two rifles sweeping the street. For a disturbing half-second, the lazy sweep of a weapon took in the window of the bar. But the afternoon drinkers let it pass unremarked as they supped their pints and swapped their gossip.

A while later, I met the man whose brother once owned a Ford Fiesta. He tried to explain how a city could cope with troops and terrorists and the constant threat of imminent catastrophe. Eventually, he found the phrase. 'Living in Belfast,' he said, 'is like living next door to the railway station. After a while, you don't hear the trains.'

For a quarter of a century the ordinary people of this city and province have existed by a similar code; a mixture of quiet desperation and an insistence that things are never as black as they seem. But after all these years, that decent pretence is becoming impossible to sustain.

The recent, barbarous killings on the Shankill and at Greysteel have reinforced a feeling that events are passing beyond civilised control. These days, it is not only the fearful visitor who hurries past parked cars and jumps at the slam of a door.

A senior Belfast police officer, now retired and necessarily anonymous, declared: 'This is as bad as it's ever been. You see, in this town you're Papist or Prod, one or the other. Now if one lot starts trouble, then the police can deal with them. But we can't deal with both at the same time. And that's what's happening. We're stretched, we're over-worked and we're knackered. I'll tell you, it's a hell of a time to hold a football match, so it is.'

Which brings us to the matter at hand. On Wednesday evening the city will offer a range of competing attractions from the Chinese State Circus on Laganbank, through Brecht's *Mother Courage* at Stranmillis College to a musical tribute to The Carpenters at Whitla Hall. Yet the truth, as Belfast and the whole of Ireland will tell you, is that there is really only one game in town.

Any match between Northern Ireland and the Republic carries the potential for tribal conflict. But a match played at such a time, at such a venue and with so much at stake raises the forthcoming contest to a hazardous level of intensity.

The sporting issues are simple: the Republic have to win on Wednesday in order to qualify for the World Cup finals. A home victory would leave Northern Ireland with nothing more than the satisfaction of having scuppered the dreams of their neighbours. It is a prize they dearly covet.

If the dramas could be confined to the football field, how happy we should be. Sadly, there was never a chance that sport would prevail. The Republic's football authority, the FAI, set a depressing tone by their ham-fisted efforts to have the game moved from Belfast. They sent a delegation to a FIFA meeting in Zurich to drop clumping hints about the new levels of violence in the province and how much better things would be if the two Irelands could settle their argument on neutral territory; preferably Manchester, but anywhere other than Windsor Park.

These machinations had nothing to do with a fear of playing in Belfast – as one or two witless scribblers swiftly suggested – but everything to do with seizing an advantage. Any game outside the six counties would be effectively a home game for the Republic, so desperate are their fans to see them qualify.

For a time, it seemed that FIFA had agreed to the switch. Travel agents in Dublin took out options on more than 5,000 aircraft seats. A meeting was held at Old Trafford to finalise catering arrangements for the big match. The Northern Ireland football authority, IFA, would be compensated by profits approaching half a million pounds. They were confidently expected to leap at the chance.

And they failed to oblige. Taking their lead from the IFA Secretary David Bowen, they fought their corner, swallowed their financial loss and insisted that Windsor Park was the only venue. Faced with such spirited resistance, FIFA succumbed.

Bob Catterson agrees with the decision. The 60-year-old chief steward has organised Windsor's security for the match. He knows the risks and believes they are worth running. 'Moving the match would have been a terrible blow,' he says. 'This is our World Cup final. If the time wasn't right for this game, when would it have been right? They had to let us play it here.'

He concedes that the Republic have helped the situation by declining to take up their allocation of 400 tickets and advising their fans not to travel. But he knows that his real problems may arise from northern nationalists turning up to cheer for the Republic. 'If there's a load of fellers waving Union Jacks and another feller pulls out a Free State Tricolour, well, we'd have to make decisions,' says Bob.

You smile at the instinctive use of 'Free State', a term which lost its meaning some forty years past. But you understand his difficulties. Windsor Park lies in the Protestant heartland. The graffiti on the little footbridge behind the old stand are crude commendations of loyalist paramilitaries: UVF, UDA, UFF.

The people of these parts did not follow Northern Ireland to their first qualifying match in Dublin, and they are not expecting Republican visitors on Wednesday.

The Republic's players will have little time to absorb their surroundings. They may not spot the Windsor Gospel Hall or the Churchill Dry Cleaners, certainly they will not seek a welcome in the Sandy Row Glasgow Rangers Supporters Club, housed in the huge blue building a mile down the road. Instead, they will come into the city, play their hearts out for Jack Charlton and country, then head straight back for Dublin. If all goes to plan, they should be in a hotel nightclub before midnight.

The result will determine their mood; victory bringing elation, defeat the bleakest despair. The same will be true for the people of Belfast, but only for a while. Their concerns are more sombre, more pressing and infinitely more important than the outcome of a football match. For they live next door to the railway station. And they can no longer ignore the roar of the trains.

A Town Called Alex

Mail on Sunday, 5 December 1993

A T ONE MINUTE PAST ten on a cool and cloudy morning, Walter Masemola heaved a huge breath, hitched his trousers and shuffled forward to accept his place in history.

History, it must be said, had prepared a sobering welcome; a sixteen-pace run and a whirl of arms culminated in a short, fast and extremely wide delivery. No matter. Walter, an 18-year-old son of the Alexandra township, had healed a rift in Anglo-South African cricket relations which had endured for 29 years. And the healing gesture had taken place on the green oasis which lies at the troubled heart of Alexandra. The symbolism was both poignant and profound.

The English cricketers wandered wide-eyed into this distressful sprawl which is home to 350,000 people on the north-eastern edge of Johannesburg. For five days, they had practised at the Wanderers Club, the ancestral home of apartheid cricket, and enjoyed the facilities of their hotel in Sandton, a suburb of high fences and elegant lawns; a place where poverty is a distant rumour. And all the while, reality was a ten-minute drive away.

Now they passed through the area known as Beirut, where shell and bullet have slaughtered indiscriminately down all the bloody years. They travelled along the route they call 'Death Row' where, only two months ago, killings were conducted without motive or mercy. They saw the shacks and the shanties, the gaunt hostels, the grinding misery of the streets.

And, unlike all their blinkered and grasping predecessors, who not only resented the South African boycott but breached it with infamous and unofficial regularity, this group of modern Englishmen were exposed to a different, more sombre truth. They reacted to the revelation with decent dignity.

Hugh Morris, the captain of England A, was prepared for the experience by a private visit he made on Thursday afternoon. Like so many of his confrères, he once had spent his winters in South Africa in defiance of the boycott. 'All that time, and I never came into a township,' he said. He stood in the middle of the Alexandra Oval, taking it all in with a long, sad stare. 'You know, it really is an honour to be involved in something like this. I hope it does some good, I really do.'

Yet the prevailing mood yesterday was not one of well-meaning platitude or idle regret. The past was another country, the future was the important challenge. So to celebrate the official restoration of good relations, Alexandra threw a magnificently curious kind of party.

A mid-morning stroll around the boundary offered an array of bewildering images. Down at third man, two funerals were being conducted fifty yards from the boundary fence; the wails and chants of two or three hundred mourners mingling incongruously with the clamorous appeals from the cricketers of the Transvaal Invitation XI.

Walking on, beyond cover, you encountered a wedding group emerging from a flat-roofed church. Jiggling and shuffling, plainly intent on raucous celebration, the guests came spilling down the steps, their songs supplementing the sounds of the morning.

On, on, to long on, and a marching band appeared around a corner, complete with clattering drums and high-stepping majorettes. They marched up the hill to the cricket ground, intent upon entertaining the patrons, mutely willing the players to vacate the turf so that the real fun might begin.

There was laughter and music; the sweet sounds of mild madness. It was rare and wonderful. Indeed, the only truly familiar sound of the day was the clatter of English wickets. A perceptive township follower noted that the MCC flag had fallen inexplicably to half-mast. He did a little dance. 'Pull that thing up,' he demanded. 'England, they ain't beat yet!'

John Jefferies looked on with a smile which never left his face. A 70-year-old white man who has coached in Alexandra for eight years, this day represented the answer to an impertinent prayer. Three of the young men he has coached were out there playing against England. 'Can't believe it,' he kept muttering. 'Just can't believe it. I mean, they were so raw, man. They didn't have a technique, didn't have an idea.

'And we are talking about real deprivation. No water, no electric in their homes. Get up at four in the morning to wash in a communal block; study by the light of the moon. They'd never even been over the hill, to the white side of town. We got them playing, took them to Durban, Cape Town in a plane. A plane! They'd never been on a double-decker bus before. Cricket did that for them. And now they're coming through to pay their dues.'

He pointed out his men with paternal pride. There was a batsman named Justice, whose brother, Peace, had been named as twelfth man. 'There's another guy called Harmony,' said Jefferies. 'We couldn't play him today, but he didn't make a fuss about it.' You try to imagine young Harmony causing trouble, but you abandon the attempt. In any case, John Jefferies is far too happy for trivial jokes. 'You know, two months ago I wouldn't have driven through here,' he said. 'People were getting shot all over, no reason. It seems to have stopped now. Times are changing.' And you pray that his optimism is not unfounded.

A sign of those changing times sat in the marquee reserved for distinguished guests. Thabo Mbeki, chairman of the African National Congress and the potential successor to Nelson Mandela, took his ease and swapped smiling small talk with black and white alike. Like so many things which happened naturally and easily yesterday, it would have been simply unbelievable a few short years ago.

The world is not a cricket field and of course there will be problems and worse when South Africa achieves her democracy next April. But, for the moment at least, the note is one of qualified optimism, a feeling that everything will come right in time.

Yes, it was a very good day. With victory secured in the afternoon, England returned to their Holiday Inn, where the muzak in the elevators dribbles out 'Deck the Halls With Boughs of Holly' and white-coated waiters never run short of sustaining drink.

Young Walter Masemola came over to consult the scorebook. 'Three for 25! That is quite a good show, I think?' Indeed it was, after an unpromising start. And old John Jefferies kept on smiling and slapping backs and telling tales of 'his boys' to all who would listen.

We should not forget this country's recent and terrible history. Neither should we forget the manner in which sportsmen all too often fell short of their responsibilities to the cardinal virtues. Yet, as the brooding clouds parted and the African sun came beaming through, it was good to listen to the old man.

Justice had done very well, he said. Harmony was waiting, uncomplaining, in the wings. And next time, who knows, the people who make the big decisions might consider giving Peace a chance.

'He Always Made Me Laugh . . .'

Mail on Sunday, 12 December 1993

MR BARRY FRY, A FOOTBALL manager of modest repute, is moving from Southend United to Birmingham City. The reason, or so he tells us, is that he: 'Welcomes the chance to rouse a sleeping giant.'

With its combination of hilarious cliché and unconscious parody, that should have served as the week's most fatuous utterance. But along came Mr Derek Partridge, to mount a thundering challenge. He is the spokesperson for something called the Forward With Franny campaign, a movement which seeks to replace Peter Swales with Francis Lee as chairman of Manchester City. And he takes his position rather seriously.

'I urge Swales and Lee to get round a table and talk,' said Partridge. 'They're doing it in the Middle East, they're even doing it in Ireland. Why on earth can't they do it at Maine Road?'

Since a minor managerial idiocy cannot compete with a man incapable of distinguishing Gaza from Gazza, the preposterous Partridge takes the prize. I fancy Danny Blanchflower would have approved.

Danny had a wonderful ear for the absurd, and football constantly fed his fancy. He used to revel in its nonsense. I once saw him chuckling his way through the Spurs car park: 'Feller just told me I was a good player going forward, but I didn't look so clever going backwards,' he said. 'Did y'ever see a footballer who looked better going backwards?'

On another occasion, he had managed to offend one of the earnest worthies on the Tottenham board. 'The trouble with you,' said the affronted director, 'is you think you know all the answers.' Danny beamed. 'Ah, God love you,' he said. 'You don't even know the questions.'

It's a sad truth that we never properly acknowledge our heroes until they have passed beyond reach of praise. Danny Blanchflower was a personal hero, with his style and his laughter, his lightly-worn wisdom and his casual decency. He was happiest when the hour was late and the argument fierce. It was then, without benefit or need of strong drink, he would argue his corner on everything from the effective symbolism of the Irish Border to the respective merits of Best and Finney.

He once, late at night, quoted something he had written for his column in the New Statesman. (Incidentally, how many contemporary footballers have contributed columns to the New Statesman? Names on a postcard, please.) Anyway, boldly and foolishly, I suggested he might be name-dropping. 'Hey, I used to play with Dave Mackay,' he said. 'Now *that's* name-dropping.'

The modern player, steeped in the banal blasphemy that winning is everything, would occasionally stare at Danny as if he had just popped in from another planet. That made him different; it didn't make him wrong. And certainly he was a different manner of manager. 'I tell them it's better to lose a game they should have won than win one they should have lost,' he said. 'The first way you have to think about it and learn from it. The other way you say: Thanks very much. And forget it.'

He could always brush aside defeat – 'If you never have bad times, how will you recognise the good?' – and when he took his turn as manager of Northern Ireland, that philosophical acceptance was frequently employed.

I recall his Irish team losing four-nothing to England in a midweek match at Wembley. 'Will that affect them?' Danny was asked. 'Not at all,' he said. 'Come Saturday they'll be off getting hammered somewhere else, and this'll go right out of their heads.'

For all that, his players loved him. 'I always told them the truth,' said Danny. 'When I started managing Northern Ireland, one of the lads asked me about the size of the bonus. "Bonus?" I said. "We've got no money and we don't win matches. Therefore there's no bonus and no problem." He went off giggling and I never heard another word about it.'

For Danny, the real wonder of the game lay in playing. He saw no great mystique in management: 'A lot of them are wrongfully sacked,' he said, 'but a fair amount are wrongfully employed.' Yet he revered the best of the breed; Arthur Rowe, the gentle purist who signed Blanchflower; Busby, Shankly, Stein and his own, irascible Bill Nicholson.

Ten years after his double-winning team broke up, Nicholson

looked back in gratitude. 'Maybe I didn't realise it then,' he said, 'but it was sheer pleasure. Most of all, I used to love talking with Danny; talking and arguing. He had such a lot of style, and he always made me laugh. I don't half miss it now.'

The talk and the argument, the style and the laughter. Above all, the glory. Much loved and much missed; it is the way that heroes ought to be remembered.

1994

An old man died, and the nation mourned. Like Billy Wright, who passed away several months later, Matt Busby represented the best of his breed. His very name invoked memories of a time when the game seemed to belong to men whose spiritual home lay on the terrace rather than in the boardroom. These days, matches at the highest level tend to be contested by conflicting groups of millionaires, with victory going to those with the deepest pockets.

But not always, as the Irish discovered one glorious afternoon in Giants Stadium. Not always.

Sir Matt of Manchester

Mail on Sunday, 23 January 1994

N THE CITY HE LOVED, in the stadium which is his memorial, they came by their thousand to mourn Matt Busby. And images both powerful and poignant swirled across a bright winter afternoon as a great man was respectfully remembered.

Two hours before kick off, a silent crowd gathered beneath the Munich clock, adding their tokens to the garden of flowers and favours which sprawled across the forecourt. Old men stood, sombre and bare-headed, as the memories came crowding in. Fathers brought their small sons; whispering explanations, urging them to remember the day. An elderly lady muttered a silent prayer, crossed herself and shuffled away, dabbing her eyes with a small lace handkerchief.

There were no extravagant outbursts, no mawkish gestures; just ordinary people remembering an extraordinary individual in the manner of their choosing. And all the more moving for that.

Dignity has been the hallmark of United's tribute these past few days, since they broke the news of the old man's death. Denis Law, who loved Sir Matt as dearly as any, went straight to Old Trafford. 'There were hundreds of people there. Hundreds!' he said. 'And nobody spoke to me. None of the usual joking and cracking. Just a few nods, and silence. Very eerie. Very impressive.'

The official gestures yesterday were equally impressive. The lone piper leading out the footballers of United and Everton. The referee's whistle signalling a minute of mute remembrance, as 44,750 people stood in a silence as bleak and as deep as a grave.

And then, something wonderful. The second shrilling of the whistle, unleashing a roar of relief and exaltation. The public address thanking the Everton followers for their respect. The players breaking ranks, starting to stroke the ball about the field. A joyous normality soothingly restored. Matt Busby faithfully remembered.

That was what Sir Matt's daughter, Sheena, had in mind when she asked that her father be recalled with a smile instead of a tear. Busby would willingly have endorsed that request. The passing of a man who has enjoyed a life of sublime achievement and serene fulfilment through four score years and four demands to be observed with celebration rather than sadness. And when that man has left such a dazzling legacy, with family grown, grandchildren reared and club established beyond argument or challenge, then joy should not be confined.

Even those of us who knew him on deferential terms, as the elderly parish priest who pats your head and calls you 'Son' and grants you absolution without censure, even we have been elevating slight acquaintance into minor friendship this week. Matt Busby had that effect on people.

A year or so back, I helped to make a film to mark the silver jubilee of European Cup victory. United had put the team bus at our disposal, and middle-aged legends with names like Law, Crerand and Charlton climbed aboard at Old Trafford for the journey to Wembley.

Sir Matt sat in the front seat, the manager's seat, puffing his pipe and watching the motorway slide past. Discreetly, without show or fuss, his old boys would take turns to keep him company; reminding him of shared deeds and familiar jokes.

When we arrived at the Wembley hotel, there was a queue at the reception desk. Law marched him straight to the front. 'Key for Sir Matt Busby, please,' he ordered, and it was swiftly produced. Bobby Charlton guided him to his room, and half an hour later, I met him in the corridor, his arm resting lightly on the shoulder of Pat Crerand.

'Our bloody luck,' said Crerand, who revered him like a father. 'The Boss's room's on the same floor! We won't be getting out tonight.' And Sir Matt smiled at the memory. 'Ah, Paddy,' he said. 'All that was years ago, eh? Years ago.'

I last saw him walking off the Wembley pitch in the company of George Best; the pair of them moving slowly, deep in conversation. At the mouth of the tunnel, a couple of Irish construction workers spotted Best and shouted a raucous greeting. Then they saw his companion, and they straightened their backs and removed their hard hats.

Some of those players sat in the Old Trafford stand yesterday; Charlton, Law and Crerand among others. Not all of them held back their tears, yet, to a man, they relished the game which had marked Busby's passing.

To hold a season ticket to Old Trafford these days is to win a lottery every fortnight. They are truly a magnificent side, a team in the richest tradition of Busby's club; elegant, inventive, adventurous and beset by the decent conviction that the game is first and last about glory.

Eric Cantona, Ryan Giggs, Roy Keane; they are forever threatening to do something extravagantly dramatic and enthralling, while in Alex Ferguson, United are led by a manager who speaks Busby's language.

To Everton's absolute credit, they battled the odds with marvellous persistence; shrugging off every escape, every miss, every chance which seemed about to unleash the avalanche.

The fact that they limited United to a single goal – a thing of thrilling movement, bewildering pace and a conclusive header from Giggs in the 28th minute – says everything about a resolute rearguard movement.

But, on this day above all other, United's victory was not to be denied, just as their championship will not be surrendered. For they owe it to that gentle, decent man who established their standards. To the man whom a city mourned yesterday. To the man whose memory the grand old game will forever celebrate and cherish.

To Sir Matt of Manchester, the last and best of his breed. May he rest in peace.

The Stench of Scandal

Mail on Sunday, 6 March 1994

THE MALADY WHICH CURSES British athletics took an ominous turn for the worse this week . . . when the most powerful man in the sport produced a sick note. The note declared that Andy Norman, promotions officer for the British Athletic Federation, was too ill to attend a disciplinary hearing of the BAF. The inquiry has been suspended, and the stench of scandal continues to pervade Britain's most successful sport.

The details of the Norman affair are tolerably well known. In a taped telephone conversation, Norman accused Cliff Temple, the athletics correspondent of the *Sunday Times*, of sexually harassing a women athlete. The allegation was vigorously denied by both the journalist and the athlete in question, and Norman gave his employers assurances that 'such activities would cease forthwith'.

But the charge, coming at a time when he was suffering severe personal problems, left Temple acutely distressed. On a January evening eight weeks ago, he took his life on a railway track near his home in Kent.

The widespread grief at Temple's passing reflected the quality of his contribution to the sport. But grief was laced with anger. For all his power and influence, Norman has never been a popular figure in athletics; indeed, he is commonly regarded as a vulgar bully with a talent for blustering abuse. And yet for more than twenty years he has worked hard to secure his place at the summit of the sport. As one senior official told me recently: 'He's vindictive, he's got a long memory, and he knows where most of the bodies are buried. A lot of people are frightened of him. But don't quote me on that.'

The disciplinary hearing was seen by many as a way of holding Norman to account, of confronting his methods with rigorous, reasoned inquiry. Professor Peter Radford, the executive chairman of the BAF, has completed a painstaking investigation and has assembled a case for Norman to answer.

Strangely, Norman has forsaken his normal policy of getting his retaliation in first, although Brendan Foster, with whom he enjoyed a long and occasionally profitable association, has apparently observed: 'It's a Press-led bash for Andy. He has ruffled their feathers over the years.' It was a trite and insensitive reaction from a man whose biography Cliff Temple had once crafted with decent distinction.

In fact, the nearest Norman has come to telling his side of the story – so far as I am aware – was through an approach made to this newspaper by a third party some three weeks ago. We were invited to interview Norman, and we agreed on certain conditions: that we reserved the right to publish our own views on the answers he would give, and that the exercise would, in no sense, degenerate into a 'whitewash' of the subject. Having kicked my heels for several hours on the morning of the appointed day, I was not wholly surprised when the interview was cancelled. Lawyers had examined the proposition and had decided that no good could come of it.

In the meantime, inertia reigns. The clubs, who represent the heart and soul of the sport, grow increasingly frustrated as justice drags its feet. The four Temple children, ravaged by their loss, await their father's final vindication. And the noblest of sports yearns for a conclusion to the shabby and shameful affair.

Let us wish Andy Norman a truly swift recovery. For all sorts of reasons.

Strange Home for Soccer Football

Mail on Sunday, 19 June 1994

I N MICKEY MANTLE'S SPORTS bar on Central Park South, they are showing some of the finest goals the World Cup has ever seen. It is a stunning collection which includes two or three flashes of the vintage Pele, Geoff Hurst's final flourish against the Germans and that darting, jinking, shuffling masterpiece from Maradona in Mexico.

These are goals which would bring the average British pub to a halt, but here nobody cheers, nobody applauds, nobody seems to notice. Instead, Mantle's patrons continue to drink and gossip, oblivious to the stirring deeds. After all, it's only football; soccer football.

A couple of blocks away, in a café on 57th Street, the waiter cleans your table and notes your accent. 'You from London?' he says. 'You here for the soccer? That's what I figured.' An amiable man, he is anxious to please his customer. 'Me, I love soccer. Hey, I'm gonna watch all that World Cup stuff. An' you wanna know who I think's gonna win?' He lowers his voice as he offers his forecast. 'England, that's what I think. Yeah, England. Why not?'

You raise an eyebrow and resist remarking that Tottenham have rather more chance of winning next year's FA Cup. In its currently unhappy state, English football can ill afford to reject the kind words of a New York waiter. And yet, however trivial, the incidents in bar and café are depressingly typical of America's attitude towards the world game. For all their humour and their zest and their free-hearted hospitality, the citizens of this great Republic know little and care less about the sport they call soccer.

Even the incomparable Pele, who worked harder than most to make football acceptable in the States, remains baffled by the level of ignorance. 'People come up to me and ask me if I'm going to play for Brazil,' he said this week. 'They really think I'm still playing!' Pele is 54 years old.

Football is not a popular television sport in this country. Unlike basketball, which is played by towering freaks, offers instant gratification in the shape of points by the hundred and is therefore ideal fodder for the small screen, football is rather more subtle and cerebral. As such, its audience ratings have been on a par with those for beach volleyball. The television commentators are acutely aware that the game must be set in an American context, hence the explanation in the opening match that Lothar Matthaeus is 'the quarter back of the German team'.

Yet had the World Cup been given a clear run this week, then it might have surprised the agnostics with the scope of its support. Instead, Sod's Law prevailed, and the activities of men like the quarter back Matthaeus and that animated Colombian with the Vera Duckworth wig were seriously overshadowed by ice hockey's Stanley Cup, the US Open Golf tournament and the attempt of the New York Knicks to win the NBA finals. Above all, they were swept aside by the ongoing tragedy of O. J. Simpson, with the extraordinary live coverage of the pursuit and capture of one of America's most important athletes of the twentieth century.

When the Los Angeles police chief announced, during the opening match between Germany and Bolivia, that his men were 'actively searching for Mr Simpson', you could hear the channel switches clicking all over America as the nation sought news of one of its favourite sons. Even the ESPN sports channel, which has bought the football and will screen if for a full month, was patently itching to launch itself at the biggest story in years instead of covering the inadequacies of a bunch of Bolivians.

Since the success or failure of USA '94 will be judged by the size of the television audience, rather than the numbers who will pack themselves into the various stadia, the Simpson saga did football no favours. Indeed, long before the week's end, one American administrator could be heard tinkering with the idea of building bigger goals so that goalkeepers might be beaten on a more regular basis.

In fairness, there have been one or two flickering hints that an American World Cup might make the beginnings of a real difference. The profile of American soccer is of a game played in the affluent suburbs by boys and girls who are neither sufficiently large nor sufficiently demented to play American football. They then drop the sport upon leaving high school. Now, and partly as a result of the current activity in these parts, attempts are being made to sow a few seeds in the ghetto. It is a long shot, of course, but if they should take root and blossom, then the world game really would embrace the world.

But the fact is that few people are holding their breath, for the likelihood is that this World Cup will make little or no difference to the advancement of the sport. Already, we have seen that its audiences are benevolent, inquisitive and amazingly ill-informed; like a Lord's crowd condemned to watch a baseball game. It is here because the men who mishandle the affairs of FIFA wanted to make large and easy profits by appeasing sponsors, advertisers and television producers. It was the wrong decision, taken for the wrong reasons.

If you doubt me, then drop in at Mickey Mantle's bar over the next few weeks. Hear the silence, feel the apathy . . . and watch England win the World Cup.

'And All the Other D'Oliveiras . . .'

Mail on Sunday, 17 July 1994

THE LORD'S WELCOME for the cricketers of South Africa will be warm and fervent this week. Hands will be pumped, backs will be slapped and the legacy of three decades of bitter separation will dissolve in the mood of the moment. And, amid all the emotion, one name will not be mentioned. For fear of offending new friends.

Basil D'Oliveira smiles at the turn of events. 'I've got no animosity, no malice,' he says. 'It's good to have them back. But I've been reading about the fantastic welcome they've already been given, and it's made me think. I mean, all that agony; it did happen, didn't it? And they were in the wrong, weren't they? Surely I'm not imagining everything?' He pauses, shakes his head. 'People say I should forgive and forget. Well, that's fine. I can forgive. But don't ask me to forget. Because I can't.'

To understand the depth of his feelings, you have to return to those days when D'Oliveira was not simply a person but an 'Affair'; the innocent victim of an injustice so vicious and cynical that its echoes still resound down the years.

Born at Signal Hill in Cape Town in 1931, and deemed by South Africa's apartheid constitution to be of 'coloured' race, he was unable to test his talent against white cricketers and was forced to pursue his career in this country. After playing for Middleton in the Lancashire League, he joined Worcestershire in 1965 and was selected for England a year later.

In 1968, he was brought into the side for the final Test of the Ashes series at the Oval. He played an epic, match-winning innings of 158, which appeared to ensure his place on the forthcoming tour of South Africa. But there was uncertainty about the South Africans' potential reaction to the selection of a 'coloured' player and, shamefully, the selectors left him out of the squad. John Arlott, who had been instrumental in bringing D'Oliveira to England, spoke for many when he declared: 'No one of open mind will believe that he was left out for valid cricket reasons.'

Two weeks later, the bowler Tom Cartwright withdrew through injury and D'Oliveira replaced him. The South African Prime Minister John Vorster immediately announced that D'Oliveira was unacceptable as the English team was being picked 'for political reasons'. The tour was called off. Effectively, the years of boycott had begun.

'I cried my eyes out when they told me,' he says. 'God, I desperately wanted to go on that tour. And I wanted to play so bloody well. Above all, I wanted to play at Newlands. And now I wasn't going to get the chance.'

Newlands in Cape Town was the cricket ground of his childhood, the ground where the white people played. For a shilling a day, he would train his father's pigeons and collect the money for his weekend treat at Newlands. 'I had to walk ten miles there, ten miles back,' he says. 'The money only covered my entrance fee. And when I got there, I had to sit in a small section of the ground with the rest of the non-whites. Sure it was demeaning, but I loved the cricket.

'I remember going there once and paying my money, just in time to see Johnny Wardle, the old Yorkshire spinner, end the game around lunchtime. I watched the last couple of overs, then I left. I told him about it years later. "Great day," he said. "Yeah," I said. "But you didn't have to walk home, did you."'

A deep yearning for the Cape lasted down the years of exile. 'The most beautiful place on Earth,' he says. 'I never lost the longing for it. And even if I hated the system, I couldn't hate the people.'

When he left South Africa, with a pregnant wife and a £450 contract to play for Middleton, one white businessman, Gordon Innes, arranged a testimonial match for him. 'I told him he'd need a permit. He said "Bullshit," recalls D'Oliveira. 'He went round with a collecting bucket and raised £154 for me. I'll never forget him. How could you hate people like that?'

He remembers the kindnesses. When he won his first cap, against the West Indies at Lord's, he pulled on his blazer and walked out on to the players' balcony. 'I was just thinking how much I wished the people at home could see me,' he says, 'when Kenny Barrington came past and tapped my arm. "It's all yours, Baz," he said. "And they can't take it away from you now."'

He remembers, with a vast grin, that innings of 158 at The Oval, when it seemed that his tour place was secure. 'Charlie Elliott was the umpire,' he says, 'and he really wanted me to do well. I flashed at a couple of balls early on, and he said: "Baz, get your bloody head down!" Then I got fifty and he said: "Hey, Baz. You're in the team." Then I got a hundred and he said: "You're in the arrivals lounge at Johannesburg bloody Airport." Then he suddenly realised what it all meant. So when I got one hundred and fifty, he said: "And now, Baz, you've just set the cat among the f****** pigeons!"'

Yet even his laughter does not disguise the lingering sorrow. 'The whole question bothers me to this day,' he says. 'I ask myself: Did you stop a series between England and South Africa? Did I hurt good friends in the England side? Am I to blame for all the things that followed? But then I say: I'm sorry it had to happen, sorry it had to be me. But look how things have worked out. I see events I never dreamed could happen in my lifetime. I see Nelson Mandela in charge of his nation. And I just say: "Thank God it's all over. Done. Finished."'

D'Oliveira's last ambition is to meet Mandela: 'Giant of a man. A statesman. All that grace, and no bitterness. Amazing.' But his goodwill towards the President does not extend to supporting the cricket team of his native country.

'England took me in when the people running South Africa said I wasn't good enough to live with them, let alone play cricket with them. They told me I was second class, and that hurt me very badly. So England's my team, it has been for a long time, and I hope they win this series.

'I wouldn't back them, mind. They scraped through against New Zealand, and South Africa's a whole lot stronger than them. Not that it really worries me. I've had no contact with these South Africans, they haven't asked to meet me or invited me to a Test, so I've no great desire to watch them. Really, they're just another touring side as far as I'm concerned.'

He doesn't mean it. In fact, he doesn't even try to sound convincing. His history and background decree that the South Africans can never be 'just another touring side'.

But his roots lie deep in Worcestershire, that county in the heart of England where his talent was brought to memorable fruition. For the past thirty years, he has lived in his pleasant semi, a mile from the New Road ground. He visits that beautiful ground, set snugly between river and cathedral, almost every day, winter and summer, to gossip and drink and debate. He played until fifty, coached until sixty and now, a portly figure with steel grey hair and plastic hips, he fills the role of general pundit.

And yet the past will always sit upon his shoulder, needing only a nudge to bring it to life. He muses upon the changes of recent years, and suddenly he grows intensely serious. 'You know what those changes mean?' he asks. 'They mean that South African teams have to be picked from the whole of South Africa. They mean that every black child in that country now has the chance to win his place. That's the most important thing for me. It's the only important thing. Always has been.

'Strange, really. You often hear white South Africans talk about the people who missed out on big careers; the Pollock brothers, Barry Richards, Eddie Barlow, players like that. Well, I'd like them to swallow their pride and take a deep breath and say: "And all the other Basil D'Oliveiras, who could have been wonderful . . . but never had the chance to show it."'

A Handful of Dust

Mail on Sunday, 31 July 1994

DIDN'T START LAUGHING until Raymond Illingworth solemnly revealed that he had inspected the contents of Michael Atherton's trousers last Saturday evening. After an urgent search and an anxious silence, the conclusion was announced. 'There was,' reported Illingworth, 'nothing untoward.' Now if you can stifle your mirth in the face of that revelation, then, as Illingworth also remarked in the course of the week: 'You're a better man than I am, Gunga Din.'

It was as if the chairman of selectors had decided that even the tackiest farce would be incomplete without the ceremonial dropping of trousers. And, after a week rich in absurdity, he may well have been correct.

Macaulay, that most eminent of Victorians, once observed that: 'We know of no spectacle so ridiculous as the British public in one of its periodical fits of morality.' Recent events have simply reinforced that sagacious judgement.

The saloon bars of the nation are abuzz with indignation. The rent-a-quote ranks of ancient Test players are, once again, ashamed to be English. The tabloid back pages, becalmed on the silent sea between the World Cup and 'The Big Kick Off', are salivating over a rousing scandal. And Jonathan Agnew, the cricket correspondent of the BBC, has issued a demand for the head of the England captain. Pity about Aggers. A distinguished cricketer, a fine broadcaster and an engaging companion, he managed to sound like the resident prig of the Lower Fifth with an abjectly pompous performance.

And what, precisely, were the offences which engendered such heat? They were (a) that Atherton carried a small amount of dirt in his trouser pocket, and (b) that he chose to keep this curious quirk to himself rather than confide in the match referee. From those bare facts, we may draw one of two conclusions. Either Atherton was cheating by altering the condition of the ball, or he was telling the truth when he said he was using dirt to dry his sweaty fingers.

My own belief is that the second explanation is so unlikely, so bizarre and so difficult to credit that it is almost certainly true. If an intelligent man like Atherton had been up to something more sinister, then five minutes' creative thought would have furnished him with a far more convincing excuse.

In any case, the conclusive piece of evidence is surely the condition of the ball. After what we now know were several inspections, the umpires agreed that the ball was unchanged. However suspicious Atherton's actions may have seemed, there was therefore no valid charge to answer. Case dismissed. Well, not quite. He had still to face the unnerving ordeal of being defended by the chairman of selectors. Now, all things being equal, I should much prefer to be abused by a whole bluster of Fleet Street tabloids than be defended by Raymond Illingworth.

Sweating gently in the afternoon heat and surrounded by predatory scribblers, he bore an uncanny resemblance to Sir Bernard Ingham in the days when he would attempt to rationalise the latest aberration of the 'Leaderene'.

He started to blame the press for the captain's mess, the instinctive reaction of the haplessly bewildered. He announced Atherton's fines: £1,000 for deceiving the match referee, a penalty which was entirely justified, then a further £1,000 'for using dirt'. Now this was entirely incomprehensible. If the skipper was innocent, as the chairman accepted, and if the condition of the ball was unchanged, then how could Illingworth justify a fine for an offence which, by definition, had not been committed? He later offered the view that the punishment was 'harsh', an admission so extraordinary that you suspect that Illingworth does not fully understand the meaning of the word.

No, he couldn't discuss England's 356-run defeat by South Africa, since he hadn't seen a ball bowled all afternoon. The fact that the hammering had taken place over four days was apparently irrelevant; the chairman had missed the final hours and therefore was unable to comment. It was a deeply unimpressive performance.

While Illingworth retreated to polish his alibi and Atherton retreated to consider his future, the horrified nation abandoned itself to a collective fit of morality. The absurd delusion that cricket is somehow a metaphor for life was once again paraded, and a charming game was once more expected to bear an unrealistic ethical burden.

So the phone-in callers grew more demented and the pundits became impossibly shrill. An England captain had cheated at cricket and the barbarians were at the gates, ran the charges. The fact that he hadn't cheated and that, anyway, the barbarians had spent these past several seasons wining and dining in the corporate hospitality boxes was neither here nor there. Heads, or at least one head, must roll.

Why, I have even seen it seriously suggested that the England captaincy should be offered to Mike Gatting, the man who, in his time, led a rebel tour to apartheid South Africa, poked and abused a Pakistani umpire and lost a brief and furious argument with a dressing room window. As another great sportsman once said: 'You cannot be serious'.

No, the real answers all involve Michael Atherton, and in my view two courses of action are open. The first, and preferred, option is to accept that he has been foolish but not venal. This being the case, he should continue to captain his country for as long as his abilities allow.

The second option is rather more savage. We could mollify the skipper's critics by burning him at the stake behind the Warner Stand. His charred remains could be collected, placed in an urn and mounted in the Long Room at Lord's. Above the urn, we could place a plaque, regretting the demise of a gifted but misguided cricketer and announcing that, from this day forward, England and South Africa will play for 'The Athers'.

A drastic solution, I agree. But it might hold a certain appeal for the likes of Jonathan Agnew.

The Passing of the Captain

Mail on Sunday, 4 September 1994

BILLY WRIGHT DIED YESTERDAY at his home in Barnet, North London. He was seventy years old and loved by all who knew him. He would have settled for that obituary, although he might have offered a quibble over that last phrase. But we shall not spare him, because it is undeniably true. In his dignified decency, Billy was loved in a way that few sportsmen have ever been loved.

William Ambrose Wright: the very name unleashes the memories. Steam radio and *Sports Report*, Charles Buchan's *Football Monthly* and CWS football boots, as worn by Stanley Matthews. Molineux, lit by new-fangled floodlights and full to bursting to entertain the likes of Spartak and Honved. And Wright at the centre of things; fair-haired, spring-heeled and brimming with an enthusiasm which never deserted him, from earliest youth to three score years and ten.

We of a certain age knew everything about the man who became captain of England at the age of twenty-three. We even knew the name of his landlady, the kindly Mrs Colley, to whom he turned in tears after Major Frank Buckley, the manager of Wolverhampton Wanderers, had told him he was too small to make the grade in professional football. For we had read the story over and over again in our *FA Book for Boys*; sharing young Bill's disappointment, then his blessed relief as Major Buckley gave him a second chance. He never forgot that day, never forgot the agony of the moment.

And, in truth, English football would have been immeasurably poorer without Wright's bustling presence. In later years, usually after the Footballer of the Year dinner, when glasses clinked and stories were told, Wright could be persuaded to speak of his glorious days.

'I wasn't a great player,' he would tell you. 'But, hey, I didn't half play with some great ones.' And the names would come pouring forth, from the early, post-war days of Lawton, Mannion, Carter, Finney, Matthews and Swift, through to Edwards, Haynes, Greaves,

Shackleton and Charlton.

He kept that kind of company through one hundred and five caps, eighty-five of them as captain. And if the bare statistics do not stagger, then consider this: during that entire span, from Northern Ireland in 1946 through to the 8–1 victory over America in 1959, Wright missed just three matches. Records, they say, are made to be broken, but this is a record which will never be approached. And yet the modesty was never impaired. Bill could still blush when somebody reminded him of his best days. With him, modesty was an instinctive and uncalculating virtue.

He would much prefer to celebrate the deeds of others than dwell upon his own achievements; indeed, his fondest party piece was to quote at length Geoffrey Green's wonderful account of England's 6–3 defeat by Hungary. In particular, he would dwell upon the description of the famous goal from Ferenc Puskas, when he turned and spun and shot while Wright, in Green's words, 'rushed past like a fire engine going to the wrong fire'. Billy would chuckle and blush, nodding at the memory, relishing the skill and acknowledging his role as victim. And the great Puskas would pat his back and smile his understanding. There is another who will mourn his loss today.

For Billy, as for most of the great ones, the real joy of football lay in the playing. He managed Arsenal for a time in the sixties, but there was never the same fulfilment, the same sense of fun.

Strangely, television was far more to his taste, and he assembled a distinguished sports career in Independent Television, first as a commentator, then as an executive. Even in that hard-boiled world, people responded to a genuinely nice man.

So far as football was concerned, he did it all; from lifting the FA Cup in 1949, in those happier days before the family silver was sold, to serving as director of his beloved Wolves. I well remember his pride at being asked to join the board. 'Who'd have thought it?' he said. 'I used to clean the boots at that place, now they've asked me to sit in the boardroom.' And he shook his head, amazed that life had dealt him such a lavish hand and insisting that his fortune was undeserved.

The truth was that Billy Wright was the best and most deserving of his breed. And the tribute he would have appreciated most of all came from a man whose name will be mentioned in the same respectful breath. 'England has had no better or more loyal servant,' said Tom Finney. 'Billy Wright was as solid as a rock. He was also a very nice guy.'

May the very nice and greatly loved guy rest in peace.

Getting Laminated with Big Ron

Night & Day, 9 October 1994

K
EEP SPREADIN' THE NOOS, Ah'm leavin' today,
Ah wanna be a part of it, Noo Yark, Noo Yark
Midday in mid-town, and Ron Atkinson is in splendid
voice. Outside, the citizens of Gotham are sweating
through a hundred degrees of high-summer heat. But here, in the
cool depths of the limousine, the darkened glass repels the glare of
the day while the air conditioning hums along with Ron.

It is a large car, only marginally shorter than Fifth Avenue and
almost half as wide. No matter; it suits Ron. From time to time, the
chauffeur calls back over his shoulder to point out places of interest.
'Dat's Tiffany's!' he bawls at a window studded with diamonds.
'Dat's Gucci's!' he yells, as Gucci slides by. Then up looms St
Patrick's Cathedral, and he is briefly puzzled. 'Dat,' he says, 'is one
helluva big choych!' Ron chuckles: 'Go on, my son,' he says. 'You're
playing a blinder.'

An hour later, we are kicking our heels in a small shack in New
Jersey. It is situated close by the gates of Giants Stadium and it serves
as the collection point for World Cup media credentials. A photo-
graph is taken and the result is processed to form the plastic ID card
which journalists and commentators are required to wear. Ron, who
is covering the competition for ITV, is growing impatient, and as a
young woman official hurries past he taps her arm. ''Scuse me, luv.
Any sign of our pictures?' he asks. 'Sir,' she says, 'you are being laminated, even as we speak.'

He is hugely impressed by the word. 'Laminated!' he says. 'That's
a word an'alf, that is. Bloody *laminated*!' He repeats it over again.
So we strike a bet. A Manhattan dinner says that Ron cannot sneak
'laminated' into his broadcast comments on the Republic of Ireland
v Italy match. 'No danger,' he says. Later that afternoon, as the
game begins, the commentator Brian Moore asks Ron about the
things which have impressed him in the World Cup so far. Ron

starts to mention the small innovations which most people don't notice. 'Like those new numbers they're wearing on their shirts; those laminated numbers.' Moore, who is in on the bet, digs him in the ribs. Ron climbs to his feet, turns to the press box and punches the air.

An hour after the match, we hurry back to the cool of Ron's limousine. He is clutching a bottle of beer, presented to him by a celebrating Irish fan. His mahogany tan has deepened in the heat of the afternoon, and his brow is glowing like an antique sideboard. The tan has always played a part in his legend, right back to the days when he managed United. 'I can't understand it,' Terry Wogan once remarked. 'Does the sun only shine on his part of Manchester?'

Ron gulps at the beer as his improbable chariot glides back to mid-town. The driver is tirelessly informative: 'Broadway! Radio City! Down that street, the best Italian restaurant in Manhattan. Would I lie?' Eventually, we approach Ron's hotel: The Plaza. 'Good gaff, this,' he says. 'Known it for years. We used to stay here when I was with Kettering.' He smiles as the eyebrows shoot up. *Kettering* at the Plaza! 'Certainly,' he says. 'Mind, it was a bit different then. I mean, there was thirteen of us. In one room.'

The limousine edges the last few yards along Central Park South; past Mickey Mantle's bar, past that patch of pavement where Streisand bade farewell to Redford in *The Way We Were*. Ron takes it all in with a besotted beam, and he doesn't even try to resist the cue:

'If I can *make* it there, I'll make it *any*where
It's up to You, Noo, Yark, Noo-ooo Yaaaark!'
DUM, DUM, DA-DA-DA!
DUM, DUM, DA-DA-DA!

Mid-morning in Bodymoor Heath, off the A4091 near Tamworth. The footballers of Aston Villa troop in from the training ground to demand tea and toast from the lady in the kitchen. One player calls his agent on a mobile phone and begins a soft mumble of percentages before he realises that others are listening. Dean Saunders, the multi-million pound striker, wags a coyly disapproving finger. 'Off-the-field interests have ruined better players than you, son,' he says, neatly sending up one of the game's hardiest clichés. Unshaven for the most part, they are flecked with mud and streaked with sweat, yet they have trained at no more than half-pace as tonight they play

Wigan in an early round of the Coca-Cola Cup.

Atkinson has named his team, and 'the Gaffer's' choice is avidly discussed. The Gaffer. For all their extreme wealth, English professional footballers still speak of the club manager as if he were a nineteenth-century mill owner and they a bunch of loom operatives. Yet in practice they can assert a robust independence, and that impression is reinforced when a head pops around the kitchen door to inform a player with a famous name that the Gaffer would like a word. 'Is it a row?' asks Famous Name. The head nods. 'A £10 row or a £5 row?' asks Famous Name. The head indicates the smaller sum. 'Sod it,' says Famous Name. 'In that case, I'll finish me toast.'

When decks have been cleared and squabbles settled, the Gaffer is ready to talk. The tan has retreated since its New York heyday; no longer mahogany, more a kind of light oak. And the urge to sing has subsided, since nobody could confuse Bodymoor Heath with the city that doesn't sleep. But, at fifty-five years of age, Ron Atkinson seems as happy as a man could reasonably be.

'Terrible job, this,' he says. 'Bloody awful job; getting out in the fresh air and pinging footballs about and doing all the things you've ever wanted to do. I can appreciate it, 'cos when I was a kid I worked in a factory for a couple of years. Hard work, it was. BSA Tools; clocking in and clocking out and do what you're told and don't argue and who d'you think you are, anyway? No, I've had all that, so I don't complain about managing football clubs.

'There's anxieties, sure. A defeat's never easy to stomach. I've never got used to it. You know, winning doesn't compensate for losing. You get a buzz, but it's nowhere near as powerful as that niggly feeling you get when you lose. Losing's horrible, but even that doesn't make it a bad job. If you're a football man, you love it. Simple as that.'

The fact is that Atkinson is a football man to his bones. Born in Liverpool, raised in Birmingham and educated at both Oxford and Cambridge (United), he adores the game with a consuming passion. Rumour insists that his latest contract is worth around £250,000 a year, and he concedes that he is 'well looked after'. Yet you actually believe him when he says that money is not his motivation. 'I've never looked on it as a job,' he says. 'For me, it's a way of life. I'm like most managers; if I wasn't working in the Premier League, I'd be looking after a Sunday morning team. That might sound right phoney, but it's the truth. Rewards are a bonus; being involved in the game is the joy. I'll tell you, if I ever got to the point of working for wages, I'd pack it in. Honest.'

Listen carefully, and you may hear the derisive laughter of young footballers whose salaries do not remotely approach a quarter of a million pounds and who therefore feel unable to espouse such high-minded principles. Atkinson understands. 'I swore I'd never be one of those who said that the game was great in our day but that it's been steaming downhill ever since,' he says. 'Nonsense, that is. But I do sometimes wonder if they really appreciate it nowadays. I was at Billy Wright's funeral recently. I looked around the place and there were people like Tom Finney, Stan Matthews, Peter Broadbent. Hey, they weren't terrible players, were they? I'm not sure I could justify the enormous gap between what they earned and what people are getting today. There's huge money to be made now, and maybe there should be. But it's not just the top players who are making it; the ordinary players are also getting big money, and I don't think the game's always better for it.'

When he gets into his stride, the deepest convictions rise to the surface. And those of us who were raised on a similar football diet find ourselves agreeing with every word. 'Maybe one or two players have got precious,' he says. 'I don't think they take criticism the way they should. People tell me I ought to give 'em a cuddle. A *cuddle*! God help us! The best players I ever knew didn't need a cuddle. Maybe their wives might have done, but they didn't.'

He begins to reel off his heroes, the way old footballers do. 'Bryan Robson, Dave Mackay, Jimmy Scoular. Great men, the lot of 'em. Men's men. Mackay, he was a class apart. Scoular, he used to frighten me. I could tackle a bit, but he'd come in growling. Urghhhh! Completely bleeding fearless. And Robson. Probably the most complete player I've ever handled. Real thoroughbred, he got the course and distance.'

Atkinson is one of those relatively rare managers who suffered dismissal from Manchester United and survived to tell the tale. 'Biggest club of the lot,' he says. 'Can't argue with that. And they just go on getting bigger. But me, I tried to look on the positive side. I mean, I was there for five or six years, and most of them were good. When I got the sack, I was upset. Then I had a bloody good party and got on with the rest of my life. Que sera, sera.'

He was far more angry when he was sacked by Atletico Madrid, after a tenure which resembled an extended Spanish holiday. 'It was one of those jobs I really thought I could crack,' he says. 'I'd only been there four months and I'd taken them from bottom of the

League to second. Then it happened. I got a phone call saying don't bother coming back.' He was massively compensated for his disappointment, but the indignity still rankles. 'I'll never understand what went on there,' he says. 'Four months! Do me a favour.'

His flow is interrupted at regular intervals by a gaggle of callers; an anxious player, an agitated physio, and, most entertainingly, a persistent salesman who persuades him to purchase a mobile phone for his daughter. Atkinson hesitates, but the patter is appealing. Official forms are flourished. 'I'll need your post code,' says the salesman. 'No idea,' says Ron. 'I only went to a secondary modern you know.' 'I'll also need one of your regular bills. Like a gas bill,' says the salesman. 'Perhaps you could bring it this evening?' Ron explodes. 'Gas bill? You must be bloody joking. Look great, wouldn't it: Coca-Cola Cup, the champions start their defence, and here comes the Villa manager. With his gas bill. Sod off, willyer.'

Ten minutes later, an old gentleman delivers a bulky package. Ron rips it open to expose three bottles of pink champagne. He hands a bottle over the desk. Across the label, in ornate italic script, is printed the legend: 'Specially bottled for Ron Atkinson'. 'Go on, take it,' he says. 'You can pay me back when we have that dinner you never bought in America. Bloody reporters!'

Unlike most people in sport, and certainly most people in football, Atkinson possesses an acute sense of the ridiculous. Self-mockery is his most attractive trait. In the eighties, he attracted a good deal of flak for his jangling jewellery and his habit of dressing like Mr Derek Hatton. Yet you sense that the tongue was never far from the cheek.

He does not deny the charge. 'I've always played Jack the Lad,' he says. 'When I was seventeen, on the Villa ground staff, I bought meself a car. Ford Anglia. Paid thirty-four quid for it. I used to drive to training in it, and some mornings I'd see Jackie Sewell and Peter McParland at the bus stop. Now they were real big time; I mean, Sewell held the British transfer record and McParland had won the Cup for Villa practically on his own. "Jump in," I used to say. "Mind the upholstery." They might have thought I was a flash little bugger, but they never said a word.'

Unlike so many of his managerial contemporaries, Atkinson enjoys the high profile conferred by his calling. 'I never understand blokes complaining about being bothered by the public,' he says. 'If they can't take the attention, they ought to be doing something else. Anyway, my missus says that if people don't recognise me in the street, I go back and tell 'em who I am.' His 'missus' is Maggie, for whom he left his first wife ten years ago, when he was manager of Manchester United. It was an acrimonious separation, heavily chronicled in the tabloids, but it swiftly faded from public consciousness as other, more exotic football scandals pressed for space in the public prints.

It might have been different had Atkinson been in charge of the national team at the time. In truth, and had he put himself forward more vigorously, he might well have secured the post of England manager, with all that means in terms of a high profile. He shrugs the thought aside. 'It didn't appeal to me; simple as that,' he says. 'Of course, I'd have loved the matches, the big tournaments, all that stuff. Anyone would. But I couldn't have taken the waiting time, the months between games. That would have driven me mad.' He doesn't add that he couldn't have tolerated the blazered battalions of the Football Association. But then, he doesn't have to.

In any case, it's hard to be one of the chaps when you're manager of England, to be in on the gags and pranks and the whole blokeish phenomenon which even men of middle age love most of all. 'My brother Graham, he played good-class football for years,' says Ron. 'He doesn't go to games now, but when I went to Wembley with Sheffield Wednesday, he came along on the team bus. We're just getting near the stadium and I look at his face and it's kind of alight. "This is what I miss, Ron," he says. "The good mates, the crack, the lovely nonsense of it all." And it's the same for me.'

In Atkinson's case, the blokeish aspect of football is no affectation. His male chauvinism is instinctive and unchanging. 'I can't stand women talking about football,' he says. 'I don't know why, but it grates on me. They shouldn't interfere. I'm at the ground one day when Terry Cooper walks in. He's managing Birmingham at the time and he's got this young girl Karren Brady with him, who's just been made managing director of Birmingham City, God help us. She's very pleasant and she says what a nice ground it is and what a good team we've got and how I must be really proud of them all, but particularly proud of my son, who's playing so well for me. Now this throws me a bit, and I say: "My son?", very casual. And she says: "I've seen a lot of good reports about your Dalian." Now that's what I mean about women and football.' For the uninitiated, Dalian Atkinson is young, extremely gifted and indisputably black.

He swings back in the chair and thumps his feet on the desk, still chuckling at his story. 'Not a bad life, is it?' he says. 'I mean, that

World Cup was bloody marvellous, wasn't it. I went to Dallas with Jack Charlton, you know. We did the lot: all the JFK bit, the Texas Book Depository, Dealey Plaza, all that. Then we went to South Fork, where the Ewings lived. We did all the telly bit there. I bought a JR hat. Great big ten-gallon job. I covered the World Cup final in it. Great laugh, it was; a really great laugh.'

As his laughter boomed out across the training ground, Atkinson was unaware that he was scarcely a week away from the most satisfying night of his career. Inter Milan would come to Villa Park, leading 1–0 after the first leg of the UEFA Cup. The team that Ron built would retrieve the goal, play the Italians off the pitch and win, deservedly, on penalty kicks. The manager would react emotionally. 'Marvellous. Bloody marvellous. Never had a team play that well. Marvellous.' But all that lay ahead. For the moment, in the office at Bodymoor Heath, he was content to contemplate the task at hand.

Aston Villa beat Wigan by five goals to nil in their Coca-Cola Cup match that evening. Dalian Atkinson scored two of the goals. Ron was ever so proud.

A Brave Face for Bruce

Mail on Sunday, 20 November 1994

T HE MATCH WAS ALMOST an hour away, but in a corner of the Upper East Stand, the visitors were in full voice. Their choice of song was a breezy little ditty, sung to the tune of 'My Old Man's A Dustman'. And, give or take a few aitches, it went: 'Grobbelaar is dodgy, he wears a dodgy hat, And when he saw that forty grand, he said: I'm having that.' You wanted to tell them that they were repeating damaging and wholly unproven allegations which, in due course, may well be tested at law. But they weren't listening.

On a mild November afternoon at The Dell, Bruce Grobbelaar was offering the kind of target which no football follower could resist. And the Arsenal fans took full advantage. They were only 1,500 strong in a crowd of more than 15,000, but they made themselves heard without effort. Songs, chants, insults; most of them unprintable, some of them sufficiently witty to draw chuckles from the Southampton stewards. To sit among that crowd was to wonder at their fierce determination to rattle the ears of the celebrity in the home goal. Merrily they absolved their own goalkeeper, David Seaman, from any taint of scandal: 'Seaman's paid by Arsenal, Seaman's paid by Arsenal,' they chanted. Reassuringly.

When the Southampton full back Jeff Kenna almost headed into his own net in the first half, he was taunted with: 'Are you Brucie in disguise?' When their target went flapping haplessly at a cross, all fifteen hundred bellowed: 'Dod-gy keeper!' Over and over again.

And, inevitably, from time to time, small bunches of the Arsenal fans would leap to their feet, waving wads of banknotes and yelling cheery obscenities. Of course, Grobbelaar would have experienced this kind of insult in his days at Anfield. In the pitiless eighties, it was common practice for London football fans visiting Northern grounds to brandish bundles of tenners while singing songs about the dole. Indeed, some of us were rather surprised when Lady

Thatcher failed to incorporate that lingering image in her coat of arms.

Now there were those who praised Grobbelaar's courage in choosing to face the music at The Dell. Others, myself included, believed that a more sensitive man might have shrunk from the ordeal, allowing the heat of the allegations to subside before making his return. But sensitivity is not Grobbelaar's strongest suit. Far from shrinking, he seemed to revel in the attention, his ego seemingly flattered by the thought that he was the man on everyone's lips.

Of late, he has communicated by prepared statement or impromptu cliché. Why, only yesterday morning he was declaring that he had 'Been to hell and back in the past ten days', a lurid phrase which may not endear him to the Zimbabwe Tourist Board. Yesterday, he conveyed his message by more conventional methods; taking a string of little bows, returning the crowd's applause, clapping colleagues upon the back and generally behaving like the all-round good egg who is embarrassed by the sleazy allegations and merely wants to get on with playing football.

The home fans understood immediately. They awarded him an ecstatic reception, cheered his every move, produced a Union Jack bearing the message: 'Bruce is Innocent' and chanted abuse at the newspaper which had accused him. 'The Sun is full of shit,' they sang, like so many literary critics.

In truth, they do not look kindly upon the fourth estate in this corner of Hampshire. As a bunch of jovial hacks stood chatting in the forecourt before the match, they were accosted by a lone Southampton fan. 'Press scum!' he roared, his knuckles not quite scraping the ground.

In fairness, the employees of Southampton Football Club were far more amenable. Indeed, they did their level best to pretend that this kind of blanket attention was nothing very new. The lady distributing press tickets did not bat an eye when the tall American in the queue announced the name of his newspaper. '*Herald Tribune*,' she said. 'That'll be under H.'

The match, of course, was an anticlimax. Assailed by injury and suspension, Arsenal fielded an essentially makeshift side; the kind of team whose grandest ambition is a goal-less draw. For most of the time, they seemed likely to achieve that modest ambition, failing to rouse Grobbelaar even to minor heroics. But, on the hour, Jim Magilton ran through the visiting defence to secure an unlikely goal, and Southampton began to celebrate.

Grobbelaar punched the air and, from fully one hundred yards distance, took another bow. A fan ran on to congratulate him; the keeper seemed shocked by the trespass. Then, six minutes later, came the penalty. Arsenal's Paul Dickov was upended by Francis Benali in the Southampton area and took the resulting kick himself. Grobbelaar dived the wrong way, but on such a day it really didn't matter. The ball sailed high and very wide. And Bruce took another bow.

And then it was over, and the goalkeeper milked every moment. He embraced his team-mates. He cuddled David Seaman. He blew a kiss to the Arsenal supporters. He kissed his Southampton jersey. He punched his heart and offered it to the fans. He bowed to every corner of the packed ground. He actually seemed reluctant to leave his stage. You were irresistibly reminded of that lady who used to come out at the close of the Morecambe and Wise show; the one who had to be dragged away.

And yet, it had been a considerable performance; a clean sheet on a dirty day, firm assurance under intense pressure, a rigidly professional achievement. Even the Arsenal fans gave him a small cheer, before getting on with taunting the Saints supporters – 'Where's yer tractors?' – and cheering the downfall of Tottenham – 'We love you Gerry, we do.'

The story still has some time to run. The allegations have yet to be aired, either before the Football Association or in a civil court, and we may be sure that there will be twists and turns along the way. But, for the moment, Bruce Grobbelaar can breathe easily once more. As Arsenal's George Graham observed last night: 'The script was already written. And it was Bruce who wrote it.'

Mickey – Maker of Matches

Night & Day, 18 December 1994

L UNCHTIME IN KNIGHTSBRIDGE, and Mickey Duff is in maudlin mood. 'You wanna know how old I am?' he says. 'I'm sixty-five. And d'you know the worst part? The worst part is, you're not surprised. You didn't say: "No, Mickey! Sixty-five! Never!" You just nodded. People do that all the time. I say: "I'm sixty-five," and they nod.' He shakes his head: 'Let me tell you something, I didn't realise how young sixty was till I got to be sixty-five.'

The mood lasts for perhaps thirty seconds, as Mickey sits silently and remembers what it was like to be young. Suddenly he snaps out of his gloom, and a terrible grin splits his face. 'Listen,' he says, 'I've got a joke. Listen.' He thrusts his arms high above his head and furiously wriggles his fingers. 'Who am I?' he bawls. 'Come on, who am I? Give up? D'you give up?' I give up. 'Frank Maloney,' he says. 'Playing the piano.'

His cackle carries across the restaurant. Four tables away, a lone diner in a Garrick Club tie turns to stare at the source of the din. You want to explain that Mr Maloney is a vertically-challenged boxing entrepreneur whose interests do not invariably coincide with those of Mr Duff. But the moment has passed, and anyway, Mickey has launched into his next story. Most of his tales involve boxing and boxers, which is perfectly understandable since the fight game has been his life for more than half a century. It has given him considerable wealth, a measure of fame and a grievously abused nose. It has also given him a name.

He was born Morris Pragier, the son of a Polish rabbi who settled in London's East End before the war. Pragier became Prager as the family grew more anglicised, and the children at Deal Street School, just off the Whitechapel Road, changed Morris to Mickey. The real problem arose when he wanted to enter the Amateur Boxing Association's junior championships.

'You had to get a letter from your parents or schoolteacher, giving you permission,' he says. 'Now my father would have killed me if I'd even mentioned boxing, so I nicked a letterhead off the headmaster's desk, and I got one of the older kids to write the note for me. Obviously I couldn't use my own name, or my Dad would have found out. But I'd just seen James Cagney in *Cash and Carry*. He played this character called Jackie Boy Duffy, and I sorta liked that. "Mickey Duffy" didn't sound right, so I fought in the junior ABA's under the name of Mickey Duff. And, d'you know what, I got beat out of sight in the very first fight.'

He has told the story a time or ten down the years and he may well have given it the smallest lick of paint, but essentially that is how it happened. Later he turned professional under a manager named Al Jacobs, a man whose political incorrectness was such that he would only manage Jewish fighters. But success remained a stranger. 'What was I like?' he says. 'Listen, even I wouldn't have paid good money to watch me fight.'

The message was not ignored. At 19, he became a matchmaker: 'The youngest for God knows how many years; most likely ever.' From now on he would wheel and deal and hustle and rant, while others took the blows. Some call him 'pragmatic', others are less kind. 'I don't paint myself as a paragon of virtue,' he says. 'It's not always easy to be fair, but I've never set out planning to be unfair. There's a difference.' He sets no great store by popularity, which is probably just as well. Even in an industry whose leading lights tend to communicate through m'learned friends, Mickey is renowned for the sharpness of his tongue.

'Sad about Lennox Lewis,' he says. 'Potentially, he was great. But he tried to be the Pope *and* the Chief Rabbi. Can't be done. He wanted to be manager, trainer, promoter, everything. If you'd stuck a broom up his arse, he'd have swept up as well. And that trainer he had. What about him, eh? When Lewis went out against Oliver McCall, for the round he got knocked out in, his trainer said: "Just go out there and forget everything I ever taught you." I remember thinking to myself: "That won't be too f****** hard."'

Chris Eubank receives similarly short shrift. 'I met him some time ago,' says Mickey. 'He reminded me that he came to see me once, when he was looking for a manager. He said I kept him waiting, didn't make a big fuss of him, that sort of thing. He said: "I bet you regret it now." I said: "Tell the truth, I wouldn't have you now. I'm not rich, but I've got what I call 'f**k you' money. That means I can do without an asshole like you." '

In fact, the size of Duff's fortune is a matter of some speculation. I put it to him that one newspaper had recently estimated his wealth at £44 million. He corrects me quickly. 'Matter of fact, they said it was £44.4 million,' he says. 'Listen, the week that came out, my brother goes to the synagogue. Now the *Jewish Chronicle* has reprinted the story about me being worth £44.4 million, so because it's in the JC, everyone believes it. "Lot of money," they say. "Mickey must be doing very well." My brother says: "Will you stop it! The story's not true. Absolute nonsense." And just for a moment there's silence. Then someone says: "All right, it's not £44 million. So maybe it's only £24 million." Marvellous, eh? I'll tell you, there's a *lot* of smoke without fire.'

Whatever is said about him, and even as a senior citizen he still merits a place in most boxing debates, nobody has ever suggested that he lacks courage. I once listened for more than an hour as a promoter castigated almost every aspect of his rival's private and professional life. Yet as he rolled up the charge sheet, he felt obliged to add: 'He's got some bottle, though. Mickey's never been short of that.' That reputation was reinforced during the sixties, when his efforts to establish himself as a major promoter brought him into conflict with two men who harboured similar ambitions. Even today, he shudders a little as he tells the story.

'I was always looking out for a good venue, and one of the best was York Hall in Bethnal Green,' he recalls. 'Unfortunately, it was only available for amateur boxing. Anyway, I had this feller working for me who used to mix with the Krays. Nice guy, he was, but very naive. He comes in one morning and says: "I was with the twins last night. They reckon they can get York Hall for professional boxing." So I say: "Well, if they can, then I can." I called York Hall and I got it. And they didn't like that.

'Then we opened the Anglo-American Sporting Club at the Hilton, and a feller applies for membership who's got a gambling club, a spieler in the East End. I'm a bit suspicious, but I'm told: "Don't worry." So he sends his fifty guineas and he joins. Well, we send out invitations to the opening night. Great show. Sugar Ray Robinson on the bill, as I remember. And the reply cards come in. And this feller, the one I'm not to worry about, his card comes back and it says: Guests – R. Kray and R. Kray. So I call him and I say: "They can't come. People don't want to belong to that kind of club." And he says: "Do you wanna tell 'em they can't come?" And I say: All right. Well,

I knew them a bit. They boxed for me as kids. So I go to a pub in Vallance Road, Bethnal Green, and I talk to the twins. I have to talk hard, mind, but in the end they accept it. And I'm a bit relieved.'

Next day, the London *Evening Standard* ran a picture of the Krays beneath the headline: 'Don't Come To The Hilton'. For Duff, the game was up. He was still holding the newspaper when the phone rang. ''Allo, Mickey. Reggie here.' 'Reggie who?' asked Duff, brightly. 'You f****** know who,' said Kray. 'What did you have to go and do that for in the *Standard*?' Duff started to say that he tried to get the story blocked, but Reggie wasn't listening. 'Well,' he said, 'we're putting it down to you, Mickey. And none of your friends can help you now.' Duff shakes his head at the memory. 'A bad time,' he says. 'Only me and my laundry will know how I was feeling.'

Shortly after, he had to travel to Miami on boxing business. Each day, he called his wife in London. One day, she sounded off-hand. He pressed her for a reason. She told him that the postman had brought a parcel wrapped in Christmas paper. It was addressed to Mr and Mrs Duff and family. Inside the parcel were four dead rats. 'They must have thought I had two children,' says Duff, chillingly. He flew home and called a contact at Scotland Yard. The house was guarded, Mrs Duff was given protection and the Krays were pulled in and warned that all of their clubs would be closed down if the Duff family was harmed. The warning was accepted, but the twins had left their mark.

A few years later, a barrister friend invited him to watch the closing stages of the Krays' murder trial. Duff smiles at the memory. 'I had a good seat right behind the jury. Ronnie looked like he wanted to kill me. Reggie saw me and he mouthed: "All right?" I pointed at myself and put my thumb up. "*I'm* all right," I was saying, "cos I'm here." Then I pointed at them. "But you're over there. And you're going down." I don't like revenge, don't believe in wasting time on it. But for those two I made an exception. Rotten bastards.'

For a few moments, he is silent. Then he shakes his head hard, and the jaunty smile returns. 'Here, I read a good line this morning. Everyone's arguing about Tyson's first fight when he gets out of jail. Will it be this guy or that guy or the other guy? Ed Schuyler, American reporter, good friend of mine, he said: "Never mind his first fight; who's gonna be his first date?" He cackles uproariously. 'First date! What about that one, then?' Four tables away, a man in a Garrick Club tie is requesting his bill.

* * *

At the civic hall in Wolverhampton, Richie Woodhall of Telford is fighting Art Serwano of Uganda for the middleweight championship of the Commonwealth. Now the Commonwealth may contain sports lovers by the million, but precious few of them have made their way to the civic hall. There are scores of empty seats, and the shouts of the small crowd echo through the auditorium. As promoter, matchmaker and manager of Woodhall, Mickey is not worried. For the cameras of BBC Television are present and the finances of the evening are therefore underwritten.

Woodhall is tall, slim and anxious, and sports the colours of the West Bromwich Albion football team. Duff is neither tall nor slim, but he knows the value of local allegiance, so he wears a WBA tracksuit. Together, they trudge through the overwhelmingly male audience as a blaring fanfare marks their arrival.

Duff looks down from the ring and nods. I ask him, Reggie-like, if he is all right. 'Me?' he says. 'I don't need to be all right, do I? It's him.' He jabs a finger at Woodhall, who is standing at his side. The fighter forces a tight little grin. He knows that Serwano should not present a serious problem. At thirty, his best years are behind him and he is, moreover, a substitute, brought from his adopted California to replace an English challenger. But he is fit and strong and, as Duff has written in the programme: 'Boxing's a funny game.'

In the event, the contest is thoroughly one-sided. Woodhall dominates every round with fluid movement and stinging jabs. Duff sits by the corner, his crumpled face staring into the spotlights, consumed in concentration. You sense a kind of proprietorial concern, the way a nervous owner might watch his racehorse. But Woodhall is winning by several furlongs.

A stranger in the civic hall would swiftly discern the difference between the televised, sanitised version of the noble art and the stark reality of a ringside seat. The small things make the greatest impact. The sounds of the punches; hollow thumps to the body and sharper, more worrying thuds to the head. The rope burns on Woodhall's white back; not serious, of course, but you know that he'll sleep on his side tonight. Always the small things: the muffled grunts of pain when a short blow jolts into the solar plexus, the sudden, violent jerking of the head when the combination punches find their mark, the globules of saliva in Serwano's corner, shimmering in the arc lights and flecked with blood.

Mercifully, the referee stops the fight in the eleventh round to spare Serwano excessive punishment. Mickey is satisfied. He congratulates the referee on his admirable decision, congratulates Serwano's manager, Sam Norman, for bringing him all the way from California. Finally, he congratulates Woodhall on a job efficiently done. Then he walks to the dressing room, reflecting upon the fight. 'What a game bastard that kid was. Didn't know how to quit. So *game*!'

At the door of the dressing room, he bumps into Sam Norman again. He gives him the hint of a meaningful look. Norman seems briefly quizzical, then he reaches into his pocket and hands over a thick wad of notes. I look on, puzzled, but Duff chuckles. 'It's all right,' he says. 'He told me he strongly fancied his feller tonight. So I laid him £1,000 to £500.'

He stuffs the £500 into his back pocket. 'It's all right,' he repeats. 'No problem.'

An hour after midnight, and Mickey is holding court in the residents' lounge of his Wolverhampton hotel. He works his way through a small mountain of sandwiches, washing them down with Campari and soda. Above him, unheard and unheeded, 'O Little Town of Bethlehem' oozes from a loudspeaker.

These are the times when he comes into his own. He tells tales of the fifties, when sport attracted an entertainment tax of thirty-three and a third per cent and only charities were excepted from the general levy. He flashes that terrible grin again: 'I promoted more shows for more synagogue building funds . . .' He accepts that boxing, propelled by television, is turning into a circus. He doesn't like it, but he recognises a dilemma: 'You can't do a foxtrot when everyone else is doing a tango.' He will not countenance any argument which questions the validity of boxing: 'It'll outlive me and it'll outlive you. It's in people's nature. Full stop.'

In fact, boxing is in Mickey Duff's nature. 'It's my way of life,' he says. 'If they outlawed professional boxing tomorrow, I'd find a couple of amateurs and manage them.' You sense that his life can be lonely. He has lived apart from his wife for three years or more and his apartment at Marble Arch is large and usually empty. 'Some nights I come in and stick something in the microwave,' he says. 'I never cook, though. That wouldn't seem right. One day, someone's gonna buy the place and get a kitchen that's never been used. I'll tell you, without boxing, there wouldn't be anything to do.'

He munches a sandwich and asks about the evening's football results. I inform him that Millwall have won at Nottingham Forest.

His jaw drops. 'Millwall! At Forest! Honest? Listen, if that had been a fight, people would have said it was crooked.' He takes another bite of the cheese and tomato, then he smiles a small, mischievous smile. 'Mind you,' he says, 'if it had been a fight, it *would* have been crooked.'

He sees me reach for my pen and he throws up his hands. 'Leave off!' he says. 'That was a joke. Don't start turning me over at this time of night. Not at my age.' And he wakes half of Shropshire with his laughter. The night porter bids him farewell as he climbs the stairs. The loudspeaker plays 'Have Yourself A Merry Little Christmas'. It is three o'clock, a wickedly late hour for a man of sixty-five.

1995

I stood and watched AS the rapist was released from his Indiana jail, and felt more than a little foolish in the process. The lady at the car rental office had put it in perspective: 'Mike Tyson's gonna come out, he's gonna walk to his car and they're gonna drive him away,' she said. 'And you've come all the way from London, England, to see that?' I found myself nodding. 'When you put it that way . . .' I said.

But the year contained far more than Tyson. There was the tumultuous success of the Rugby World Cup in South Africa, the yearly farce of Wimbledon and the annual glory of the Open. And there were the great names: Greaves, Finney, Piggott. Any one of them would have made it a rewarding year, but all three . . .

The Rapist Returns

Mail on Sunday, 26 March 1995

THE PROFILE WAS FLEETINGLY framed in the prison door, and the explosion of flash bulbs brought a bleary Indiana dawn to dazzling life. Michael Gerard Tyson was free, and America was trembling.

For the past three years, the nation's most volatile icon had been out of sight and out of many a mind as he served his sentence for violent rape. But at 6.16 yesterday morning, he walked from his prison cell at Plainfield to begin a new and entirely unpredictable journey. His companions on those first few steps were members of that same Muslim sect which adopted and exploited Muhammad Ali.

At a time when America's cities are poised upon the edge of anarchy, when its President is politically impotent and its Congress bitterly divided, the prospect of its most charismatic athlete preaching and proclaiming radical fundamentalism to youthful minds is the stuff of nightmares. But the movement's authority over its most glittering convert was emphatically demonstrated in the first moments of freedom.

Eight Muslims surrounded the boxer as he walked down the four steps of the jail. The largest of them stood in front of him, his coat spread like a cloak to shield him from the cameras. In the background, high in the prison building, the silhouettes of serving prisoners were poignantly etched at every window. When their time came to leave, you knew that they would not be met by a grotesquely stretched limousine, they would not be clad in a custom-tailored suit, and their departures would not be attended by a prison guard, shooting a home video for posterity. And yet you sensed that they might conclude their time with far more grace and dignity than Tyson managed yesterday morning, hiding behind his bulky confrères with the air of a man who was beginning rather than terminating his sentence.

The waiting press started to boo and hiss. The bodyguards simply glared. Above the hubbub came the shrill, incongruous voice of an

English woman journalist. 'You rotten buggers! You rotten, miserable buggers!' she cried as Tyson, unheeding, ducked into his swollen car. He wore a white prayer cap upon his head and, so far as one could ascertain, he seemed a good deal lighter than his fighting weight.

But soon he was away, speeding in a nine-car motorcade to the North American Islamic Center, close by the jail. After forty-five minutes in prayer, the vehicles set off for Indianapolis International Airport, the police obligingly closing roads to allow the cavalcade to reach 110 mph along the freeway, where the legal limit is 65. On they sped, screeching past all formalities and driving across the runway to a parked Lear jet. Still hiding their recruit from public view, they ushered him on to the plane and out of the state of Indiana, his home these past three years.

Ms Naomi Troop, a rape counsellor, spoke for the decent majority of Americans when she reflected: 'It's like he was coming home from the war. They're treating him like a hero, and it can't be right. It says something about our society.' Indeed it does. It says that fame is the cardinal virtue, that shame and remorse are for wimps and losers, and that when a former heavyweight champion seeks instant gratification, a woman's role is to lie back and think of Indiana.

In fairness, the media had been willing accomplices in Tyson's latest exercise in indecent exposure. We had travelled in numbers from Germany and Japan, from London, England and from station WDTN in Springfield, Ohio. And for hour upon silent hour we had kept our weary watch, as the clock ran down for the prisoner.

The night had been strange beyond experience. A thin frost dusted the ground, sparkling in the prison spotlights. Guards clustered in the watchtower in the corner of the compound to stare down upon a parking lot awash with the fourth estate. There were ten television trucks, dishes yawning at the night sky. There was a cluster of radio jeeps and a fleet of press cars; windows steaming, heaters throbbing, reporters dozing. The photographers had claimed their places on the previous afternoon, marking them with ladders and tripods. Untended, a platoon of cameras was trained upon the prison door like some ethereal firing squad.

Plainfield, on the south-western fringe of Indianapolis, had found all the fuss quite amusing. It embodies worthy, unremarkable, small-town America. According to its road sign, it is: 'A Community of Values'. Plain and simple folk living plain and simple lives. A local hotel is staging a convention of basket-makers, unworldly people who say 'Howdy-doody!' and 'Gosh darnit!' A clapboard store

Patrick Collins

advertises 'Patriotic Fireworks'. A prominent estate agent, and I am not making this up, is called Mr Randy Keys.

Another road sign strikes a slightly sombre note: 'Prison Area – Do not pick up hitchhikers'. But while Plainfield has learned to live with that, it never really learned to live with Tyson. Early in his sentence, he said: 'If you want to see the dregs of society, just come to prison and see the changing of the guards.' Perhaps understandably, the prison officers did not love their celebrity convict. Two days ago, the guard at the gate grunted at my greeting. 'Ain't a good morning in my book,' he said. 'Won't be a good morning till he's outa here.'

Don King would agree with that. The promoter's role yesterday was to cling to Tyson as a man might cling to a meal ticket when others are trying to tear it from his grasp. It was he who signed autographs for the guards, this man who killed two people in his former life as a numbers racketeer in Cleveland. While in jail, King acquired the rudiments of a classical education. I once heard him react to an English accent with the line: 'As yo' great Bard of Avon truly said: "To be or not to be – that's what they askin', baby".'

Some see the shameless huckster as a jovial, almost lovable, diversion. They recall the time when he pleaded the Fifth Amendment three hundred and sixty-four times in the course of a single case. They quote with a snigger his wide-eyed remark on the eve of Tyson's release: 'I just want him to be free to come out and have intercourse with society.'

Others can find no hope for the ex-champion while he remains entangled with his promoter. One condition of Tyson's probation is that he must not associate with anyone who is likely to lead him off the straight and narrow. That condition possibly outlaws the entire world of professional boxing. Certainly it would seem to exclude Don King.

At the slender age of 28, Tyson has experienced enough for a dozen lifetimes, and he still possesses the potential for untold wealth. Just how much depends upon whom you ask. 'Leastways, fifty million; bestways, three hundred million,' I was told. Foolishly, I asked if the financier was talking in pounds or dollars. He sniffed. 'When it's that much, it don't matter,' he said. It doesn't matter. Nothing matters in America except money, power and celebrity. And the greatest of these is celebrity.

At some stage of the night-long wait, I remembered Tyson talking of the squalor of prison; of the shared cell with its stainless steel commode; of the brawls, the drugs, the male rape, the mental and physical torture. 'The place is a zoo,' he had said. 'A crazy, lousy zoo.'

At sixteen minutes past six yesterday morning, Mike Tyson put the zoo behind him. Now only the hostile, uncharted jungle lies ahead. Small wonder that America is trembling.

The Bloke from the Telly

Night & Day, 9 April 1995

THE MAN ACROSS THE lunch table is plump and comfortable. He has a silver shrub of a moustache and, when he tries, he can remember the war. It's hard to believe that we used to pick him alongside Pele in our World XI to play Mars. But we did.

You see, Jimmy Greaves really was that good; swift and intuitive, with sublime control and a quirky, high-stepping stride, he brought the simplicities of the playground to a mean and complex game and his fifty-seven matches for England yielded him forty-four goals. Suggest that he might well have been one of the finest footballers of the century, and he gives a modest little shrug. 'Very nice of you to say so, mate. But I honestly don't think about it. I mean, I can't remember how it felt to be a decent player. No, if people recognise me these days, they say: "It's the bloke from the telly." That's all right by me.'

With two programmes currently showing on the ITV network – *Saint & Greavsie's World of Sport* on Monday evenings and *Sport in Question* on Tuesdays – Greaves has become an engagingly familiar figure to millions who never saw him kick a football. The first show is little more than a nostalgic canter through ancient footage. The second has reinforced his popular status as 'the bloke from the telly'.

Sport in Question is a tracksuited version of *Question Time* which provides Greaves with a pulpit for some locker room jokes and state-of-the nation punditry. Now you may not chuckle at all his jests and you may not recognise the nation he describes. Frankly, he doesn't give a damn. After the agonies he has endured, he is effusively thankful that he still has the nerve to perform in public. 'I'm amazed at my way of life,' he says. 'I hadn't catered for all this telly stuff. When I left football, all I had was a small packaging business and a couple of little sports shops. Then I really started drinking, and everything went.'

In time, the details of his disease would become public knowledge and Greaves would win approval for his courageous candour. Yet even today he shudders when he recalls the way things were. 'Funny, these days it's fashionable to have a drink or drug problem,' he says. 'It bloody wasn't in 1978. And people still don't realise the complex nature of alcoholism. It's a lot more than just loving a drink. To this day, people say to me: "Can't you have just one drink?" Nobody understands it. I didn't understand it myself. I realised I had a problem in 1975, and it was February 1978 before I solved it. Three years of trauma. I remember coming out of Warley mental home and saying to myself: "F*** me: what year is it?" Terrible. I saw psychiatrist after psychiatrist; all I learned was that they were more potty than I was.'

The road to recovery took a few improbable twists. An East London businessman gave him a job selling ladies' knitwear. 'Used to go round with a case. Didn't sell too much, but it helped my confidence,' says Greaves. He then collaborated in a book about his drinking experiences, *This One's On Me*, and acquired an occasional sports column in the *Sun*. He had been sober for two years when ATV, the Midlands television company, were looking for a successor to Billy Wright as football analyst. An executive spotted Greaves's column in the *Sun*. 'What about him?' he said, and picked up a telephone.

'I was scared for a while,' recalls Greaves. 'I'd never done anything like that. But my wife Irene, she told me to get off my arse and get up to Birmingham, 'cos I might never get another chance like it. Dead right, an'all.' So he found himself in a television studio, and his worries dissolved. 'I thought of what I'd been through, and I realised that nothing could really bother me after that,' he says. 'I mean, when I was playing, I was frightened of being a failure. But when you've hit the floor and skidded a few thousand miles, it don't really worry you very much. Mind, I couldn't do what I do now if I hadn't gone through that. I'd have been too self-conscious. Strange, innit?'

Strange, indeed. But his strength lay in refusing to be seduced by the mysteries of the medium. He simply sat there, said his piece, thanked the floor manager and collected his cheque. True, he didn't push back the frontiers of television, but neither did he strike poses or pull faces or behave in any way which wasn't completely natural. He was Jimmy Greaves; he had been to the bad places and he had emerged with his sanity. And if they didn't like him, well, that wouldn't break his heart. In fact, most of them loved him enough to transform a hopeful experiment into regular employment. He joined the ITV panel for the 1982 World Cup, became involved with children's programmes, then he found Saint. And the earth moved.

Ian St John had been a tremendous player. Unlike Greaves, his talents had never been touched by genius, but he had played a crucial role in the development of Liverpool Football Club. Slim, Scottish and relatively serious, he represented a credible Stan Laurel to Greaves's Oliver Hardy. Greaves started to contribute to St John's Saturday football show, and within two years *Saint and Greavsie* acquired an independent life of its own.

Different men with different interests, they tended to meet only in television studios. But the chemistry worked well enough and the show drew an audience of four million each Saturday lunchtime. It survived and flourished until, several years later, ITV lost the major football contract to a joint bid from BSkyB and BBC. 'Nobody told us about it,' says Greaves. 'I read it on the front page of the *Sun*.'

You observe that the *Sun* constantly nudges its way into his story, and he becomes quite misty-eyed about 'the old Currant Bun'. You then make an idle remark about that newspaper being the house magazine of Essex Man, and his tone changes. A chord is touched. The amiable philosopher becomes agitated, and a remarkable outburst ensues.

'Listen,' he says, 'I'm Essex Man. Proud of it, too. And the one thing Essex Man doesn't have is a voice. He goes to work, pays his taxes, brings up his family . . . and gets shat on by everyone in the entire bleeding country. The Church tells him he's got to be more charitable to the likes of gays and lesbians. Wonderful, that is. People don't want their vicar banging on about all that. They want him singing "He Who Would Valiant Be"; that stuff. Not going on about gays.

'And privatised industries. Look, we're paying through the nose for water, getting well ripped off, right? But we've had five billion trillion gallons of the stuff dropped on us these last few months. And we're still paying a fortune. Now does that make sense? Then there's the judiciary. Problem with crime? Send all the yobs on holiday. That's their answer. No, don't laugh. It's true. They're taking us all for a ride and nobody makes a fuss about it.

'I just can't take the way things are. Why should you always have to lock your car, eh? I was born in "Hope and Glory" time in the East End. D'you ever see that film, *Hope and Glory*? That's just like it was in Manor Park. You could go out and leave your back door open. People had standards. No money, but standards. There's no standards now. Look at all the filth, all the graffiti in the inner cities. 'Course, your left wingers'll tell you that's because people are poor and deprived. Bollocks! There was no rich people where I came from, but they used to polish their front door steps till they were gleaming. You didn't dare tread on them. I used to jump up, grab the knocker and swing in through the front door, terrified I'd fall on the step. See, people had pride then. These days they walk around in rags. I was at Gatwick Airport, picking up my Irene last summer. There were people getting off planes with no shoes and socks on! Straight up, that was how they travelled! No standards.

'So, yes, I'm *Sun* Man. And Essex Man, Surrey Man, Wiltshire Man; all the ordinary people who don't have any say in the way they lead their lives. The minorities get all the say 'cos they make the most noise. But the ordinary punter who goes to work and brings up his family has seen everything eroded. Anyone who ever bought a house knows that. And anybody who sends his kids to school. I mean, what are they learning, what are they training for? There ain't a lot out there, is there?'

Gently, you ask him which political party has presided over the decline and fall of 'all we hold dear' these past sixteen years. It is a fruitless interruption, swiftly swatted. 'You can't blame everything on the government. Don't give me that,' he says. 'I mean, you've got women today saying: "I don't have to get married to have a baby." And I say: "Fair enough. I don't mind that, love. I just object to paying for it." Can you blame me?'

In view of the foregoing sentiments, it should surprise nobody that Greaves once attempted to become a Conservative parliamentary candidate. 'I went before the selection committee in Hornchurch,' he says. 'I was on the piss at the time, funny enough. It was between me and Robin Squire and he won it, thank Christ. He's been there ever since. Won't be there after the next election, mind.

'Don't get me wrong, I'm a Conservative, dyed-in-the-wool. I'll hold up my hands in horror when that Blair walks into No. 10. That's the worst thing that could happen to this country. But at the moment, there's no real leadership. Now Maggie Thatcher, she wasn't everyone's cup of tea but the one thing she did was to make up her mind. And we miss that. I know. You're thinking I'm a daft old git, and you might well have a point. Sure I could be wrong. But it's what I feel. I reckon the old values have gone. And I'm sad about that.'

At last he pauses, with the breathless air of a man who has just delivered a year's supply of *Sun* leader columns. And the face breaks into a faintly sheepish smile. 'Sorry about the whinge, mate,' he says. 'I got a bit carried away for a while there.'

In truth, it would be a great mistake to judge Greaves by his occasional 'Hope and Glory' eruptions, for he possesses deep shrewdness and a natural ability to ask sharply incisive questions. On an earlier series of *Sport in Question* he gave Terry Venables, the England football coach, perhaps the most uncomfortable public interrogation that gentleman has ever experienced. Now most sporting interviewers tend to approach Venables on their knees, lobbing him a docile diet of slow full tosses. Greaves bustled in like a hungry terrier, barking a barrage of pertinent inquiries about the events which led to Venables being dismissed as chief executive of Tottenham Hotspur.

Venables, plainly furious, writhed in his chair. At one stage, he could be heard grunting: 'I don't believe it!' as the tenacious inquisition continued. Rumour has it that Venables did not hang around for the customary cheery chat when the closing credits rolled.

Greaves is utterly unrepentant. 'What happened was that we had Alan Sugar, the Spurs owner, on the show the week before. It was strange, but I felt genuinely sorry for him. I mean, he comes to the club, spends fortunes, rescues it, then he gets spat at and abused by some of the fans because he's sacked the chief executive. It didn't seem right. Then we were told that Terry was going to come on and explain everything, but it didn't happen like that. He was asked why Sugar sacked him and he sort of shrugged and said: "You tell me."

'Well, I wasn't having that. I wasn't going to have us used for propaganda. Maybe Terry thought we were there to massage his ego, but that's not the purpose of the show. The purpose is to get to the bottom of sporting issues. We're trying to do what *Question Time* never does; get a few honest answers. All right, it didn't work out like that, but we're still friends, me and Terry. At least, I think we are. I haven't seen him since.'

The fact is that Greaves has never considered himself a member of the back-scratching freemasonry of former footballers. When he tells you he has forgotten how it felt to be a player, he is patently speaking the simple truth. 'I know I did it,' he says. 'It's there, on tape, in the record books. Chelsea, Spurs, Milan, West Ham, all that. But I just can't remember. When I went into Warley last time, I reckon I must have swapped bodies with someone else. Not only do I look different, but I've got no memory of playing football. No, I swapped bodies all right. And the other feller got the better of the deal.'

But, even with his body-transplant, Greaves still attempts to understand modern footballers. 'I can empathise with them as players,' he says. 'People suffer, they lose their form; I can go with that. I saw that Andy Cole some time ago. He was having a bad spell and he didn't know where the next goal was coming from. And I thought: "In a minute, a ball's going to hit him up the arse and go in, then he won't be able to stop scoring. It used to happen to me."

'What I can't understand is their money. There's such a vast gap between what they get and what we used to get that you can't sort of take it in. Someone told me that Jurgen Klinsmann's earning £22,000 a week from Spurs, and what did I think about that? I said it took me nine seasons to earn what he gets in a fortnight. It was the only way I could explain it. It's a different world.

'Years ago, when I played, footballers were people you might very well see on a bus. I know some of them had cars, but most mornings you'd see groups of professional footballers walking from the bus stop to the ground, going to work. Most players today wouldn't recognise a bus. And we all used to try to dodge paying the fare. When I was a kid at Chelsea, we'd sit in that three-seat place by the door, ready to dive off before the conductor came. And he'd try to whack us as we jumped.

'There was a feller at Spurs, first-team player, who got caught for fare-dodging. Bill Nicholson, our manager, said that when he came up at the magistrates' court in Edmonton, he shouldn't let them know who he was or what he did for a living. Our feller wouldn't have that. He turned up in club flannels, club blazer and club tie; trying to impress them that he wasn't the sort of bloke who'd knowingly jib at a twopenny fare. Funny, I thought of him recently when that Dennis Wise was charged with kicking in a taxi and walloping the driver. And turned up at court dressed like a tramp.'

For all the fame and for all the attendant fortune he has since discovered, you sense that Greaves was most deeply content in those distant, laddish days at Tottenham, when he was earning sixty pounds a week and taking his football from the gods. Once again, the eyes mist over: 'We'd go in the Bell and Hare after matches,' he says. 'Load of players, few fans, bunch of press lads. All in the back room of the pub. We'd have a good few drinks, knowing the fans'd be no trouble and the press wouldn't turn us over. Sometimes we'd stay there till gone nine o'clock. We knew how to live, eh?' He chuckles nostalgically, recalling the capers and the cracks, the songs and the smoke-filled rooms and all the Saturday evenings of his youth, before his grandest pleasure became his heaviest cross.

And are there regrets? He thinks for a moment. 'Yeah,' he says, 'I finished playing too early. Gave it all up when I didn't really need to. I was at West Ham, a bit unhappy, and I needed someone to say: "Don't retire, Jim. Have a few months off. Sort yourself out." But nobody said a word. So I stopped playing football and went down the pub.' He gives another, sadder, chuckle, then he drains his glass of Coke and strolls out into the London afternoon. The hotel door-man recognises a familiar figure and throws a brisk salute. Greaves waves a breezy response.

And as he disappears down the Strand, you do not see a 55-year-old man with a few surplus pounds at his waist. No, you see a young, slim athlete, with a quirky, high-stepping stride. A man who might have kept company with Pele. And beaten the Martians out of sight.

All Changed; Changed Wondrously

Mail on Sunday, 28 May 1995

MIDNIGHT IN A JOHANNESBURG hotel and the stereotypes are out in force. The Irish at the bar, arguing about horses and religion. The English, Old Fartonians in striped blazers, are braying their banal hymn to a chariot, while the Scots are giving heartfelt thanks to the obliging losers of the Ivory Coast.

But over in the corner, a small Welshman who claims he once played outside half for Llanelli Schools is stepping quietly out of national character. 'You want to know what's the best thing about the World Cup?' he says. 'The best thing about the World Cup is being invited to it.'

It wasn't quite on a par with the Olympic motto about not winning but taking part, yet essentially it was saying the same thing. There are some sporting events which are so moving, so timely and so captivating that simply being there is sufficient. The rugby World Cup, sprinkled across what Nelson Mandela calls 'this rainbow nation', is such an event.

From the moment that the President welcomed the world, lifting the curtain upon that impossibly dramatic collision of South Africa and Australia, we knew that the game had a hit on its hands. And so it has proved. Among all its troubles and all its self-inflicted strife, rugby union retains a beguiling capacity to enchant and inspire, and already those qualities are raising their voices.

It is difficult to exaggerate the significance of that opening match. A heavy home defeat or a fury of fists and boots could have stripped the tournament of all its optimism. But the Springboks did full justice to the occasion and the cheers exploding at Newlands were to roll across the entire Republic.

Now there are liberals of a certain age who can never feel completely comfortable supporting a side made up of Stranskys and Mulders and Krugers, just as we can never feel entirely at home in a

281

city which names major roads in the memory of Vorster and Verwoerd and other high priests of apartheid. No matter. The past is another country, even if it does have the occasional ability to rear up and dig you in the ribs. How else to explain the nostalgia evoked by the sight of the great J. J. Williams, taking his ease and telling his tales in the jumbo bound for Jo'burg?

JJ played for the Lions of 1974, the team which beat the Springboks in the temple of Loftus Versfeld. Steve Tshwete was a political prisoner on Robben Island, exiled with Mandela. 'We had very few opportunities to get back at our captors,' recalls Tshwete, 'but one way was to cheer for the opposition whenever the Springboks played a Test. We loved those Lions because they showed the Afrikaners that they were not invincible. When JJ went over for his second try, we went crazy.' On Thursday afternoon, Steve Tshwete, South Africa's Minister for Sport, sat with his mentor and cheered his heart out for the Boks. Times have changed.

In fairness, the game has not yet taken a universal hold on South African affections. While the rest of the nation's media abandoned themselves to ecstasy after beating Australia, the Sowetan, the newspaper of the vast township on the fringe of Johannesburg, awarded the event a front page picture and ten sparse paragraphs on the back page. The enduring farce of the Paul Gascoigne transfer deal rated similar space, and you were obliged to accept that soccer will take a deal of supplanting in the hearts and minds of black South Africa.

In equal fairness, ordinary South Africans have problems rather more pressing than their country's failure to win its share of line-out ball. Johannesburg's status as the most dangerous city on the planet is now a matter of perverse local pride. They speak of the crime rate in the way that New Yorkers used to boast of muggings and shootings. You point to a picture in the local paper of a detective brandishing a charred hand which had been found in a box during a police raid. 'Yeah,' they say, 'but you should have been here last week . . .'

Of course there are terrible problems, but there is also a curious, almost tangible sense of optimism. Partly it lies in the mere presence of Mandela, the benign colossus who radiates hope and reassurance. Partly it derives from the heady novelty of democracy, the feeling that so much has already been achieved that nothing is truly impossible. And partly it stems from a genuine, collective determination to make this rainbow nation worthy of its own aspirations.

Victory in the World Cup may appear a trivial sideshow, yet it would work wonders for the nation's self-respect and enormously assist the process of reconciliation. Of course, it is far too early to think in such terms. Indeed, the Springbok captain, François Pienaar, actually trotted out the beloved cliché about 'taking each game as it comes'.

Ah yes, the odds are long and the opposition is fierce. But it could happen; South Africa could become champions of the world. Time was when the very notion would have appalled us, but no more. For times have changed. Changed wondrously.

Jeff and the Last Tarango

Mail on Sunday, 9 July 1995

O NCE UPON A TIME, a mild-mannered reporter became embroiled in argument with a steward at Wimbledon. The steward, a sensitive fellow, reported the squabble to the authorities and a committee of inquiry was convened. After a long, pompous and frequently farcical hearing, the reporter was informed that he would be suspended from the championships for one week and was asked if he had anything to say. 'Certainly,' he replied. 'A week's nowhere near long enough. I demand a life sentence!' The remark did not go down well with the dullards who enforce the rules at the All England Club, but those of us who do not love the place often quote it with approval. For a few, precious moments, it almost succeeded in puncturing Wimbledon's insufferable air of smugness and self-regard.

But now Mr Jeff Tarango has spoken and, for quite different reasons, his line will be cited in all future Wimbledon debates. Goaded beyond endurance by an outside court crowd of saloon bar subversives and primary school *provocateurs*, our Jeff rounded on his tormentors with an immortal squeal of: 'Oh, shut up!'

Now I ask you, is there another sporting venue on this planet in which a competitor could seriously utter those words? 'Oh, shut up!' Can you imagine him using that phrase at, say, Millwall's Den, Wigan's Central Park or Glasgow's Kelvin Hall? Why, had he behaved in such a fashion at the rugby clubs of West Wales, then sheer ridicule would surely have rendered him the 'Last Tarango in Powys'.

But Wimbledon is different; pathetically so. The umpire, another sensitive soul, construed the outburst as an 'audible obscenity' and issued the code violation to set off the chain of events which will spring to mind whenever we need cheering up: Jeff pouting his way off court; Mrs Jeff, a French person, slapping the umpire then bawling: 'Je ne regrette rien!'; endless discussions involving people in blazers; the amateur psychologist who interpreted Jeff's performance as, yes, 'a cry for help'. It was all too wonderful for words, too perfect for parody. And it all sprang from that single yelp of: 'Oh, shut up!'

In fairness, there was a time when Wimbledon could stage a convincing tantrum. You may recall that voice in the crowd beseeching Connors to: 'Keep trying, Jimmy,' during his match with Arthur Ashe. 'I *am* trying, for Chrissakes!' screeched the incensed Connors.

You will certainly recall the outbursts of John Patrick McEnroe, the last truly interesting tennis player. 'You cannot be serious!' has already taken its place in the Dictionary of Quotations, but 'This is the pits of the world!' deserves its place in the pantheon, along with McEnroe's inspired description of the umpire who sat in his chair: 'Like a frog on a log'.

McEnroe, teetering on the brink of middle age, now insists that Tarango's outburst warrants exemplary punishment, but that probably conceals his contempt for the limp-wristed nature of the offence. 'Oh, shut up!' is a phrase which young John Mac could never have conceived.

Yet the paucity of original invective merely reflects the tedium of the tennis. The game has become boring beyond reason or belief; serve and volley, yawn and slumber. And on Wimbledon's grass, the boredom is all-consuming. In both men's and women's singles, the four semi-final places were occupied by the top four seeds; such is the mundane predictability of the competition. And nothing has so well demonstrated the prevailing poverty of British sport as the unseemly enthusiasm which attended the entrance of a carpet-bagging Canadian.

Add to this list the Agassi factor (the fact that the top seed has the appearance and personality of a laundry bag) and the Spanish factor (the fact that scarcely anybody can tell their Conchita from their Arantxa, and what's more they don't care) and you may deduce that tennis is currently on the crest of a slump. But none of this really matters to Wimbledon, since Wimbledon is not primarily concerned with tennis.

Wimbledon is getting the best seat for your chairman or the best price for your tickets. Wimbledon is being the last voice to scream 'C'mon, Steffi!!!' before the umpire says: 'Quiet, please,' and everybody giggles. Wimbledon is queuing all night to watch a sport you wouldn't cross the road to look at if it wasn't being played at Wimbledon.

Wimbledon is Virginia's voice; wistful and whining, as if somebody had just driven over her pet cat. Wimbledon is boozing and cruising and Britons bravely losing. Most remarkably, Wimbledon is an irascible little Woody Allen clone with thinning hair and a chip on both shoulders, standing on the dregs of his dignity and squeaking: 'Oh, shut up!' to the silliest crowd in the whole of sport.

And today, it comes to an end. The last drunk will stagger away from the corporate hospitality trough, the last ticket tout will take his lucrative leave of the car park, the last blazer will swallow his last free lunch.

Sure there are those who wish that Wimbledon would never end. Personally, I am of the school which believes that the whole thing goes on for too long. About two weeks too long.

An Open from the Gods

Mail on Sunday, 30 July 1995

THERE WAS A MOMENT yesterday afternoon when it really did seem that St Andrews was trying a touch too hard. The sun was fixing the Old Course with an unblinking stare, Tom Watson, the noblest of golfers, was proceeding down the eighteenth fairway and a teeming gallery was cheering its collective heart out to honour the occasion.

You found yourself thinking that this was utterly perfect; sport shamelessly stolen from the gods. Then you realised that the same thought had been scampering across your mind on the hour, every hour of this staggering event. Truly, we have been spoiled by the wonder of it all. For a divine conspiracy of climate and venue, warm nostalgia and glittering promise has made this a vintage Open, with a quarter of its course still to run.

The images come flickering by like leaves in the wind. Palmer, taking his tumultuous farewell with the practised perkiness of an ancient trouper. Weiskopf, unleashing that immortal swing in the still of a summer morning. Daly, twisting and grunting and launching the ball through entire postal districts. Sevvy, eking out the remnants of a glorious talent and sailing through the encouraging roars of a raucously pro-European crowd. Campbell, the coming man who may arrive before this day is done, working a piece of jaw-sagging magic from the bunker by the Road Hole.

And Gordon Sherry. Especially Gordon Sherry. Now he looks, if he will forgive the comparison, like one of those big, daft Scottish second-row forwards; broad of beam and heavy of leg. His face is an open book; frank and engaging. And his potential has no obvious limits. But more important by far is the fact that he enjoys sport the way that sport is meant to be enjoyed. He pops in a hole in one while practising with Nicklaus. He faces up to the Old Course while his elders tremble beneath its gaze. He cruises the fairways with Watson and Norman and just happens to bump into ex-President Bush. And always the expression says: 'Is this really happening to me? You bet your life it is!'

The meeting with George Bush was an occasion worth remembering whenever sport and sports people become too serious. Norman was worldly-wise: 'Hi, Mr President! Great to see ya!' Watson was more sober: 'Great pleasure, Mr President. You're very welcome.' Then Sherry came lumbering over to be introduced. 'Hell-ooooo!' he said, sounding like Iain McCaskill introducing a sunny spell. Pleasantries done, he teed up his ball, swung the wood like an axe and swatted a drive clean over the roof of the Old Course Hotel. Utterly perfect . . . again.

Later he would tell us how Tom and Greg had helped him sail through the round. 'Norman kept saying: "Come on, big man. Hole the putt!" And Tom called me "partner" all the way round. Wasn't that something!' He also confided that the wise old pair had told him that he must complete his university studies before taking up the professional career which is his obvious destiny.

He spoke of his coach, Bob Torrance, who has been working on some remarkable material in Sherry. He spoke of Torrance's kindness, his enthusiasm, his support and the fact that his wife, June, makes excellent bacon rolls. And never, not once, did he lapse into that joyless jargon which characterises the obsessive technocrats who are over-represented in golf as in every other major sport.

In short, he was a delightful chapter in a marvellously memorable week. And today, the final chapter will twist and turn and ultimately unfold. Wise men and women will not miss a single shot. This incomparable Open deserves no less.

God Save Our Gracious Team

Night & Day, 30 July 1995

SPORT WAS DECLARED 'a good thing' in the Downing Street garden on a morning in high summer. Speaking with rare passion and genuine authority, the prime minister announced his intention to move sport into the mainstream of national life. School sport would be revived, participation would be encouraged and a British Academy of Sport would be established. In short, sport was being given official permission to stay up late and mix with the grown-ups; with opera, ballet and the other performing arts.

And as the applause from an overwhelmingly sporting audience clattered around the garden and drifted out over Horse Guards, you found yourself wondering if it might possibly be heard a few hundred yards away; in the big house at the end of The Mall.

Probably not. You see, the House of Windsor tends to regard popular sport as the regrettable diversion of the great unwashed; like the *Sun* or extra-strength lager. It is true that their names frequently appear on the notepaper of countless sporting organisations, usually with the job description of 'Patron'. It is equally true that they are occasionally moved to honour the leaders of the said organisations: 'Arise, Sir Bert, thou good and faithful servant.' But there endeth their interest.

The royal attitude towards popular sport was most eloquently expressed by the Prince of Wales at last season's FA Cup final between Everton and Manchester United. Never in the history of Wembley Stadium has anybody been so patently bored. He twisted and turned, shuffled and squirmed, stifled several yawns and studied his watch. And all the time, his body language screamed: 'How the hell did I let myself in for this?'

Sure, he had encountered a degree of irreverence from the customers; when the national anthem was played before the start, the Everton fans sang 'God Save Our Gracious Team', while the United supporters chorused 'Ooh, Ah Cantona!' in memory of the absent Eric. But even that could not excuse the prince's glazed expression.

You were reminded of that look which invades his father's face when he is required to endure four hours of folk dancing by the occupants of remote Pacific islands.

Charles cheered up when the game ended. A sweaty fellow in a football shirt came trudging up the stairs. Better give him the Cup. He picked up the trophy and was about to present it to Steve Bruce, when somebody told him that these days the losers came up first. And Bruce was the captain of Manchester United. Who had, sort of, lost.

Charles pulled a face. He'd sat in the best seat in the house, yet he was one of the few men in England who did not know the result of the FA Cup final. But he didn't seem particularly bothered. 'Ah, well,' said his thin smile, 'better wait for the chaps in blue shirts to turn up. Then, thank God, I'm off. I'll tell you, things'll be different when I'm King. They won't get me within twenty miles of this bloody place.'

I suspect that his views on popular sport owe a good deal to his parents. The Duke of Edinburgh once played cricket to village green standard, rarely misses Cowes Week, drives carriages and still brings his brand of bluff covery to sporting politics, to no great effect. Other than that, his major contribution to sport in general consists of shooting small bundles of feathers.

As for Her Majesty; well, she adores her horses, and there is precious little more to be said. In fairness, she always turns up at the Commonwealth Games and stares at the various events, from bowls to badminton, with no obvious enthusiasm. Rumour suggests that her postcards home carry the message: 'Loved the Commonwealth – Hated the Games'.

She often attends Lord's on the Monday of the Test match, usually at a time when England require around 550 runs to avoid the follow-on. But, again, she is not what you might call a fan. She once arrived at a Lord's Test against the West Indies and chatted with the old Surrey spinner, Pat Pocock. He looked across the ground, at the capering cavalcade of West Indian supporters, and a thought occurred. 'Have you ever watched a match in the Caribbean, ma'am,' he asked. 'No,' she said. 'I suppose the closest I ever came to it was when I knighted Sobers.' Yet she is believed to count the weeks and days leading up to Royal Ascot, that annual orgy of Ruritanian excess, where bands play and corks explode and massed ranks of chinless chancers raise their rented toppers as the sovereign's carriage trundles past in daily procession.

And that's when you find yourself remembering the London Marathon, the best idea that British sport has ever had. In its fifteen-year history, the marathon's vast army of foot-soldiers has raised some £60 million for charities by a doggedly determined shuffle from Greenwich to the heart of the capital. Every Spring, the journey takes the runners past Buckingham Palace, but the curtains never twitch, for the lady of the house is never at home. Well, not at *that* particular home. While her subjects are trotting past in their tens of thousands, she is off walking the corgis at Windsor and worrying about the going at Wincanton.

Her children, by and large, have followed her example of indifference towards popular sport. Charles plays polo, whose followers would not recognise Monsieur Cantona if he kicked them in the chest. Anne, it must be said, was a brave and gifted horsewoman. Why, in a frenzy of forelock-tugging back in the early seventies, BBC viewers actually voted her 'Sports Personality of the Year'. She is also a member of the International Olympic Committee, although her forthright views have not made her a popular member of that dubious assembly. Andrew pursues the solitary vice of golf, while Edward plays real tennis, of which it has been said: 'About as many people play real tennis as have a chance of ascending to the throne.' I have not mentioned Diana; in the gym or on the slopes. Nor have I cited Fergie, who used to turn up at Wimbledon to scoff strawberries and leer at the legs of Scandinavian seeds.

But my point is a simple one. If John Major is correct and sport is indeed 'a good thing', capable of interesting and involving enormous numbers of ordinary people, then would it not also be 'a good thing' if the royal family supported his efforts to make sport more accessible?

Polo, skiing, sailing and carriage-driving are all very well, but they cannot be said to reflect the sporting interests of most people on these islands. The royals would surely benefit by experiencing those occasions which excite and inspire the populace. And in turn, even in an age which has seen the death of deference, royal patronage could do much to enhance the esteem of popular sport.

We should therefore hope that Charles can swallow his antipathy and force himself to savour the delights of Elland Road or Ewood Park. We should hope that the Duke might seek enlightenment at, say, Wigan's Central Park. Above all, we should hope that next year Her Majesty will give a lead, reject the temptations of Windsor and watch the London Marathon from the balcony of Buck House. So the humble trudgers, nearing the end of their agony, will raise their eyes, wave their hands and mutter in breathless gratitude: 'Gawd bless yer, Ma'am. It's a pleasure to see you in the Mall on Sunday.'

'Even Paranoiacs Have Enemies'

Mail on Sunday, 17 December 1995

M R RECORDER WILLIAMS IS an engaging gentleman with a disarming smile and a mind as sharp as a guillotine. Chances are that he has no great desire to be known as the man who changed the face of English football. Yet that, I fancy, may be his fate.

In the course of a rigorous and dispassionate judgement, he left Terry Venables financially poorer and ethically bankrupt. Having ruled against the England coach in a squabble over an unpaid bill at a London night club, he used phrases such as 'wanton' and 'not entirely reliable' to describe some of his evidence under oath. He also dismissed out of hand Venables' claim to have been the target of a 'conspiracy' and he pointed out a certain glaring contradiction between the coach's evidence in court and his assertions in a published autobiography.

Now in football terms, these may seem like a series of slaps on the wrist. Why, many a manager would consider that to be thought not 'entirely reliable' was a fairly benevolent description of his truthfulness. Certainly the Football Association has reacted with typical decisiveness. 'The position is unchanged,' says an FA spokesman. 'Terry is still the best man to be coach of the England team,' says Graham Kelly, with scarcely a hint of self-parody. And Sir Bert Millichip, with the air of a man who cannot face the consequences of an abjectly misguided appointment, tells this newspaper today that he expects to offer his discredited employee a contract until 1999. Walter Mitty rules at Lancaster Gate!

But then, Walter and his chums were not present in Court Three of the Central London County Court for the action Fugler & Fugler v Scribes. They did not hear the evidence, watch the reaction of Mr Recorder Williams or endure the studied indignation of Terry Venables as he stood in the witness box, hand on hip, and declared: 'What you can't take is when people say "He is a shady character"

. . . I defy anyone to be looked into by the Fraud Squad, by the DTI, the FA, the Premier League, the Inland Revenue . . . I've had to live with it, and it's all been unfair.'

For an irreverent second, you thought of that old music hall joke: 'Infamy! Infamy! They've all got it in for me!' But then you reflected that this was what the FA, or at least its more thoughtful members, had dreamed of in their worst nightmares: the England coach in the witness box, under oath, scarcely a dozen hours after leading the national team into its match with Portugal.

You closed your eyes and tried to imagine some of Venables' predecessors in a similar situation. Could you seriously contemplate a Winterbottom, a Ramsey or a Greenwood, to name just three, complaining of investigation by the Fraud Squad or the DTI? They would be horrified by the very suggestion. And yet, with Venables, we accept such bizarre intrusions as par for his particular course.

Strangely, for one who is starting to make more court appearances than Horace Rumpole, Venables seemed a trifle uncertain. He made the mistake of patronising Shane Dougall, counsel for his opponent, as he searched for a document. 'I'm sorry,' said Mr Dougall. 'Take all the time you need,' burbled Venables, with the misplaced confidence of a man stroking a shark.

And he attempted the odd joke, which was another mistake. You see, Venables is a poor comedian; he gets the timing all wrong and he has to laugh to signal the punch-line. Now his usual sycophantic audiences always manage a chuckle to order, but the technique did not work in Court Three. On a couple of occasions Venables burst into 'Whoa! whoa! whoa!' only to see his mirth returned by a bank of blank faces.

His tone throughout was one of defensive indignation, like the Essex car salesman whose vocation is to supply used Jags and Mercs to the glitterati of Billericay: 'Your honour, it was running like a dream when it left our premises. Why it should choose to blow up upon reaching Basildon, I really cannot say.' And yet, when the reporters gathered at an Italian restaurant at lunchtime, the consensus was that the worst thing that could happen to Venables was a messy draw, rather like that which his England team had procured from the Portuguese the night before.

Venables had dashed away as soon as his evidence was over, back to those places where people laughed at his jokes and shared his sense of indignation. He left behind his chum, the eminent financial adviser Eddie Ashby, whose evidence, Mr Recorder Williams was to say, needed to be treated with: 'More than a pinch of salt, more likely a handful'.

Back in court three, Shane Dougall was saying: 'Mr Venables says he may be paranoid. Well, so what if he is?' The judge nodded and murmured, with exquisite timing: 'Even paranoiacs have enemies.'

Outside the courtroom, in winter-dark London, tour buses rumbled towards Madame Tussauds. Three workmen clambered over the scaffolding across the window, occasionally flashing the court an incurious glance. A solicitor's clerk fell into a light snooze, bored to a dozy distraction by the dreariness of the contest. And, as the arguments were presented and the evidence was assessed, Recorder Williams made up his mind.

Venables was not only defeated but, if reports are accurate, faces a legal bill of up to £150,000. A more damaging result for the standing and credibility of the England coach could scarcely be imagined. His departure from the post was no longer a matter for argument but rather a matter of time. Later, and entirely in character, Venables declared that he felt 'significantly vindicated'. It was easily his worst joke of the week. Yet it won the loudest laugh.

The Proudest Man in Preston

Mail on Sunday, 24 December 1995

T HE MAN IN THE box-office queue explained that he wasn't just buying a ticket, he was purchasing a piece of history. In years to come, he would tell his grandchildren that he had attended the birth of the Preston grandstand on the last Saturday before Christmas in 1995. He thought that the elegant construction was quite perfect, and I remarked that the club had made an inspired choice in calling it 'The Tom Finney Stand'. He frowned at this statement of the obvious. 'This is Preston,' he said. 'What else would they have called it?'

A few moments earlier the man himself had passed through, with the bow-legged bowl of the old pro and a face stolen from a cigarette card. Now he was out on the Deepdale terraces, posing for a picture on the very spot where his dad used to lift him up to watch Alex James back in the twenties, before the wee man broke their hearts by signing for the Arsenal. 'I couldn't understand anyone wanting to play for any club but Preston,' says Finney, smiling at the innocence of childhood.

He spoke with the authority of one who remained faithful to his first and only love in the course of a glittering career. He signed for Preston at the age of 15, played 76 times for England and scored 30 international goals. And when he retired, 23 years later, he was still turning out in the white shirt of North End.

'I only seriously thought of leaving once,' he says. 'It was 1952 and I'd just played for England in Florence when the president of Palermo asked to see me. He said he wanted me to join them and he'd pay me £10,000 for a two year contract. Well, I was getting fourteen pounds a week at the time, so I had to be tempted. We had this chairman at Preston called Nathaniel Buck. Broad Lancashire, he was. When I got back I told him about the offer, and he went mad. "I'll tell tha now," he said, "if tha doesn't play for us, tha doesn't play for anyone else." And that was it. I had to stay.'

Being Finney, and as decent a man as ever played the game, he has long since forgiven this feudal rejection. 'Probably all for the best,' he says. 'I mean, all my friends were here in Preston and I had two youngsters to educate and maybe Italy wouldn't have suited my wife . . . No, I don't regret it. Really I don't.'

There are those who will tell you that Tom Finney was the greatest player that England ever produced; certainly he would find a place on any short list for that distinction. Yet at a time when the game turns out millionaires by the dozen, it is instructive to remember the way things were just two generations ago.

'What with the war and one thing and another, I never played a League match for Preston until I was 24,' says Finney. 'I retired at 38, so my career lasted fourteen years. All that time, the most I earned was twenty pounds a week or a thousand a year. Sure the value of money's changed, we know that, but I worked out the other day that Alan Shearer gets more in a week than I earned in my entire career.

'Good luck to him, too. I mean, what's he supposed to do; tell 'em it's too much and turn it down? No, things had to change. I remember my first cap for England, against Northern Ireland in Belfast. We all met up in Liverpool to catch the boat, and big Frank Swift said he'd do my expenses for me. He put down five bob for a meal on the train and the FA struck it off. They said I wouldn't have had time to eat between Preston and Liverpool! But we just accepted those things.'

When Preston reached the 1954 FA Cup final, the players asked Finney to squeeze some extra money from Mr Buck. 'He pretended he didn't know what I was on about,' says Tom. 'But I went back next day and he said he had good news: "We've 'ad a board meeting," he said. "And to reward your efforts in getting us to t'final, your wives will be getting an 'andbag. Each."'

He chuckles at the tales, yet he remembers the sense of insecurity. 'I was lucky,' he says. 'I had a trade. I built up the plumbing business down the years and it's done well by me and my family. But other pros used to worry about what they'd do when they finished. Most of them took pubs or sports shops or found a job as a brewery rep. A lot of great names fell on hard times, I'll tell you.'

He resists the temptation to dwell in the past, but he scoffs at the notion that the game has changed for the better. 'I watch the Italian football on Sundays,' he says. 'Wonderful players. They all seem so comfortable on the ball, the way they should be. Then I turn over to Division One when the adverts are on. Chalk and cheese, I'm afraid.'

He relishes the gifts of moderns like Steve McManaman and Jamie

Redknapp, looks forward to the return of Darren Anderton, believes that Robbie Fowler has genuine potential, insists that Shearer would score stacks of goals if he played for a good side like Portugal and regrets the self-inflicted waste of Paul Gascoigne's talents.

But the mildest of men only becomes truly annoyed when his contemporaries are sold short. 'I say to people: "Look, I'm not going to argue. But to say that those players couldn't have played in today's game is a joke."' He reels off the names like some blissful litany: 'Leave Stan aside, 'cos Matthews was out on his own. Just think of forwards like Carter, Lawton, Mannion, Doherty. Ball-players like Mitchell and Shackleton. Half-backs like Burgess, Blanchflower, Wright and the rest. I really believe the game was about skill then. Now it seems to be about formations.'

Straight-backed, in blazer and club tie, drinking a gin and tonic 'because it's Christmas', Finney glows with his recall of the days when footballers went to the match on the bus, when they married girls with names like Elsie and Beryl, and when television didn't tell them which day they must play and what time they must start.

There are more tales of the great ones, of the time Bobby Charlton played his first match for England and scored from Finney's cross. 'Never seen a volley hit like that. Tommy Younger, the Scottish keeper, said the first he saw of it was in the *Sunday Post* next day.' And Stan; always Stan. 'They'd never tell the papers when Matthews was out with an injury. They knew they'd lose 6,000 people off the gate.'

He smiles in fond memory of Bill Shankly, a Preston colleague who was besotted by Finney's talent. 'Someone told me that a bunch of reporters were once talking to Bill about Tony Currie, and they asked if he'd rank him alongside me. And Bill thought for a moment, then he said: "Aye, I'd rank him with Finney . . . Mind, Finney's turned sixty-years-old these days!"' More chuckles and a modest blush. So you hazard an impertinent question: Would a knighthood, richly deserved and long overdue, round off his story in the grandest manner. The loudest chuckle of all: 'Oh, please! I wish people would forget that. I'm more than happy with my lot, really I am. I don't need anything more.'

He looks out across Deepdale as workmen in hard hats beaver away on the stand which bears his name. 'D'you know,' he says, 'I'm thrilled to bits about this. I shouldn't say it, but it's a fact. "The Tom Finney Stand" . . . who'd have thought it?' And his face shines with ageless wonder. Just like that small boy all those years ago, who perched on his father's shoulders and cheered for the men in white and prayed that Alex James would never stray far from Preston North End.

'I *Have* Won Nine Derbies . . .'

Night & Day, 31 December 1995

ONE BRIGHT MORNING IN Newmarket, a young trainer meets the great man. 'Morning, Lester,' he says. Piggott grunts. 'Bit of a problem, Lester,' he says. 'Thought you might be able to help.' Piggott grunts again; dubiously. 'My old school's asked me to go and speak to the boys. They want me to tell them what I know about racing. What should I say?' Piggott thinks for half a second, then he grunts again. 'Tell 'em you've got flu,' he says. And walks on.

The scene moves to a Northern racecourse, where a small-time trainer has found a horse which he thinks might win the Derby. At considerable expense, he has engaged Piggott to ride his horse in a Derby trial. The trainer has placed large bets on his protégé; worse, he has encouraged his friends to make similar investments. After six furlongs, Lester decides that the horse has nothing to offer and he eases to a canter. The trainer is outraged and retreats to the bar with his newly impoverished friends. Heads nod in agreement as the word 'betrayal' is muttered. Suddenly, the object of their anger hurries past the bar door, *en route* to an evening meeting in the Midlands. 'Piggott!' booms the trainer. 'You will never ride for me again!' Lester considers his list of patrons; all those sheiks, moguls and mercantile princes, the kind of people who command large corporations and small countries. 'I s'pose I'll have to pack it all in then, won't I?' he grunts.

When you ask him about the truth of these tales, he replies with a slow smile and a small mumble. If they are not true in every dot and comma, well, they're pretty close. At this stage of his life, Lester Piggott seems to enjoy the notion that some people find him a bit of a card. There are those who suggest that he may be mellowing, but that is almost certainly wishful thinking. The raging self-belief which drove him through his extraordinary career did not subside simply because the old chap had decided that there was more to life than riding large horses at improbable speeds.

In truth, 'extraordinary' is a wholly inadequate description of the most astonishing career that British sport has known. It began on the afternoon of 7 April 1948, when he climbed aboard a horse called The Chase to contest an apprentice handicap at Salisbury. I once encouraged him to place the date in historical context: Clement Attlee as prime minister, England awaiting Bradman's Australians, John Major recovering from the celebrations of his fifth birthday; that sort of thing. He gave one of his famous grunts. 'I remember my horse got beat,' he said. 'Does that help?'

In fact, the mere statistics convey an amazing tale: twenty-nine English classic victories, including nine Derby successes; eleven times champion jockey; more than five thousand winners around the world. The figures speak of genius, but the nature of the achievement is even more breathtaking. At five feet seven inches, he was immoderately tall for a jockey. Now he found it easy to devise a riding style which would accommodate his height, a vaguely incongruous posture with his legs tucked into ultra-short leathers and his bottom thrust high in the air. The training purists warned their young riders against copying such wanton unorthodoxy, just as boxing trainers dismissed the Ali shuffle and cricket coaches counselled caution to those who would slog like Botham.

But if height was one thing, then weight was quite another. To meet the demands of his profession, Piggott made a coldly deliberate decision to spend some forty years of his life at two stones below his natural weight, and he suppressed his appetite with black coffee and cigars. He makes light of the sacrifice: 'Nothing hard about that,' he says, 'I'm just not a big eater. Doesn't bother me, eating.' But Walter Swinburn, himself the rider of three Derby winners, tells a revealing story. 'When I came from Ireland he took me under his wing,' he says. 'I used to stay with him at times and I learned from his amazing discipline. D'you know, he used to lock away his stock of Yorkie bars. And when he unlocked the cupboard, he'd take out one piece of a Yorkie at a time. One piece at a time!'

Some might regard such self-denial as evidence of consuming ambition, while others might speak of unhealthy obsession. But it is a compelling image, the great jockey breaking off a single chunk of chocolate then pushing aside the rest of the bar and perhaps wincing a little as he turns the key in the lock. And all because he wanted to be the best there was, the best there has ever been.

His features are testimony to this voluntary deprivation, the skin stretched tautly across the striking bone structure, the deep trenches running from cheek bones to jaw, the forehead lined as a London street map. One racing sage described Piggott as having 'a face like a well-kept grave'. Lester nods his approval of a deft phrase.

The motives which underpinned this relentless sacrifice are less clear. It seems too easy to speak of simple meanness, that miserly streak which looms all too large in his legend. Those who have known him for many years will tell of the early days when his love of ice cream was matched only by a firm refusal to pay for his treat. And a lady who has studied his life and times down the decades tells of the days when he was dashing around in his first motor car: 'He was always turning up to give people lifts with an empty petrol tank,' says the former trainer Mrs Helen Johnson Houghton. 'And if they didn't fill it up, they never got anywhere.'

But others tell of kindnesses freely given; of small, unconsidered acts of charity which flatly contradict his image. Lester seems not to care, he shrugs indifferently when the subject is raised. It may be more accurate to see him as an outsider, cut off from the mainstream of his sport by his impaired hearing and laboured articulation, yet determined to command a price which defined his true worth.

In his early riding years, he offended everybody. Most particularly he offended Sir Gordon Richards, whose charge that Piggott had ridden recklessly brought the young man a protracted suspension from the turf. Lester accepted the penalty with that familiar shrug; you win some and lose some, but you never, ever let them hurt you. Still less do you allow them to short-change you. So he piled up the winners, both mundane and classic, and he worked upon his list of Derby victories until it acquired the lilt of a litany: from Never Say Die, which he rode as an 18-year-old in 1954, through Crepello, St Paddy, Sir Ivor, Nijinsky, Roberto, Empery, The Minstrel and Teenoso.

The greater his success, the more money he demanded; in winks and nudges and tax-free 'gifts'. He knew his price, and he knew that rich men would pay it. Yet when the inevitable reckoning came, it was Piggott alone who paid the price. He had retired from riding at fifty, persuaded that the game belonged to younger men, and he had been training for a couple of years when Inland Revenue investigations established a tax debt of some £2.5m. The Revenue made at least three attempts to have him put his house in order before they lost patience and prosecuted. In 1987, he was sent to jail for a year on charges of tax evasion.

Some believed the sentence was right and fitting. After all, taxes fall upon rich and poor alike, and if a multi-millionaire like Piggott could avoid and evade, then what hope for the rest of us? Others, surely the majority, were shocked by the simplistic severity of the sentence. Even after all these years, Lester finds it difficult to discuss. His head drops and he speaks slowly, almost jerkily: 'I suppose they wanted to make an example of someone,' he says. 'Maybe they thought that if they started jumping on well-known people, then everyone else would think twice. I dunno. I just wonder if it did any-one any good, me going to prison? Yeah, I was punished and I accepted it. But did it really do anyone any good? I wouldn't have thought so . . .'

A dozen years earlier, he had been awarded the OBE. Now, as he shuffled off to the Highpoint Prison in Suffolk to start his sentence, the Establishment took away the honour. The family packed it up in a box and sent it off to the Central Chancery at Buckingham Palace. They say it broke his heart, and he does not deny it.

Yet the public kept faith, sending him shoals of letters and imploring him to return to the trade he knew best. Wise men chuck-led, but Piggott took the impossible decision. He came back to the track. 'It's what I know, it's what I do best,' he said. 'And, anyway, I missed it.' The media were inquisitive and plied him with technical questions: 'Have you changed your technique,' they asked. 'No,' said Lester. 'It's still the same; one leg each side.' Twelve days later he was riding Royal Academy for Vincent O'Brien in the Breeders' Cup Mile at Belmont, New York. He had been out of the game for five years, yet he had not lost his taste for the miraculous.

Brough Scott, the racing writer and broadcaster, recalls it with genuine awe. 'You have to remember that he was fifty-five. Fifty-five!' he says. 'That's like a George Best or a Barry John coming back to play today. Sure, it was the horse who did the running, but it was Lester who took all the decisions, dropped him in on the inside, held him back, then rode the kind of finish only he could ride. And, do you know, we all knew beyond question that he was going to win it. Beyond question. The great ones inspire that kind of certainty in an audience. And the old boy's the greatest one we've ever seen, isn't he?'

The American press were anxious to instruct Lester in the immen-sity of his achievement. How did he feel about winning such a prize at such a track? Overawed, perhaps? Lester stroked his chin and gave his shrug, then observed in those splendidly slurred tones: 'No, not overawed. I mean, I *have* won nine Derbies . . .'

While his career enjoyed its Indian summer, his private life grew curiously complicated. Anna Ludlow had worked for the blood-stock agency run by Lester's wife Susan for almost fourteen years. Just over two years ago, she gave birth to Lester's son, Jamie Charles. Piggott registered the birth himself at the local register office. She now lives in a bungalow four miles from the Piggott home, and while he continues to live with Susan, he is a frequent visitor to the bungalow. All the parties involved are said to be at ease with the arrangement.

In similar circumstances, many a lesser celebrity might find himself hounded by packs of prurient scribblers. Yet there is something in Piggott's personality which discourages unwelcome intrusion, a scorn so abrasive that it scars even the thickest skin. His independence is utterly formidable. I once asked him how he coped with the weight of public expectation, how his presence in a big race would inevitably shorten the odds as the money poured on to his mount. 'Doesn't affect me,' he said. 'It never did. I've always known that winning means as much to me as it does to them.' His voice was flat and his logic irreproachable.

Inevitably, he is at his best when he speaks of the art and practice of horse racing. So you confess your ignorance – which he has long since detected – and throw yourself on his mercy. He is indulgent, laughing more easily than his image would allow. And he has a fine, spare way with words. What does it take to win a Derby? Piggott explains: 'You have to have enough pace to lay up in the first eight early on; the right balance to cope with the twists and contours; the strength to hold a good position; the stamina to stay the trip and the turn of foot to kill the opposition at the end.' Simple, the way he tells it.

And he has a feeling for a phrase. Why was Sir Ivor the best horse he ever rode? 'Because he just did everything you asked him to.' And what made Epsom on Derby Day his spiritual home? The face lights up and, almost instinctively, his hand flicks against an ear: 'Because it was the only place I ever heard the crowd.'

Although he affects indifference to public acclaim, you sense that he feels that his contribution to British sport has been consistently undervalued. The BBC 'Sports Personality of the Year' award has yielded some unlikely winners down the years, from snooker players to ice dancers. Yet the votes have never fallen for the most consistently excellent performer of all. Peter O'Sullevan, that prince of sports commentators, drew pointed attention to the lapse when awarding Piggott a form of 'retirement' present at this year's ceremony.

Had things been different, then he would certainly have been knighted in the twilight years of his career. Sadly, the prison sentence ensured that the sword would never descend upon his shoulder, but his dearest wish is that some way may be found to restore his OBE. There surely would be no great surge of disapproval if simple justice should usurp stale custom, and certainly there would be no objection from a racing monarch who has been present at so many of Piggott's triumphs.

And there have been so many triumphs, so many memories, so many marvellous horses since that distant day at Salisbury. There is no secret to his extravagant success, or so he tells you. 'I just worked at it,' he says. 'I watched all the best jockeys, and stole their best bits and pieces.'

But the jockeys, the men who understand better than anybody the true dimension of his genius, they paid him the highest tribute of all. A year or two back, they presented him with one of the racing industry's Oscars. Then, as the man they call the 'long fellow' stood with head bowed, every jockey in the country rose to applaud him for fully ten minutes.

Then somebody had a brilliant idea, one which was adopted by acclaim. So nowadays, when the annual awards dinner comes around and the finest jockeys in the land are called up to receive their prizes, they are no longer given an Oscar. Instead, and as a stirring tribute to the greatest of them all, they are handed a Lester.

1996

From time to time, the roving scribbler finds himself undertaking an assignment which is quite unsuitable for a grown man. I remember thinking as much when I stood outside a gymnasium on the wrong side of Las Vegas and waited for Mike Tyson to arrive for training.

Tyson was boorish and his hired hands were even worse, but I stuck to my task until he gave me the interview I had come for. It amounted to a grand total of 33 words. Each of them exclusive.

The Matoority of Mike Tyson

Mail on Sunday, 11 February 1996

T HE BIG MEN ARRIVE soon after lunch, tumbling from a fleet of station wagons. They switch on their short-wave radios, scowl at a couple of unwelcome guests and start to search the building. In truth, the building is scarcely more than a glorified tin hut so the search is brief. Eventually, they are satisfied.

The leader, and largest of all, lifts a crackling receiver to his lips: 'The place is clean!' he declares. 'Sterile! All set for The Man!' And so, in a cloud of dust and a blast of rap music, the green Range Rover carrying Michael Gerard Tyson arrives at the door of the Golden Gloves Gymnasium: Prop: Lt Hal Miller (ret).

The gym is in downtown Las Vegas, and so far on the wrong side of the tracks that, as the old phrase has it, you can't even hear the whistle of the train. It is a strange place for neo-presidential posturing. And the visitors, myself and our photographer Michael Brennan, offer no obvious threat to Tyson and his wide-bodied chums.

No matter; the lads have seen the secret service movies, and they know precisely what they must do. As their woolly-hatted meal ticket climbs down from his vehicle, one gentleman begins to bawl: 'No pictures! You *hear* me, man?' At the same time, his friend places a hand as large as a soup plate upon my chest and drawls: 'Not another step. *Sir*.' Tyson seems quite unconcerned at this fatuous flexing of muscle. 'Hi!' he growls. 'How ya doin'?' And he disappears into the gym.

Inside, there are garish portraits of a man who looks vaguely like Mike Tyson. There is a list of gymnasium fees: 'Main event boxers, $100 and up'. There is a large American flag. And there is a covering notice, in case the authorities come a-calling: 'All boxers not born in the USA *must* present their green card as proof of identity.' I can describe the scene in some detail because I visited the site before Tyson arrived. Sadly, I cannot describe his activities once inside, since 'Soup Plate' has slammed the door shut behind him.

All I can offer is a list of indistinct sounds; rap, thuds, grunts, yelps of 'You the Man!', more rap. In truth, I couldn't tell you much more even had I seen him train, since watching fighters in the gym is rather like watching racehorses in the paddock; unless they are actually limping or frothing at the mouth, then observers can learn little about their health or form.

But I gather he is working well, sparring for six rounds then completing a further four rounds on the punch-pads. And all this after rising at 3.30 a.m. to run four miles through a park near his home, devouring a hearty breakfast and enduring a conditioning session. Strange, 3.30 is roughly the time he used to drain his last drink and set off in search of other distractions. But those were the distant days when he was heavyweight champion of all the world, and before those 'other distractions' caused him to serve three years in an Indianapolis prison.

Being desperately short of alternative attractions, professional boxing awaited the return of the rapist with the kind of anxious impatience which used to be reserved for veterans of foreign wars. When he reappeared he was allowed a couple of toby jugs for target practice, but next month he resumes authentic hostilities with a fight for Frank Bruno's world title. Now if you or I were managing the challenger, we should present him as New Tyson, a man who has learned from his mistakes, has put his old ways behind him and has discovered a menacing sense of purpose.

Enter Rory Holloway, in a scarlet Jaguar. His links with Tyson go back to New York's Bed-Stuy ghetto. Now he is co-manager, the roly-poly gentleman charged with keeping the man-child in decent order. 'Mark my words,' he says, 'the world is gonna see a new Mike Tyson. Sooo fit! Sooo willing! Sooo focused! He don't drink, he don't hang out, he don't do none of them things that got him in trouble. No more. He's done his time, and he's learned.

'Sparring partners, he knocks 'em out. All the time. Better still, he sends 'em to hospital. One day, he knocked out three guys in the first round. Hey, we're talking 270 lb men here. Big men. All fallin'. The man is *awesome*. Know what; I'm proudda him. Remember how he was at his best, against Tyrell Biggs, Tony Tucker, guys like that? He's back there now. Right back. He weighs 224 lb 'cos he's eating right, exercising right. Last time he fought Bruno, he weighed 280 lb six weeks before the fight. Yet he still took care of the guy. Is Bruno better now than he was nine years ago? I don't think so. But Tyson is.

'The other day, I showed him a film of Bruno and Oliver McCall. He watched maybe two minutes, less than a round. Then he told me, he said: "Don't show me this stuff, man. This is, like, embarrassing." That's what he said. Listen, I don't wanna put your guy down, but this is not gonna be a late night. Two, maybe three rounds. Bruno's not the most elusive fighter. He's easy to hit, and when he's hit, he'll go. That's the way it is.'

Two hours later, New Tyson emerges from the gym. Gold teeth glittering in the winter sun, he launches his charm offensive. 'Whaddya want?' he snarls. I ask him a few docile questions about his physical condition and learn that he is 'in great shape'. I mention the Bruno tape, and he sneers. 'I don't watch no tapes. I don't do that stuff. Why would I watch Bruno? I know what I need to know, you know?'

New Tyson turns towards his vehicle, the exhaustive interview at an end. Brennan starts to take pictures. Soup Plate explodes: 'I said no photographs. Forbidden! Sonofabitch!' Holloway intervenes: 'It's all right, leave him.' Soup Plate is not placated: 'I was just doing my f****** job, for f***'s sake,' he says. 'Guys wanna take pictures, I stop them. It's what I'm f****** here for.'

By now, Tyson's Range Rover is heading for the freeway. Holloway watches it out of sight. 'Twice the man since he came out of prison,' he says. 'He's gotten a new matoority. He's more . . .', he searches for the word, and arrives at one which is so unlikely that you suspect he is joking. 'He's more *humble* these days,' he says. 'Yeah, Mike's a very humble person. That might surprise you, but it's true.'

And you find yourself smiling as the wagons stream away from the parking lot. For this is professional boxing, where words mean whatever you want them to mean, and one man's truth is another man's slander, and everybody lies all the time. And nothing can ever surprise you.